COMMUNITY-BASED CORRECTIONS

VERNON FOX

Florida State University

PRENTICE-HALL, INC., Englewood Cliffs, New Jersey

Library of Congress Cataloging in Publication Data

Fox, Vernon Brittain (date)
    Community-based corrections.

    Bibliography: p.
    Includes index.
    1. Community-based corrections. 2. Community-based
corrections—United States. I. Title.
HV9275.F67   364.6   76-6879
ISBN 0-13-153254-5

Dedicated to my three children,
now grown and with their own families

Karen, Vernon, and Loraine

© 1977 by PRENTICE-HALL, INC., *Englewood Cliffs, New Jersey*

Printed in the United States of America

10 9 8 7 6 5 4 3 2 1

PRENTICE-HALL INTERNATIONAL, INC., *London*
PRENTICE-HALL OF AUSTRALIA PTY. LIMITED, *Sydney*
PRENTICE-HALL OF CANADA, LTD., *Toronto*
PRENTICE-HALL OF INDIA PRIVATE LIMITED, *New Delhi*
PRENTICE-HALL OF JAPAN, INC., *Tokyo*
PRENTICE-HALL OF SOUTHEAST ASIA PTE. LTD., *Singapore*

Contents

Chapter 7

Community Services Management   *99*

Employment.   Legal Aid.   Personal Affairs.   Personal Budget Counseling.
Welfare Problems.   Health Problems.   Other Helping Services.
Agency Coordination.   Technical Assistance.   Conclusions.

Chapter 8

Chemical Dependency Programs: Alcohol and Drugs   *123*

Chemical Dependence in Historical Perspective.   Alcohol Programs.
Drug Programs.   Treatment Strategies.   Conclusions.

Chapter 9

Governmental Programs in the Community   *150*

Vocational Rehabilitation.   Veterans Administration.
Department of Justice Programs—LEAA.   Department of Labor.
Department of Health, Education and Welfare.
Department of Housing and Urban Development.
Department of Agriculture: Food Stamps.   Office of Economic Opportunity.
National Science Foundation.   Conclusions.

Chapter 10

New Careers and Ex-Offender Groups   *166*

New Careers.   Linkers.   Ex-Offender Groups Providing Direct Service.
Ex-Offender Groups Providing Indirect Service.   Ex-Offenders Working in Corrections.
Employment for Offenders.   Conclusions.

Chapter 11

Private Community-Based Corrections   *182*

Chapter 12

Group Homes, Foster Homes, and Juvenile Services   *196*

Chapter 13

The Youth Service Bureau   *234*

Chapter 14

Volunteers in Community-Based Corrections   *243*

Chapter 15

Problems in Community-Based Corrections   *260*

Behavior of Residents.   Relationship with Police.
Jurisdictional Problems in the Criminal Justice System.   Public Relations.
Political Misuse.   Funding and Support.   Competency of Personnel.
Failure of Community-Based Programs.   Conclusions.

Chapter 16

The Future of Community-Based Corrections   *270*

Dissatisfaction with Prisons.   Prevention Programs.   Diversion Programs.
Halfway Houses and Group Homes.   Work Release and Furloughs.   Volunteers.
Dependency Programs—Alcohol and Drugs.   Cost Benefit Analysis.
The Move Toward Community-Based Corrections.   Conclusions.

Bibliography   *289*

Index   *309*

Foreword

During the past decade, the term community-based corrections has become a commonplace term for criminologists and practitioners in the field of criminal justice. It has been viewed by some as a way to decrease prison populations; by others as a more humane way of helping the offender; and by still others as a less expensive method of punishment and incarceration.

Interestingly enough, it has been viewed by many as *more* successful than imprisonment; by some as *less* successful than imprisonment; and by others who say there is no difference between imprisonment and community-based corrections relative to success. Although the debate and research continue, courts and prisons are relying more and more upon the concept and will probably continue to do so until it is proven that community-based corrections is harmful, or, at a minimum, contributes little, if anything, to the offender or to the public.

In the mid-1960s, community-based corrections showed a dramatic increase as a means of assisting offenders returning from prison. It also provided the courts with an alternative to imprisonment. It was the era of de-institutionalization. Thus, as expected, there was a decrease in the prison population around the country; there was a decided increase in caseloads on probation and parole; and the population of halfway houses also took a sudden upturn. By 1974, still a different trend developed—a sharp increase in the number of persons sent to prison. Did this mean a lessening of community-based corrections? No. They, too, increased at a rapid pace. Caseloads were higher than ever; more probation and parole staff were hired; more programs had volunteer services than ever before;

and there was a dramatic increase in community-based residential programs around the country.

The obvious conclusion to be made is that community-based corrections is around to stay and will increase. It will not show the dramatic
trends that prison populations show, but there will be a gradual and
consistent addition to the correctional spectrum.

Dr. Fox's book *Community-Based Corrections* arrives on the scene at
a most appropriate time—a time when confusion and suspicion swirls
around the entire concept of treatment in the community.

The book does many things. It is the most complete historical document on community-based programs. The author reaches back into time
to provide insight into the development of the entire community-based
corrections concept and then shows what was accomplished during that
era. Few books delineate between concept and accomplishment as does
this book.

The author clearly spells out the differences between traditional community-based corrections (jail, probation, parole, and juvenile court services) and community-based services that mobilize community resources
for the offender and provide true alternatives to punishment, another
important contribution.

Community-Based Corrections presents a wide array of topics relating
to services provided for the offender by the community. It describes neighborhood projects, diversion programs, halfway houses, work release, study
release, drug and alcohol programs, and ex-offender groups. In juvenile
services, the book encompasses group homes, foster homes, youth service
bureaus, and volunteer services. Although it is not a cookbook as such,
it does provide a firm background of programming that exists in the
country.

The final two chapters in the book alone would be a valuable addition
to any library. Chapter 15, Problems in Community-Based Corrections,
brilliantly presents the many factors that have prohibited the full growth
of community-based programs. The author minces no words in discussing
relationships with the police, the public, the political aspects, as well as
the vital areas of funding and staff competency.

Chapter 16, The Future of Community-Based Corrections, projects with
realism what the future holds for community-based programming. Dissatisfaction with the ability of prisons to rehabilitate the law violator
seems destined to grow. Creative community-based programs seem just as
destined to increase in popularity and utility. The author concludes that,
while there will always be a need for prisons and institutions for some
offenders, community-based programs in the future will continue to play
an important role for more and more offenders.

Community-Based Corrections should be a part of every correctional worker's library.

JOHN "MIKE" McCARTT
Executive Director, Talbert House
Cincinnati, Ohio 45206
Past President of the International Halfway House Association

Preface

In 1973 the National Advisory Commission on Criminal Justice Standards and Goals said that although the system of community-based corrections was not organized and had no unified management, had no consistent philosophy, and no empirical evaluation, it was nevertheless considered to be a viable alternative to incarceration in the future. It was the Federal Prisoner Rehabilitation Act of 1965 that gave governmental support to community-based corrections and provided governmental participation in work release programs, halfway houses, and other related endeavors.

The beginnings of community-based corrections were at least as early as the "Good Samaritan" referred to in the New Testament and the ecclesiastical monasteries of the Middle Ages. In the modern context, community-based corrections refers to the mobilization of community resources for assistance to offenders and ex-offenders commensurate with the public safety. Although incarceration, probation, and parole take place in the community, they are not "community-based corrections" in the modern sense. Rather, they are traditional elements of the criminal justice system. Today community-based corrections programs have a function of complementing (not including or supplanting) the traditional roles of imprisonment, probation, and parole.

Studies of probation and parole activities have indicated two elements of supervision—surveillance and assistance. Surveillance is a treatment-supervision function, while assistance is a counseling function. But because of the size of their caseloads, probation and parole agencies, supervisors, and officers tend to place emphasis on surveillance; their primary concern becomes crisis intervention and crisis counseling over and above finding jobs and mobilizing community resources for their cases. Very little time is spent on such things as finding out what offenders on their caseloads do during their leisure time—whether or not they drink heavily, what are their relationships with the opposite sex, etc.—except when they are picked up by the police. Community-based corrections can and should mobilize community resources, find jobs, and perform other mundane tasks so that probation and parole personnel will be able to devote more time to the counseling and assistance function.

The President's Commission on Law Enforcement and Administration of Justice was established in 1965 to find ways of improving the criminal justice system in the United States. Its massive report in 1967 provided many useful recommendations for change to improve the system. Simultaneously, the Federal Prisoner Rehabilitation Act of 1965 made possible governmental participation in community-based corrections through such things as work release and furlough programs, pre-release centers, and designation of community services officers. The American Correctional Association's *Manual of Correctional Standards,* written in 1959 and reprinted several times, has a short chapter on community correctional centers with emphasis on the parole process and the re-entry of ex-offenders into society. From 1967 to 1969 the Joint Commission on Correctional Manpower and Training, composed of ninety-nine private organizations, focused on improvement of correctional personnel. It was during the 1960s, then, that contemporary community-based corrections programs achieved governmental participation and recognition. Although such programs had been in existence for a long time under private auspices, the Federal Prisoner Rehabilitation Act of 1965 began a new era, with community-based corrections as a major component in the field of criminal justice.

The purpose of this book is to provide a rationale and a structure for community-based corrections programs that support and complement the system of imprisonment, probation, and parole. These programs can assume a service function and release valuable personnel to provide their basic function of assistance, counseling, and treatment-supervision.

The programs mentioned in this book are examples of community-based correctional programs and constitute only a fraction of the hundreds and thousands of programs in existence. Any attempt to list all the ongoing programs would result in a voluminous directory. This book provides a survey of the *types* of programs that are in operation in many places and could be implemented elsewhere. There is no single prototype of community-based corrections. The majority of successful efforts reflect the personalities of the people who organize and operate them. In this area, people "do their own thing" more than in any other part of the criminal justice system. Although this makes the field unsystematic and disorganized, it also provides the opportunity for flexibility and for adapting programs to the needs and resources of individual communities.

Appreciation is expressed to the many people who made this book possible. Many who are operating community-based correctional programs throughout the United States responded promptly and courteously to inquiries about their programs, some of which are not to be found in the literature. Mr. Ken Demarest assisted significantly in the compilation of a bibliography. Appreciation is expressed to Mrs. Mary Harris, Mrs. Sandra Burkholder, and Mrs. Juana Hendry for the preparation of the manuscript. Any weaknesses, omissions, or errors are the fault of the author.

VERNON FOX
Florida State University

Chapter 1

Development of
Community-Based Corrections

The functions of community-based corrections programs are (1) the mobilization and management of community resources to assist in the rehabilitation of offenders and (2) the provision of alternatives to incarceration in a way that is compatible with the public interest and safety. "Corrections" refers to the agencies of social control that attempt to rehabilitate or neutralize the deviant behavior of adult criminals and juvenile delinquents for the protection of society. *Community-based corrections* refers to that part of corrections—other than the traditional imprisonment, probation, and parole functions—which is located in the community and makes use of community resources to complement, augment, and support those traditional correctional functions.

Although jails and probation, parole, and juvenile courts services are located in the community, they are not to be confused with community-based corrections functions as defined in this book. The purpose of jails is to (1) hold legally innocent persons awaiting trial, (2) hold convicted felons and other serious offenders awaiting sentence or execution of sentence, (3) hold short-term offenders, and (4) hold material witnesses who might otherwise disappear. Probation services have the traditional functions of (1) preparing the pre-sentence investigation report (PSI), and (2) supervising probationers who are under order of the court. The area of parole involves (1) the selection of persons in prison for release on parole, (2) the preparation of those about to be released on parole, and (3) the supervision of parolees. Juvenile courts provide protective supervision of those dependents or delinquents considered to be juveniles according to the law of the jurisdiction. Disposition for delinquents is

1

generally (1) unofficial probation, (2) official probation, or (3) commitment to an institution for juveniles (although there are more legal dispositions).

There is a general consensus that prisons do not do what they are
supposed to do. Prisons and penitentiaries were originally designed to
break the harshness of English penal practice, in terms of both corporal
and capital punishments. Although our current penitentiary system represents a humanitarian effort started by the Quakers in Philadelphia in
1790, many people feel that it has "gone sour" and is counterproductive.
Quakers are anxious to remedy this,[1] as are others. Joseph G. Wilson
asked in 1950 whether or not prisons were necessary.[2] In 1951, Donald
Powell Wilson scored the prison system when he discussed the negative
effect prison conditions have on people.[3] Similar opinions were later expressed by Mitford on a much broader scale;[4] and Menninger arrived
at the same conclusions from the psychiatric perspective.[5] This same
viewpoint is being expressed everywhere in the literature—in books, professional journals, and popular magazines.

Whether or not these indictments are overstated, they are consistent
with the thinking of both correctional administrators and scholars. Killinger and Cromwell believe that imprisonment has "assumed too great
a role" in dealing with offenders in the criminal system.[6] Most large
prisons are located far away from the community, thus increasing the
distance from the society men and women must eventually rejoin. How
can they make any sort of successful readjustment when they have been
forced to remain enclosed in a vastly dissimilar environment?

Not only is the prison less effective than had been hoped, it is also more
expensive. A person could be sent to America's finest universities for the
same amount of money it would take to maintain him or her in a maximum security prison. It has been estimated that 95 percent of expenditures for prisons are for custody in the forms of walls, fences, bars, and
guards, while only 5 percent is spent for hope, in the form of health
services, education, development of employment skills, and treatment.[7]

---

[1] American Friends Service Committee, *Struggle for Justice* (New York: Hill &
Wang, 1971).

[2] *Are Prisons Necessary?* (Philadelphia: Dorrance, 1950).

[3] *My Six Convicts: A Psychologist's Three Years in Fort Leavenworth* (New York:
Rinehart & Co., 1951).

[4] Jessica Mitford, *Kind and Usual Punishment: The Prison Business* (New York:
Knopf, 1973).

[5] Karl Menninger, *The Crime of Punishment* (New York: Viking Press, 1968).

[6] George G. Killinger and Paul F. Cromwell, eds., *Corrections in the Community:
Selected Readings* (St. Paul, Minn.: West Publishing Co., 1974), p. v.

[7] Ronald Goldfarb, *Ransom* (New York: Harper & Row, 1965).

The authoritarian system of a maximum security prison reduces people to a state of irresponsibility and dependency such that rehabilitation as self-respecting, wage-earning citizens is almost impossible.[8] Arch Booth, executive vice-president of the Chamber of Commerce of the United States, has said:

> The correctional process is a massive operation, receiving more than 2.5 million offenders a year at a cost of more than $1 billion. It is burdened with a performance record which would plunge any business into bankruptcy.[9]

It becomes obvious that alternatives to prison must be found. As stated in the Report of the National Advisory Commission on Criminal Justice Standards and Goals in 1973, a community-based corrections system is a desirable and viable alternative to incarceration for many people.[10]

In the brief time community-based corrections programs have been a part of the corrections system sponsored by federal and state governments, there has been some confusion and conflict between the new and the traditional services, both in educational courses and in the field of practice. The functions of mobilization and management of community resources to achieve the correctional objective and to find alternatives to incarceration have always been present. Traditionally, however, probation and parole officers have been expected to provide these services in addition to their function of control. Control primarily involves surveillance and crisis intervention, and it involves a great deal of time and energy. A recent study has shown that most traditional probation and parole supervisors know very little about their individual probationers' and parolees' personal lives.[11] But considering the huge caseloads of law enforcement personnel, it is not hard to understand how it is that the functions of assistance and guidance of prisoners and ex-prisoners has been neglected.

Today, the availability of assistance from the community-based correctional agent, manager, or program has cast the probation and parole officer into a new role. To the extent that he is adequately prepared to understand and accept the community-based system, he can more effec-

---

[8] Henry Burns, "A Miniature Totalitarian State: Maximum Security Prison," *Canadian Journal of Corrections,* 11, No. 3 (1969), 153–64.

[9] Arch N. Booth, "Foreword," *Marshaling Citizen Power to Modernize Corrections* (Washington, D.C.: Chamber of Commerce of the United States, 1972), p. iii.

[10] "Corrections and the Community," in *Corrections* (Washington, D.C.: National Advisory Commission on Criminal Justice Standards and Goals, 1973), pp. 221–36, and the Standards 7.1 through 7.4, pp. 237–46.

[11] Jürgen Jung, "The Parole Supervisor's Perception of the Parolee's Situation," *Canadian Journal of Criminology and Corrections,* 16, No. 3 (July 1974), 272–81.

tively utilize his time and efforts to better understand and guide his charges. Seen in the light of their complementary and supportive function, community-based correctional personnel should offer no threat or pose any jurisdictional problems for the parole and probation supervisors within the community. Rather, their working together can result in the bringing about of more effective corrections and a healthier society.

HISTORICAL BEGINNINGS OF COMMUNITY-BASED CORRECTIONS

The beginnings of community-based corrections were probably as long ago as 2,000 B.C., when a court scene was depicted on the shield of Achilles in Homer's *Iliad*. Ancient people had no jails, prisons, or correctional institutions as we know them. Their places of detention were dungeons in castles and towers, or even animal cages. While Jerusalem had detention places as early as the 6th century B.C., the first building erected specifically for the purpose of detaining people was that authorized by Henry II in 1166 at the Assize of Clarendon. Ancient and medieval punishments involved compensation, restitution, and retribution and vengeance. The philosophy of compensation and restitution is well stated in Exodus 22:1–9. Vengeance and the death penalty are also described in the book of Exodus. When circumstances called for punishment other than the death penalty, ancient man used a sort of community-based corrections system, although it was not viewed that way. Dispositions involved (1) compensation and restitution by the offender to his victim, (2) indenture of the offender to the victim or the victim's family when he could not provide restitution and compensation, (3) assignment to the public works, such as quarries, mines, the construction of roads and buildings, and other public services, and (4) execution or banishment. These approaches were used for criminal justice purposes until the advent of workhouses and transportation of major offenders to distant lands in the sixteenth century. The development of prisons in the late eighteenth century became a substitute for banishment and was designed to be just as secure and effective. Any recent changes have been the result of relaxation of security and the developing philosophy of reintegration of the offender back into his community.

The idea of community-based corrections goes back for centuries, but its organization has been fairly recent. Efforts have been traditionally private and at first focused on people who were mentally incapacitated. The mentally ill, the retarded, the aged, the orphaned, and the poor have historically been not only tolerated, but cared for with compassion within the community in primitive, ancient, medieval, and modern societies.[12]

---

[12] David Rothman, *The Discovery of the Asylum* (Boston: Little, Brown, 1971), pp. 440–41.

Vagrants, unemployed persons, the elderly, and minor offenders began to be cared for in community workhouses beginning in the sixteenth century. Pope Clement XI built the Hospice di San Michele (House of St. Michael) in 1704 to care for the kind of children we now refer to as "delinquent." That institution still stands in Rome and is still being used for the same purpose. The Low Countries (the Netherlands, Belgium, and Luxembourg), Switzerland, and England were the first to place persons with mental disturbances in homes.[13] These were generally in small, rural neighborhoods in a climate of reduced social pressure. In Belgium, the practice of community care for deviant persons began in the thirteenth century with the establishment of a colony called Geel. Legend has it that in the eighth century, an Irish princess was decapitated by her demented father, from whom she had fled because of his incestuous designs, but he overtook her in Geel and the town became a shrine to the memory of her sainthood. Some persons came to Geel as pilgrims, and they remained and became residents. In 1852, the government of Belgium assumed maintenance and supervision of the colony and provided an infirmary.

Prisoners' aid associations are among the oldest group of organizations concerned with offenders and ex-offenders. In 1787 the Quakers started the Philadelphia Society for Alleviating the Miseries of the Public Prisons —the name was changed to Pennsylvania Prison Society in 1887. The Correctional Association of New York was formed in 1844. The Prisoners' Aid Association of Maryland was formalized in 1869, but its beginnings go back to 1829, when the rector of St. Paul's Episcopal Church in downtown Baltimore provided food and other assistance to men leaving the penitentiary. The Massachusetts Correctional Association was established in 1889 as the John Howard Society; the first John Howard Society was established in England in 1866. Currently, there are prisoners' aid societies functioning around the world.

New York, Pennsylvania, and Massachusetts established the first halfway houses in the United States in the early 1800s.[14] Although a Massachusetts commission recommended the establishment of such facilities in 1820, the primary movement came from private groups. Early halfway houses were self-contained, relatively isolated from correctional staff, and assisted in the reintegration of prisoners back into the community.[15] They were not considered to be part of the correction system, however, and most did not flourish. A halfway house was established in Boston

---

[13] Benedict S. Alper, *Prisons Inside-Out: Alternatives in Correctional Reform* (Cambridge, Mass.: Ballinger, 1974), p. 14.

[14] Oliver J. Keller and Benedict S. Alper, *Halfway Houses: Community-Centered Corrections and Treatment* (Lexington, Mass.: D. C. Heath, 1970), p. 7.

[15] Robert H. Vasoli and Frank J. Fahey, "Halfway Houses for Reformatory Releasees," *Crime and Delinquency*, 16, No. 3 (July 1970), 293.

in 1864 and operated for twenty years. A group of Quakers opened a half-way house for women in New York City in the 1880s; this continues today as the Isaac T. Hopper House. They also opened the House of Industry in Philadelphia in 1889, which still receives parolees from Pennsylvania prisons.[16] In the 1800s, there was opposition to halfway houses from the organization now known as the American Correctional Association, which considered them to be operated by meddling nonprofessionals. Maud Booth, whose Volunteers of America had split from the Salvation Army, opened Hope Hall with her husband in 1896 in the Washington Heights section of Manhattan. This institution came under harassment from the police to the extent that Mrs. Booth appealed directly to President Theodore Roosevelt for assistance.[17]

Settlement houses began to appear in the 1880s. They did more than just work with ex-offenders. They were designed to assist in the improvement of entire neighborhoods in terms of economic security, employment, recreation, better lighting, social welfare, and other social phenomena sometimes considered to be only peripheral to efforts at control and prevention of delinquency and crime and with no ostensible or obvious service to offenders and ex-offenders.

The first settlement house in the United States was the Neighborhood Guild in New York City in 1887; it was an outgrowth of the London Movement founded by Toynbee Hall.[18] Earlier organizations had been formed for similar objectives, such as the YMCA (1851) and YWCA (1861). Their purpose was to provide recreation and counseling services to youth who needed them to "keep normals normal," thereby preventing delinquency.

Prisoners have been employed outside the prisons through various means and in various capacities almost from the beginning of the prison movement.[19] Formal work release plans began in the Irish system of incarceration by stages in 1854 under Sir Walter Crofton. Work release programs have been used in Sweden since 1937. France, Scotland, Norway, West Germany, and Great Britain have used it for a long time.[20] Work release in the United States began in Wisconsin under the Huber Law in 1913.

There are three patterns of work release programs. Some ex-prisoners

16 Edwin Powers, "Halfway Houses: An Historical Perspective," *American Journal of Correction*, 21 (July–August 1959), 35.

17 Keller and Alper, *Halfway Houses*, p. 7.

18 Herbert H. Stroup, *Social Work* (New York: American Book Co., 1960), pp. 43–45.

19 Charles R. Henderson, ed., *Outdoor Convict Labor: A Report to the Governor of Illinois* (Chicago: University of Chicago Press, 1907).

20 Stanley E. Grupp, "Work Release and the Misdemeanant," *Federal Probation*, 29 (June 1965), 7.

retain their pre-conviction jobs because of their skills and because the criminal justice system has permitted them to stay in jail nights and weekends and work during the week. Sometimes, inmates are given jobs by friends or members of their family so that they can be released early from institutionalization. The rest generally obtain work release employment while they are still confined in prisons, jails, or community correctional centers.

The support by tax funds in governmental programs of community-based corrections has been recent. Wisconsin was one of the first states to move toward this idea in an effort to alleviate problems. In 1873, the Wisconsin State Board of Charities and Reform reported:

> Here are scores of hundreds of men, some of them young and in vigorous health, who are compelled to spend from a few days to a year, and sometimes two years in absolute idleness, while the taxpayers of the various counties are supporting them. What a waste of labor! What an injury to the men themselves to keep them in a state of enforced idleness! What an unwise expenditure of public funds to support healthy, able-bodied men in such idleness.[21]

In 1913, the Wisconsin legislature enacted the Huber Law, which was sponsored by the late Senator Henry Huber for the purpose of (1) providing for the reformation and rehabilitation of the prisoner and (2) providing by means of financial support for the prisoner's deepndents.[22] The Huber Law provided that misdemeants sentenced to jails for terms of one year or less could be permitted to work at their usual jobs or new jobs that were found for them, but were confined for the rest of the time, particularly evenings and weekends. It was a jail work release plan. In 1919, women were also included under the law. In 1927, discretionary authority was given to the courts by which they could either sentence under the Huber Law or could choose to sentence people to spend all of their time in the jail. In 1945, prisoners committed to county workhouses were also included in the Huber Law and prisoners without dependents were allowed their earnings less a charge for room and board. In 1947, persons convicted of contempt of court by failure to pay support as ordered by the court were included in the law. In 1957, the requirement was that half the prisoner's saved earnings must be paid to the counties, and provision was made for payment of such savings to the prisoner upon discharge.

---

21 John R. Gagnon, "Jail Work Release Under the Huber Law," *Proceedings of the Eighty-Ninth Annual Congress of Correction, Detroit, 1958* (New York: American Correctional Association, 1959), p. 391.

22 Ibid., pp. 391–98.

When the Department of Public Welfare in Wisconsin surveyed the state in 1957, it found that every county in the state had taken advantage of the law during the 1956 calendar year. In that year, there were 26,405 male adults held overnight or longer in the county jails, of whom 7,309 were sentenced to jail terms and 2,581 were sentenced under the Huber Law. Approximately one-third of persons sentenced to jail, then, were sentenced under the Huber Law. Less than 9 percent violated the conditions of their sentence. Approximately 40 percent of their earning was used to support dependents; about 24 percent was used to offset the cost of maintaining the inmates themselves; 4 percent went to the counties; 10 percent went to the inmates to pay pre-existing debts; 5 percent was given to the inmates at the time of release; and 17 percent was used for such costs as medical and dental services, clothing, court costs, union dues, maternity fees, restitution, and other expenses during imprisonment.

In the 1950s and early 1960s, North Carolina was facing economic problems because of inadequate budget. As an economic measure, this state used work release programs and established camps for felons in several places. The social and rehabilitative benefits deriving from these early experiments through avoidance of long-term institutionalization and its effects caused officials in North Carolina to formalize the project, extending it to felons in 1959. Work release, then, was really pioneered in Wisconsin and North Carolina.

EARLY PRIVATE COMMUNITY-BASED CORRECTIONS

Private community-based corrections programs preceded those supported by tax funds. These informal services were generally provided by private individuals or religious groups. In England, the lay visitor became popular in jails and prisons in the late eighteenth and early nineteenth centuries. But his main function was to obtain jobs and provide counseling and some informal supervision after the prisoners' release. Early well-known lay visitors in England were Jonas Hanway (1712–1786), James Neild (1744–1814), Thomas Sillitoe (1754–1836), and Sarah Martin (1791–1843).[23] Probably the most famous lay visitor was Elizabeth Gurney Fry (1780–1845), for whom the Elizabeth Fry Societies in the English-speaking world were named. In the United States, lay visiting was also popular, particularly in Philadelphia among the Quakers, who provided the impetus for the development of the first pententiary at the Walnut Street jail in 1719. The service received considerable momentum when the Eastern Penitentiary of Pennsylvania was opened in Philadelphia in

---

[23] Harry Elmer Barnes and Negley K. Teeters, *New Horizons in Criminology*, 3rd ed. (Englewood Cliffs, N.J.: Prentice-Hall, 1959), p. 512.

1929, when a basic principle of the system was separate or solitary confinement augmented by prison visiting by laymen.[24]

CITIZEN PARTICIPATION IN CORRECTIONS

Until the mid-1960s, citizen participation in the correctional field included what is now known as community-based corrections. The American Correctional Association, the primary professional organization in the field of corrections, first met in Cincinnati, Ohio in 1870, as the National Congress on Penitentiary and Reformatory Discipline.[25] The last *Proceedings* of this association, in which the title "Citizen Participation" was used exclusively, was in 1966.[26] The topics were rehabilitation programs in the community, direct services to misdemeanant offenders, relief assistance, post-relief services for jail inmates, work release and preparole camps, citizen participation in workhouses, and the role of private agencies. In the following year, the *Proceedings* included the title "Community Services and Citizen Participation" to cover this area of community services, halfway houses, community mental health centers, volunteers, and vocational placement.[27] By 1968, a major section entitled, "Community-Based Treatment" covered the community treatment center concept, halfway houses, the use of electronic control in rehabilitation to replace prison, use of ex-offenders, community-based treatment facilities, volunteer agencies, and work release.[28] By 1969, the section on citizen participation had disappeared and the section entitled "Community-Based Treatment" was prominent.[29]

Citizen participation in the correctional effort has been traditional in

24 Negley K. Teeters and John D. Shearer, *The Prison at Philadelphia: Cherry Hill* (New York: Columbia University Press, 1955), pp. 161–69.

25 E. C. Wines, ed., *Transactions of the National Congress on Penitentiary and Reformatory Discipline, 1870* (Albany, N.Y.: Weed, Parsons and Co., 1871, reprinted College Park, Md.: American Correctional Association, 1970).

26 *Proceedings of the Ninety-Sixth Annual Congress of Corrections of the American Correctional Association, Baltimore, 1966* (Washington, D.C.: American Correctional Association, 1967), pp. 91–144.

27 *Proceedings of the Ninety-Seventh Annual Congress of Corrections of the American Correctional Association, Miami Beach, 1967* (Washington, D.C.: American Correctional Association, 1968), pp. 45–63.

28 *Proceedings of the Ninety-Eighth Congress of Corrections of the American Correctional Association, San Francisco, 1968* (Washington, D.C.: American Correctional Association, 1969), pp. 50–95.

29 *Proceedings of the Ninety-Ninth Annual Congress of Correction of the American Correctional Association, Minneapolis, 1969* (Washington, D.C.: American Correctional Association, 1970), pp. 27–55.

the United States as well as in other countries. It has recently moved to community-based corrections because of its inclusion in public programs supported by tax funds. Formerly, finance came from membership in the interested organizations, private donations, and other private funds. The recognition of community-based corrections as an effort equal to the traditional function of jails, probation, prison, parole, and juvenile services required formal establishment and support by public funds. Previously, citizen participation had been peripheral and included informal assistance to offenders and ex-offenders and attempts to influence public policy through legislative action (such as abolition of capital punishment, special treatment of juveniles and the mentally ill). The traditional corrections system has opposed community-based corrections.

The concept of probation was initiated by citizen participation. John Augustus introduced the practice of friendly supervsion in the city courts of Boston as early as 1841, spending much time visiting the courts, showing an interest in prisoners, and bailing out misdemeanants who could not pay the fines themselves. By 1858, he had bailed out or paid the fines of 1,152 men and 794 women and girls. Augustus died in 1859; but his work was continued by Rufus Cook, chaplain to the county jail and representative of the Boston Children's Aid Society and other less well-known pioneer volunteer "probation organizations." In 1869, Massachusetts provided for the appointment of a state agency of the Board of State Charities to investigate cases involving children tried before the courts. The Massachusetts statute of 1878 provided for appointment of a paid probation officer for the court of criminal jurisdiction of the city of Boston. This was the beginning of probation as we know it today.

It was citizen action that began parole, also. When Captain Alexander Maconochie became the officer in charge of the penal colony on Norfolk Island near Australia, he established a system of marks for good behavior. After a person had earned 100 marks, he could be released to the community on a ticket of leave. When Maconochie took over the island in 1838, there existed a practice of "assignment," in which prisoners transported from England to the Islands of the South Pacific were assigned to local citizens as laborers. Maconochie and others attacked this as slavery. When he changed the system and introduced release by ticket of leave, he was dismissed in 1844 as being too lenient on prisoners. The system was accepted by Sir Walter Crofton and Sir Joshua Jebb from 1850 to 1870, and the Irish system in 1854 provided for a system of graduated release. In fact, the Irish system permitted prisoners to go into community to work in the final stage of incarceration; this was the forerunner of work release. The first formal parole plan was in New York in 1876, when the Elmira Reformatory began to permit release before the expiration of the maximum sentence and, consequently, initiated a period of supervision under parole.

The juvenile court movement was also an example of citizen participation. In the late 1890s, there was a movement in America toward protection of children, which later found expression in the first White House Conference on Children in 1910, called by President Theodore Roosevelt, and the first child labor laws passed by Congress in 1912. The national Parent–Teachers Association was founded in 1897, at the same time the Cook County Women's Clubs were trying to establish a juvenile court in Chicago.[30] After two unsuccessful attempts, Lucy Louisa Flower summoned the founders of the PTA, Phoebe Apperson Hearst and Alice McLellan Birney of Washington, D.C. and, with Nellie Flood, who was a teacher paid from funds from the Women's Clubs, induced the Cook County Bar Association to write a law that was constitutional. It was enacted in 1899.

MODERN COMMUNITY-BASED CORRECTIONS

Modern community-based corrections can be said to have begun in about 1965. Although early community efforts in the United States began almost simultaneously with the emergence of the Auburn-Pennsylvania prison systems beginning in 1790 (more specifically, around 1830) and the formation of Prisoner Aid Societies in many larger cities after 1820, these efforts were always private and not supported by public funds. Although Wisconsin had had work release plans for jail inmates since 1913 under the Huber Law, and North Carolina had informally and administratively begun work release programs for felons in 1959 for economic reasons, these efforts on the part of state governments were isolated. The Federal Rehabilitation Act of 1965 was significant in bringing community-based corrections into the governmental organization. To improve the rehabilitation procedures and to hold down the number of inmates in prisons and correctional institutions, Congress formally sanctioned the use of residential community centers or halfway houses preceding parole, the granting of brief leaves or furloughs in emergencies or the preparation for release, and work release programs for private employment or vocational training in the community in this Act of 1965. Immediately, a community services office was opened in Atlanta and pre-release guidance centers were initiated to assist prisoners about to be paroled. Actually, the United States Bureau of Prisons had opened the Federal Community Treatment Center by administrative decision in Chicago and Los Angeles as early as 1961, with a similar center started in Detroit in 1963. The Prisoner Rehabilitation Act of 1965 gave impetus to the program and other centers were subsequently opened.

---

[30] G. Bowdon Hunt, "Foreword," in Vernon Fox, *A Handbook for Volunteers in Juvenile Court,* special issue of *Juvenile Justice,* February 1973.

Several states, for a variety of reasons, had also administratively and sometimes informally participated in various types of community-based corrections plans. In the North and West, forestry and conservation camps took prisoners into the rural areas. In the South, it was common practice for maintenance and domestic helpers to be provided to the governor, the state capitol building, and some state officials and county sheriffs, although sometimes the lines of propriety in these services were hazy. Consequently, in all sections of the country, administrative and informal policy frequently brought prisoners into contact with private citizens or the public. In 1961 the California Youth Authority began one of the best state-sponsored programs in the Community Treatment Project at the Northern Reception Center and Clinic at Sacramento.

The President's Commission on Law Enforcement and Administration of Justice was created in 1965 and published its major works in 1967, which served to make reform of the criminal justice system a major national goal. Pretrial diversion was recommended as follows:

> Bail projects should be undertaken at the state, county, and local levels to furnish judicial offices with sufficient information to permit the pretrial release without financial condition of all but that small portion of defendants who present a high risk of flight or dangerous acts prior to trial.[31]

> Each state should enact comprehensive bail reform legislation after the pattern set by the Federal Bail Reform Act of 1966.[32]

> Each community should establish procedures to enable and encourage police departments to release, in appropriate classes of cases, as many arrested persons as possible promptly after arrest upon issuance of a citation or summons requiring subsequent appearance.[33]

The President's Commission also recommended increased use of community facilities in corrections:

> Correctional authorities should develop more extensive community programs providing special, intensive treatment as an alternative to institutionalization for both juvenile and adult offenders.[34]

> Graduated release and furlough programs should be expanded. They should be accompanied by guidance and coordinated with community treatment services.[35]

---

[31] *The Challenge of Crime in a Free Society* (Washington, D.C.: The President's Commission on Law Enforcement and Administration of Justice, 1967), p. 132.

[32] Ibid., p. 132.

[33] Ibid., p. 133.

[34] Ibid., p. 171.

[35] Ibid., p. 177.

In addition, the Commission recommended more use of community resources in working with juveniles:

Efforts, both private and public, should be intensified to:

Involve young people in community activities.

Train and employ youth as subprofessional aides.

Establish Youth Services Bureaus to provide and coordinate programs for young people.

Increase involvement of religious institutions, private social agencies, fraternal groups, and other community organizations in youth programs.

Provide community residential centers.[36]

The Law Enforcement Assistance Act of 1965 provided the means for experiments with measures that might replace imprisonment. The Joint Commission for Correctional Manpower and Training, also on the basis of an Act of 1965, studied the problems of personnel in correctional programs. The 1967 report of the Commission mentioned above was instrumental in persuading the federal government to provide several hundred millions of dollars, part of which is spent on reforms in the prison system. Of the numerous programs in the various states, likewise financed by federal, state, and private funds, mention can be made of the far-reaching research done in California, where the Department of Corrections has for years been experimenting with various types and intensities of supervision and individual care in various groups of prisoners. The marked emphasis on probation and parole as measures replacing imprisonment makes it possible to treat offenders in an open community on a much larger scale than before. The work release program enables the delinquent to leave the institution and work in the free society. A similar, often parallel system releases prisoners (especially juvenile delinquents) for educational purposes. Another result is the recognized existence of stages between full institutionalization and full freedom. Under this heading come the halfway houses, pre-release centers, and various asylums for those given conditional releases. The United States has many such programs, based on a variety of legal foundations. The common denominator of all of these is that small groups of released prisoners are accommodated in homes from which they go to work or to school, always under some supervision and counseling. A pioneering effort was the foundation of four pre-release guidance centers for juvenile delinquents in New York, Chicago, Los Angeles, and Detroit by the Federal Bureau of Prisons in 1961. Congress expanded this program to adults in 1965.

---

[36] Ibid., p. 69.

Special efforts are made to prepare the society for the acceptance of ex-convicts who, rather than being rejected, should be assisted.[37]

Information from fifty states and the District of Columbia indicated that in February 1971, there were twenty-eight departments of correction with 4,143 adult inmates participating in community treatment programs designed to facilitate their transition from the institution to the communty.[38] Four of the twenty-eight programs received federal inmates, nine state programs were limited to males, one served only females, and eighteen served both sexes. Many different types and combinations of physical facilities were used in operating community programs. Only eight states reported programs operating out of noncorrectional facilities in the community without also operating work-study release out of jails and correctional institutions.

CONCLUSIONS

The community-based corrections system has become an integral and official part of American corrections. The police, courts, and corrections entities have been brought together in the community better than ever before. Up to a certain point, control agencies in the community, such as police, have become diagnostic units themselves, beginning with police discretion; agreement between police, court, and correctional workers on pretrial diversion and diversion from jail or bail; and similar types of informal processing that could not have occurred a few years ago.[39] Community-based corrections programs reduce the "social surgery" of removing a person from his social environment while attempting to help him adjust to it. They are considered to provide a more humane and economical way of dealing with people, substituting community integration or reintegration of the offender for the questionable hypothesis that people can be taught to live in society by being removed from it.

In discussing the provisions of the Prisoners' Rehabilitation Act of 1965, Myrl Alexander, then director of the United States Bureau of Prisons, replied to a hostile question about releasing convicted criminals back into the community through halfway houses and work release:

---

37 P. P. Lejins, "Modern Concepts of Imprisonment in the USA," in M. Busch and G. Edel, eds., *Education to Freedom by Deprivation of Freedom* (Neuwied, Netherlands: Herman Luchterhand Verlag, 1969), pp. 293–308.

38 Bertram S. Griggs and Gary R. McCune, "Community-Based Correctional Programs: A Survey and Analysis," *Federal Probation*, 36, No. 2 (June 1972), 7–13.

39 Eliot Freidson, "Disability as Social Deviance," in Marvin B. Sussman, ed., *Sociology and Rehabilitation* (Washington, D.C.: American Sociological Association, 1969), p. 92.

We insist these innovations prove themselves, and the test we put them to is whether they are a better way to protect the public.[40]

Many correctional administrators believe that the community-based programs are a better way to protect the public because they reduce the chance of institutionalization changing the value system of people confined there.

---

[40] Quoted by Robert Osterman, "Stone Walls Don't Make This Prison," in *Crime in America*, a *Newsbook* published by *The National Observer* (Silver Springs, Md.: Dow Jones & Co., 1966), p. 174.

Chapter 2

Neighborhood
and Area Projects

The most recent immediate forerunners of the modern American concept of community-based corrections programs are the neighborhood and area projects begun in Chicago in the early 1930s and the settlement houses that were established in 1887 in New York (the Neighborhood Guild) and in 1889 in Chicago (Hull House). It is appropriate that these movements be reviewed together because their objectives were essentially similar. It is apparent that the area projects and settlement houses have been working in the same area, though there have been different emphases, depending upon funding and leadership. Settlement houses began with a broad perspective designed to improve social conditions, while neighborhood projects began with a focus on delinquency prevention and control. By the 1930s, however, many settlement houses had focused their attention on individual potential delinquents and families, while many neighborhood projects had become more concerned with urban renewal and community improvement. Most settlement houses and neighborhood projects have recently viewed these two emphases as interrelated, however, and both have become concerned with the total problem of the effect of the community on producing or reducing delinquency.

Certainly, environmental conditions and deviant behavior are related. When crime and arrests are plotted on one map, welfare recipients plotted on another, and health problems plotted on still another, the configurations are similar, as Shaw and McKay have shown.[1] Crime and

---

[1] Clifford R. Shaw and Henry D. McKay, *Juvenile Delinquency and Urban Areas* (Chicago: University of Chicago Press, 1942 and 1969), pp. 90–107.

delinquency, then, emerge as only one index of social breakdown in a city. It's probably the most visible index, however, and it is closely related to the other indices and social problems in the community.[2]

The urban environment as it exists will inevitably produce ethnic and culture frictions. All the social and behavioral sciences, together with medicine and public health, must be included in assisting city planners. The preservation of the ethnic individuality, on the one hand, or the "melting pot" component of cultural assimilation, on the other, must be examined in the light of reduction of conflict.[3] The American concept of justice has become hopelessly confused by propaganda, sensationalism, political chicanery, inefficiency of police and court systems, emotionalism, civil rights problems, and other problems. City planners, including financiers, technicians, developers, transportation specialists, and other planners and experts, must re-examine the entire urban environment.

Neighborhood and area projects and the settlement houses had focused attention on these social problems. The effect of the environment on the individual determines whether behavior will be deviant or conforming or, for that matter, whether it will drift somewhere in between these two extremes. It is often difficult to work with extreme deviants, but there is no doubt that those drifting somewhere in between the extremes of deviance and conformity can be reached and helped.

SETTLEMENT HOUSES

Settlement houses were designed to revitalize the urban neighborhood as a "social settlement." [4] One of the significant early efforts was in 1884 when Samuel A. Barnett founded Toynbee Hall in the East End slum of London as a colony of Oxford and Cambridge graduates who identified with residents of the neighborhood. The neighborhood guild was founded in New York City in 1887. The first significant settlement house in the United States was Hull House, founded in 1889 by Jane Addams and Ellen Gates Starr, who rented a house built by Charles G. Hull at 800 South Halsted Street. Twelve large buildings were added, and eventually Hull House covered half a city block and operated a playground across the street and a large camp in the country. Many volunteers, both men

---

2 Ibid., pp. 43–89.

3 Fred Smith, *Man and His Urban Environment: A Manual of Specific Considerations for the Seventies and Beyond* (New York: The Ford Foundation, Man and His Urban Environment Project, 1972), p. 53.

4 Elmer Hubert Johnson, *Crime, Correction, and Society,* rev. ed. (Homewood, Ill.: Dorsey Press, 1968), p. 623.

Jane Addams.

Courtesy of Jane Addams'
Memorial Collection, Uni-
versity of Illinois at
Chicago.

and women, became residents of Hull House while they continued their
professions as lawyers, teachers, social workers, and business people. Hull
House became a laboratory for challenging the social problems of poverty,
labor, education, government, and many other areas. In January 1961,
the University of Illinois announced the building of a campus there.
Citizen protests were unsuccessful, and the trustees of Hull House sold
the fourteen buildings and adopted plans for decentralized operations in
other areas of the city. The original Hull House was preserved, however,
and was declared a national Historical Landmark in 1967, supervised by
a curator. The Jane Addams School of Social Work of the University of
Illinois has branches at Urbana-Champaign and Chicago Circle.

The primary goals of the settlement houses recently have been to
bring specific results of organized activity to the neighborhood—this is
exhibited in the tendency to work with underprivileged children rather
than focusing on developing community solidarity.[5] Traditional casework
and psychiatric approaches dealing with individuals or families have been
the primary approach in the area of delinquency prevention.

By the middle 1930s, urban renewal projects by WPA (Works Progress
Administration) provided jobs during the Great Depression that resulted
in concentrations of underprivileged people in public housing projects.
Many settlement houses were developed in direct connection with housing projects—for example, as with the Brewster Housing Project in Detroit
in 1939. These settlement houses were primarily walk-ins that provided

---

[5] Arthur Hillman, *Neighborhood Centers Today* (New York: National Federation
of Settlement and Neighborhood Centers, 1960), pp. 17–18.

recreation, counseling service, and other assistance to the youth in the neighborhood. They were not depicted as "delinquency control" programs, because that would have alienated the youth who needed to be reached. Rather, the emphasis was on recreational opportunities of all types; casework services were provided for individual problems as they arose.

Hull-House.

Courtesy of Jane Addams' Memorial Collection, University of Illinois at Chicago.

By the late 1930s, the objectives of many settlement houses and neighborhood projects were the same. There was some criticism of the settlement houses as compared with area projects because the focus of the settlement houses was not toward the indigenous community structure, but toward individuals and families.[6] Further, the settlement houses worked with the people who came to them, a fact that may have eliminated some serious cases who needed the service more. On the other hand, the area and neighborhood projects functioned without a physical setting, and therefore were out in the streets where the problems were, and had to work within the environment of the neighborhood. It is interesting to note in this context that the neighborhood and area projects were criticized by some traditional social workers because workers indigenous to the neighborhood were used who sometimes did not have the social

---

6 William Foote Whyte, "The Social Role of the Settlement House," *Applied Anthropology*, 1 (October–December 1941), 14–19.

20

work education, training, and casework competence thought to be desirable.[7] In some ways, then, the neighborhood and area projects and the settlement houses did complement each other while addressing the same objective with regard to delinquency prevention and control. It is interesting to note that the settlement house concept has become part of community-based corrections program as a neighborhood walk-in for youth or a type of halfway house.

CHICAGO AREA PROJECTS

The Chicago Area Projects were begun in 1932 by Clifford R. Shaw and his associates at the University of Chicago. They were primarily designed to test the hypothesis that community disorganization causes high crime rates, not to prevent or control delinquency. A series of studies beginning in 1929 had resulted in the conclusion that delinquency in the slum areas in the cities reflected the striving of youth in a social direction, rather than in an antisocial direction. Delinquency was seen to be the result of interactions with associates in a socially deprived setting where young people attempted to find status and satisfaction in their roles. If adults were indifferent or engaged in illegal activities themselves, it was believed that youth would accept delinquent behavior as a natural way to live. The Chicago Area Projects later attempted to mobilize the adults of the neighborhood to promote nondelinquent behavior and to work with youth in improving self-esteem, as well as to provide status for conforming roles, and to provide counseling by workers who were indigenous to the neighborhood and thus understood the social setting. The theory was that the local community should be an active agency in reducing its own delinquency and modifying personal relationships in gangs and among youth through the school, the church, the police, welfare agencies, and civic groups. Experiments in the control of delinquency along these lines were developed under the guidance of the sociologists from the University of Chicago and the Institute for Juvenile Research.[8] A primary principle involved in the projects was that persons

---

[7] See Solomon Kobrin, "The Chicago Area Project," in Norman Johnston, Leonard Savitz, and Marvin E. Wolfgang, eds., *The Sociology of Punishment and Correction,* 2d ed. (New York: Wiley & Sons, 1970), p. 581. Originally published as "The Chicago Area Project—A 25-year Assessment," *The Annals of the American Academy of Political and Social Sciences,* 322 (March 1959), 20–29.

[8] Ernest William Burgess, Joseph D. Lohman, and Clifford R. Shaw, "The Chicago Area Project," *National Probation Association Yearbook, 1937,* pp. 8–28. Also Clifford R. Shaw and Jesse A. Jacobs, "The Chicago Area Project," *Proceedings of the American Prison Association, 1939,* pp. 40–53. Also Shaw and McKay, *Juvenile Delinquency and Urban Areas,* pp. 442–46.

who reside in areas of high delinquency were encouraged to form organizations for the purpose of reducing their own delinquency rates. A basic hypothesis was that community disorganization causes high delinquency and crime rate, so organizing the community would help to reduce them by promoting reward for conforming behavior.

The projects were considered to be successful. By 1959, similar projects had been established in twelve Chicago neighborhoods under a central civic board called the Chicago Area Project and in a number of other cities under the Illinois Youth Commission.[9] These projects are continuing today.

THE CAMBRIDGE-SOMERVILLE YOUTH STUDY

The Cambridge-Somerville Youth Study was begun in 1935 under the leadership of Dr. Richard C. Cabot to study delinquency prevention and develop stable elements in children. The specific purpose of the Cambridge-Somerville Youth Study was to determine the processes by which persons become criminal and the application of the results in the practical situation to test their effectiveness. Cambridge and Somerville are industrialized and deteriorated areas in the metropolitan Boston Area. Two groups of 325 boys were carefully matched from a large group of referral from the Cambridge-Somerville area. The T-group or experimental group was provided sustained and friendly counseling, whether or not there was an acute problem. The C-group (control group) was provided no counseling. Although the original plan called for a ten-year study, there was considerable disruption because of World War II, resulting in fewer cases than had been planned because of the shortened time.

The treatment method was to provide personal advice and guidance through the service of paid visitors, both men and women, who knew the boys intimately, saw them frequently, and attempted to influence their conduct.

The results of the experiment are still under debate. It was apparent that the special work of the counselors was no more effective than the usual forces in the community in preventing boys from committing delinquent acts.[10] Subsequently, however, McCord and McCord re-exam-

---

9 Solomon Kobrin, "The Chicago Area Project—A 25-year Assessment," *Annals of the American Academy of Political and Social Science,* 322 (March 1959), 19–29.

10 Edwin Bowers and Helen Witmer, "The Cambridge-Somerville Study," in Johnston et al., *The Sociology of Punishment and Correction,* p. 599. Originally published as *An Experiment in the Prevention of Delinquency* (New York: Columbia University Press, 1951), pp. vii–xi, 320–38.

ined the more than 500 boys who participated in the study and found more optimistic later results.[11] Essentially, they pointed out that early counseling had better long-term results than were apparent earlier.

THE NEW YORK CITY YOUTH BOARD

The New York City Youth Board was established in 1947 by the Board of Estimated Resolution, primarily for the purpose of receiving funds from the State Division for Youth in planning and implementing youth services. The Youth Board was part of the Office of the Mayor and was mandated to analyze, coordinate, and develop policies for youth services and to implement youth programs. Originally created as a temporary agency, it is still in existence. The activity of this organization was highly energetic and very effective between 1947 and 1966. It was formulated somewhat in the same general pattern as the Chicago Area Projects, but the coverage in the city was broader. The New York State Youth Commission, which was established in 1945, helped other cities in New York State to offer similar youth services. The New York City Youth Board was well known for its "detached workers," who were generally college graduates indigenous to the neighborhood in which they worked. Subsequently, the Los Angeles County Probation Department and other cities have used the concept of detached workers. They dressed in the same type of clothes that the people in the neighborhood wore, whether leather jackets, T-shirts, jeans, shorts, or whatever attire would fit into the social setting. They knew the customs and social norms of the area. They provided counseling when possible, attempted to avoid problems when possible, and did whatever needed to be done, short of intervention and confrontation, to resolve problems, particularly on an individual basis.

On occasion, the detached workers were viewed by police as obstructing justice because they did not report impending "rumbles" between gangs or other troubles that might have permitted the police to provide preventive measures. Most detached workers considered that if they were to do this, their effectiveness in the neighborhood would be impaired or, more probably, eliminated.

The New York City Youth Board engaged in research and issued several important publications. It was also engaged in controversy on occasion, particularly regarding the use of the Glueck Delinquency Prediction Scales, which it found to be useful in the field, but which was attacked by many research sociologists as being defective in research methodology. The position of the New York City Youth Board and its

---

[11] William McCord and Joan McCord, *Origins of Crime: A New Evaluation of the Cambridge-Somerville Youth Study* (New York: Columbia University Press), p. 219.

detached workers, however, was that regardless of any methodological deficiencies, the scale worked in practice.

In 1966, the Youth Board was relegated to an advisory role and the Youth Services Agency was created, essentially as an operational agency. The Youth Board was retained as a policy-making body in theory, but its effectiveness was gone. Between 1966 and 1975, the Youth Board had no staff and served what some have called only political purposes, much as the United States Children's Bureau did after its functions were absorbed by the Juvenile Delinquency and Youth Development Administration in 1969. However, it continued to answer correspondence without an office. In 1975, Mayor Beame revitalized the Youth Board with the appointment of a new chairman and an unpaid staff of three members. With a two-year grant from the Department of Health, Education and Welfare, the Youth Board has identified 400 program sites in Bronx County, surveyed the needs of 900 youth, and is working closely with the United Neighborhood Houses, co-recipient of the grant. New staff has been paid from the grant and the Youth Board appears to be functioning again.

The Youth Services Agency continues operation, also. Administratively located in the City of New York's Human Resources Administration, it remains the operational arm of youth services in New York City. Good relationships now exist between the agencies serving youth in New York, according to reports, and the police, city agencies, Mobilization for Youth, and other agencies appear to be more cooperative than in the past.

THE PROVO EXPERIMENT

The Provo Experiment in Delinquency Rehabilitation in Provo, Utah, was one of the first efforts to provide a community alternative to incarceration for persistent delinquent offenders.[12] The Provo Experiment was initiated in 1959, funded by the Ford Foundation, to use group techniques in which delinquents were contributors and recipients in group decisions involving sociological factors. The assumptions were (1) that delinquent behavior is primarily a group phenomenon that needed an approach to treatment different from those that consider the delinquent to be "sick" or "misguided," (2) that effective rehabilitation must view the delinquent as a participant in a delinquent social system, and (3) that delinquents must be forced to deal with conflicts imposed on them by the demands of conventional and delinquent social systems, the resolu-

---

12 LaMar T. Empey and Maynard L. Erickson, *The Provo Experiment: Evaluation of Community Control of Delinquency* (Lexington, Mass.: Lexington Books, 1972), p. 321.

tion of which must involve community decision. The delinquent peer group was used as a means of perpetrating the norms and imposing the sanctions of the conventional system. Boys assigned to the Provo program lived at home and spent only part of each day at the program center. No more than twenty boys were assigned to the program at any given time. The two phases of the program were (1) an intensive group program that used work and delinquent peer-group pressure as the principal instruments of change, and (2) efforts to maintain reference-group support for each boy in community action and to find employment. The only rules were daily attendance at the center and hard work on the job. Release usually occurred four to seven months after beginning. Though there was little evidence that the Provo Experiment was superior to regular probation, there was evidence that there were fewer arrests of boys while they were in the program and during the post-release supervision. In any case, the community program was found to be at least as effective as incarceration and, certainly, more humanitarian and less costly. It was considered to be unfortunate that the state of Utah did not pick it up after the five-year funding by the Ford Foundation had expired.

MOBILIZATION FOR YOUTH

The Mobilization for Youth Project in New York City's Lower East Side was financed by a large grant from the federal government under the Juvenile Delinquency Prevention and Control Act of 1961 and by some private foundation funds. It was based on opportunity theory as presented in Cloward and Ohlin's book, *Delinquency and Opportunity: A Theory of Delinquent Gangs* (Glencoe Press, 1960), for which the authors were honored by Mobilization for Youth in 1966.[13] The Mobilization for Youth Project began operations in 1962. It is a large operation that involves a broad educational program, including arts and music, individual counseling, neighborhood service centers, antipoverty programs, and many other varied approaches to mobilization of resources for the prevention and control of delinquency in that area.

NEIGHBORHOOD SERVICE CENTERS

Neighborhood service centers are walk-ins, store fronts, or other offices in vacant building in the neighborhoods staffed by people who can provide information to the residents of the neighborhood regarding avail-

---

[13] "Cloward, Ohlin Honored for JD-Opportunity Study," *MYF News Bulletin*, 4, No. 3 (Winter 1966), 4. Mobilization for Youth, Inc., is now headquartered at 271 East Fourth Street, but the old office at 213 East Second Street is still operative.

able services and the procedures to obtain them. Typical services are assisting people in finding needed legal help, working out problems with the welfare department, referrals to centralized employment services, helping with school problems, and many other services. A neighborhood service center is not aimed at the offender, but focuses on the entire neighborhood. Many police departments, such as that in Baltimore, have maintained neighborhood service centers and walk-ins in various areas of high delinquency.

OTHER PROGRAMS

There are similar programs elsewhere throughout the country. Although this chapter has focused on the Chicago Area Projects, New York City Youth Board, and other well-known programs, there are similar programs in Minneapolis, Chicago, Detroit, Los Angeles, San Francisco, and many other American cities. Space does not permit a detailed description of each, but the general pattern can be seen from those programs discussed here.

Model Cities (developed from Title I of the Demonstration Cities and Metropolitan Development Act of 1966) has been one of the largest funding agencies for these special urban programs. By 1971, there were 147 such programs throughout the country funded by Model Cities,[14] a program under the administration of the United States Department of Housing and Urban Development (HUD). The primary goal of this program is to provide social, economic, and physical problems in selected impoverished areas. The intention is to demonstrate in a few broadly representative cities how blighted neighborhoods can be rejuvenated, physically and in lifestyle, through the pooled efforts of everyone concerned.

Several cities have developed neighborhood programs and citywide programs with neighborhood components as a result of the civil rights disturbances in the late 1960s. New Detroit, Inc., was organized after the civil disorders of 1967 to work with problems of disadvantaged and alienated people of the city. Besides general programs to improve neighborhood conditions and police-community relationships, youth programs and crime prevention programs have worked with experimental drug programs in high schools in Detroit. There is a New Detroit advocacy for widespread improvement of youth services delivery. New Detroit, Inc., has been considered to be quite successful as a citywide, community-based coordinating and service agency.

The greater St. Louis Alliance for Shaping a Safer Community is a

---

14 *Attorney General's First Annual Report: Federal Law Enforcement and Criminal Justice Activities* (Washington, D.C.: United States Department of Justice, 1972), p. 406.

citizen volunteer organization with national, state, and local alignments. Although its primary purpose is to stimulate dialogue and action among citizens and public officials, it does aid development of improved community-based prevention efforts and community-based resource assistance for ex-offenders and victims of crime. Stimulating employment is essential.[15]

In 1969, community leaders in Hartford, Connecticut, decided that nothing would be done to improve the city's racial and crime problems unless citizens coordinated their efforts and focused on developing community programs in pertinent areas. Consequently, the Hartford Criminal and Social Justice Coordinating Committee was established; it works with the Greater Hartford Community Council and the Chamber of Commerce. Having mobilized generally, special programs were then initiated. A grant was obtained from the Ford Foundation for $58,000 for the first year, and this, added to private contributions, made possible the establishment of the Hartford Institute of Criminal and Social Justice. Subsequently, grants have been received from several private foundations; and there has been a grant for a methadone maintenance program from the National Institute of Mental Health, grants from Law Enforcement Assistance Administration (LEAA), and others. The program has been considered to be most successful.

Arbitration centers appear to be helpful diversions from courts in the cases of neighborhood disputes. The Philadelphia Settlement Center has an administrative staff of five persons and uses the services of approximately forty-five professional arbitrators.[16] This program operated under a grant from the Ford Foundations and has subsequently received LEAA funds.

Settlement of disputes within and between families in the neighborhood is a service traditionally provided by police in their "domestic disturbance" category. Crisis units have been used often when police have been called to family disturbances, particularly when these complaints are frequent and from the same families and neighborhoods. One problem is that many police officers do not have the expertise of a family counselor or caseworker and have to handle such disturbances as best they can. The Family Crisis Intervention Unit (FCIU) in New York City was funded by a private foundation and became very successful, functioning as a diversion program in response to inter- and intrafamily violence. A squad of specially selected officers were provided with special training. During the twenty-two month duration of the project, many

---

15 *The Community & Criminal Justice: A Guide for Organizing Action* (Washington, D.C.: Law Enforcement Assistance Administration, 1973).,

16 B. Herbert, *Report on the Program of the Philadelphia Center for Disputes Center* (mimeographed), 1971.

families were referred to family counseling programs and arrests were substantially reduced. Unfortunately, the program expired when the grant expired. Oakland, California, began a similar Family Crisis Intervention Program (FCIP) and the preliminary assessment shows a slight improvement over the New York experience, but the results are not yet clear. The Oakland Program has gone beyond the experimental stage and has been expanded and improved.

CONCLUSIONS

The early massive efforts in community-based corrections were in settlement houses, neighborhood and area projects, and in prisoners' aid societies (the latter will be discussed at greater length in Chapter 11). The large number of programs could not be discussed here, but we have presented a few examples so that patterns will be clear. Certainly, the success or failure of such efforts are dependent upon the people in leadership and the people participating from the community. Any action program in the community needs to be motivated by (1) authority; (2) emotional contagion through news stories, campaigns, advertising, and personal contacts with key individuals; (3) reward of some type through which the community can experience tangible gain; and (4) tapping existing motivation on which to build.[17]

Settlement houses and area projects were the immediate forerunners of modern community-based corrections programs. Essentially, they demonstrated that, under the right circumstances, the community has a vested interest in itself and its inhabitants, including some responsibility for those whose behavior has deviated into crime and delinquency.

---

[17] Paul H. Bowman, Robert F. DeHaan, John K. Kough, and Gordon P. Liddle, *Mobilizing Community Resources for Youth: Identification and Treatment of Maladjusted, Delinquent, and Gifted Children* (Chicago: University of Chicago Press, 1956), pp. 113–14.

Chapter 3

Diversion
from the Criminal Justice System:
Pretrial Intervention

Pretrial and pre-hearing diversion programs for alleged adult offenders and juvenile delinquents are in compliance with recent trends toward greater use of community-based corrections programs and the attempt to avoid labeling people as criminals and delinquents. It is well known that the earlier a person is arrested and placed in the criminal justice system, the longer he or she stays in it and the more frequently offenses are repeated. Although this may be a function of selection, it is also a function of conditioning. Consequently, several training schools have been closed because of the judgment that they were doing more damage than good (e.g., the Kentucky Village at Ormsby in 1968 and Dr. Jerome Miller's training schools in Massachusetts in 1971). Further, there has been a movement toward closing adult institutions; the Wisconsin State Reformatory at Green Bay was planned to be closed; the California State Prisons at San Quentin and Folsom will be closed as soon as possible. Also, the closing of the mammoth State Prison of Southern Michigan at Jackson was announced in January 1973. With the economic recession in the mid-1970s and high unemployment, however, Michigan set a new record for its number of prisoners and other states had similar experiences. Therefore, these closings have been delayed indefinitely. To close all institutions, of course, would be unrealistic, because there exist dangerous offenders who have developed beyond the treatment resources society has available in its criminal justice system; some have to be held for the protection of society. There is general agreement, however, that the mass of institutions now in existence is more than society needs and has a deleterious effect on the many property and victimless offenders whose problems have not progressed beyond society's treatment resources.

The earliest form of pretrial diversion programs was "benefit of clergy." In the early days of the Christian church, clergy and laity emerged and were recognized by privileges and immunities granted by Constantine I (d. 337 A.D.). This was later extended and codified in the sixteenth book of the Theodosian Code in 438 A.D. The clergy was exempted from the jurisdiction of certain civil courts in 1295. The English Parliament included the clergy with the baronage or aristocracy. The power of the clergy from the thirteenth century down to the Reformation was based on the claim of Pope Innocent III that clergymen, as rulers over spiritual things, were much superior to temporal rulers. In the twelfth century, King Henry II was compelled to grant immunity from trial or punishment to all clergy accused of capital offenses. On producing letters of ordination, accused clergy were turned over to the local bishop, who never inflicted the death penalty and most frequently invoked benefit of clergy. In 1576, the practice of handing convicted clergy or laymen over to the bishop was abolished and imprisonment for one year was substituted. In 1692, benefit of clergy was extended to women, and in 1707, to all religious persons whether they could read or not. It was abolished in England in 1827. It was adopted in the American colonies by judicial practice, but abolished soon after the American Revolution, though it persisted in the Carolinas until the mid-nineteenth century.

Diversion of persons from the criminal justice system has been common in the United States for a long time. Generally, it has been part of the discretionary action of the police and prosecutors, when they did not consider a case worth following through to the criminal justice system. Screening out of less serious cases has always occurred, but it has become more widespread and publicly recognized in recent years. A primary problem has been that laws have been made by a small segment of society and applied to other segments and have placed overly restrictive boundaries on some behavior. The crisis of overcriminalization has accompanied the crisis of overcontrol, and to conceal injustices inherent in such a situation reveals a basic intolerance of diversity.[1]

Pretrial and pre-hearing diversion programs are designed to avoid the need to convict an alleged offender or reach an adjudication of delinquency in the case of a juvenile. The recommendations of the National Advisory Commission on Criminal Justice Standards and Goals, released in January 1973, include a recommendation on pretrial intervention programs as follows:

---

[1] *Diversion from the Criminal Justice System* (Rockville, Md.: Center for Studies of Crime and Delinquency, NIMH, 1971), p. 26.

The Commission recommends that community based, pretrial intervention programs offering manpower and related supportive services be established in all court jurisdictions. Such programs should be based on an arrangement between prosecutors or courts and offenders, and both should decide admission criteria and program goals. Intervention efforts should incorporate a flexible continuance period of at least 90 days, during which the individual would participate in a tailored job training program. Satisfactory performance in that training program would result in job placement and dismissal of charges, with arrest records maintained only for official purposes and not for dissemination.

Other program elements should include a wide range of community services to deal with any major needs of the participant. Legal, medical, housing, counseling, or emergency financial support should be readily available. In addition, ex-offenders should be trained to work with participants in this program and court personnel should be well informed about the purpose and methods of pretrial intervention.[2]

Pretrial diversion is an appropriate concern of community-based corrections programs because it is the correctional worker who provides the follow-up programs and supervision.

TRADITIONAL COMMUNITY PRETRIAL DIVERSION

There have been several types of pretrial diversion techniques traditionally practiced in the community. The family, school, welfare departments, police, and juvenile courts have practiced diversionary tactics for juveniles since their beginnings. Police and prosecutors have also practiced discretion regarding processing of adults. It has long been recognized that not everyone who transgresses or violates the law needs the full impact of its sanctions.

School Diversion Programs

Potential delinquents tend to appear in school as behavior problems that eventually develop into truancy.[3] Unfortunately, many schools suspend behavior problems, which is getting rid of the problem rather than solving it. Kvaraceus has suggested that special programs be developed

2 *Community Crime Prevention* (Washington, D.C.: National Advisory Commission on Criminal Justice Standards and Goals, 1973), pp. 127–28.

3 Ruth Shonle Cavan, *Juvenile Delinquency: Development, Treatment, Control*, 2nd ed. (Philadelphia: Lippincott, 1969), pp. 286–305.

for problem children in school to control the development of delinquent behavior.[4]

There are several programs in public school systems, such as St. Petersburg, Florida, and Phoenix, Arizona, where broad use of social work and other clinical assistance is made in what was originally the traditional visiting teacher program. Social workers in the schools can identify students with problems and those who are failing and about to drop out. Counseling, assistance in finding employment after school, and other services by the school personnel have resulted in reduction of referrals to juvenile court.

The United States Office of Education has been working for a number of years on models for implementing the features and components of meaningful curriculum, involvement of parents in language programs for infants and children, and other approaches aimed eventually at preventing delinquent behavior. There are Model I (school-based) programs in Los Angeles, California; Atlanta, Georgia; Hackensack, New Jersey; Pontiac, Michigan; Jefferson City, Colorado; and Mesa, Arizona. The Model II programs (employer-based) are about to be opened in Oakland, California, and New York City. Model III programs (home/community-based) are still in feasibility study stages being developed by the Educational Development Center in Newton, Massachusetts. The use of school facilities for community programs can be found in many parts of the United States. Several schools function on a twelve-month basis. Many schools open their facilities for community functions without raising prohibitions about the facilities being used for nonschool programs.

Protective Services

Protective services are child welfare services primarily designed to supervise and care for dependent and neglected children and protect abused and beaten children.[5] It has been frequently stated among social workers in child welfare work that the difference between a dependent child and a delinquent child is about ten years! The meaning is obvious. The dependent child has begun life under socially and economically handicapped circumstances and will develop behavior problems if he or she is not cared for and supervised adequately. Nationally, the average age of dependent children in child welfare programs and juvenile courts

---

4 William C. Kvaraceus and associates, *Delinquent Behavior: Culture and the Individual* (Washington, D.C.: National Education Association of the United States, 1959), pp. 62–75.

5 *CWLA Standards for Child Protective Service*, rev. (New York: Child Welfare League of America, 1973).

is about 4 or 5; but the range is from newborn infants abandoned by parents to teenage adolescents. The average age for delinquent children is approximately ten years higher; the average girl who is sent to the state training schools is about 14½ and the average boy is about 16 years of age.

Social workers in protective services frequently provide pre-hearing diversion from the juvenile justice system; child welfare workers often fail to refer children to juvenile court for delinquency hearings as a consequence of acts that could be adjudicated to be delinquent.

Voluntary Police Supervision

Police have developed juvenile aid bureaus in all the major departments.[6] Some have developed athletic programs, such as New York's PAL (Police Athletic League), but many administrators have questioned whether this is a legitimate police function. Nevertheless, many large aid bureaus have been developed to identify and supervise potential delinquents.

One of the largest and most successful such operations is the Youth Aid Bureau in Montgomery, Alabama, where 106 of a total 467 sworn officers are assigned to work with juveniles. Nationally, police departments provide voluntary supervision to more youth than are supervised in the juvenile courts. In many cities, police have offices in the school buildings and serve, in uniform, as counselors. Most have been able to develop excellent relationships with the youth, teachers, and other school personnel.

Juvenile Court

The first juvenile court was established in Chicago in 1899 so that juvenile offenders could be treated differently from adult offenders. Adults in court are subjected to an adversary proceeding with a prosecution and defense; the juvenile court was conceived as one in equity or chancery in which the proceedings would be more informal and benign—more "in the interests of the child" than the "protection of society," although there is opportunity for certifying serious juvenile offenders to adult courts. In the setting of the philosophy and procedure of the juvenile court as originally intended, probably more than half of the juveniles referred to juvenile court are never adjudicated. Rather, they are placed

---

[6] John P. Kenney and Dan G. Pursuit, *Police Work with Juveniles and the Administration of Juvenile Justice*, 4th ed. (Springfield, Ill.: Charles C. Thomas, 1970).

under informal supervision by court personnel.[7] This type of diversion from the criminal justice system still prevails in juvenile court, even though recent Supreme Court decisions (*Kent*, 1966; *Gault*, 1967; *Winship*, 1970; *McKiever*, 1971) have tended to bring counsel into the procedures so that it might, in some cases, approach adversary procedure. Nevertheless, the basic principle of *parens patriae*, traditional in the juvenile court, still prevails and the juvenile court maintains the responsibility of the state for the welfare of its children. As a result, both in delinquency and dependency, many children are still supervised unofficially and without the delinquency label.

PATTERNS OF PRETRIAL INTERVENTION

Pretrial intervention programs (PTI) represent one type of diversion strategy. PTI diverts the accused offender, typically at the time of arraignment, into a short-term community-based program with supervision and supportive services. Upon successful completion of the program, the participant receives a dismissal of criminal charges. Rovner-Piecznik's evaluation report on pretrial intervention research examines studies of fifteen demonstration programs offering prosecution alternatives to selected criminal defendants.[8]

A directory published in May 1974 by the National Pretrial Intervention Service Center of the American Bar Association identified fifty-seven pretrial intervention programs in California, Colorado, Connecticut, District of Columbia, Florida, Georgia, Hawaii, Illinois, Maryland, Massachusetts, Michigan, Minnesota, Missouri, New Jersey, New York, Ohio, Oregon, Pennsylvania, South Carolina, Tennessee, Texas, the Virgin Islands, and Washington. There were at least three programs in California, Florida, Massachusetts, Michigan, Minnesota, Missouri, and New York.[9] These PTIs are patterned after the United States Department of Labor pretrial intervention manpower services model. There are others

---

[7] Paul H. Hahn, *The Juvenile Offender and the Law* (Cincinnati: W. H. Anderson, 1971), particularly Chapter 19—"The Juvenile Court: Philosophy and Procedures," pp. 266–305. See also Samuel M. Davis, *Rights of Juveniles: The Juvenile Justice System* (New York: Clark Boardman Co., 1974).

[8] Roberta Rovner-Piecznik, *Pretrial Intervention Strategies—An Evaluation of Policy-Related Research and Policymaker Perceptions* (Washington, D.C.: American Bar Association, 1974).

[9] *Source Book in Pretrial Criminal Justice Intervention Techniques and Action Programs* (Washington, D.C.: National Pretrial Intervention Service Center of the American Bar Association Commission on Correctional Facilities and Services, 1974), pp. 1–11.

that vary from this pattern. The United States Department of Labor has financed most of these programs for a period of about eighteen months under the Manpower Development and Training Act of 1962, as amended. Two of the early ones were Project Crossroads in Washington, D.C., administered by the Administrative Office of the Superior Court of the District of Columbia, and the Manhattan Court Employment Project in New York City, administered by the Vera Institute of Justice, which had previously carried out the Manhattan Bail Project. The early results of this program can be seen in one of the first projects, in which 753 young first offenders were brought into the project. Charges were dropped for 468 who completed the program successfully, and 285 offenders were returned to face prosecution because of unsatisfactory performance.[10] The recidivism rate based on a fifteen-month follow-up was 14 percent lower for the project participants than for a control group of first offenders.

The programs include counseling and personal assistance through a community worker who is responsible for the enrollee during his or her stay in the program and also for submitting evaluation reports on performance to the appropriate court. Job placement officers arrange employment interviews for the participants until a suitable job is found. Provisions are made for individual tutoring and specialized programs, such as preparation for high school equivalency examination, remedial reading, and job-test coaching.

The Cook County Boys Court handles over 20,000 defendants between 17 and 21 years of age every year. It follows a pattern of disposition leniency that includes frequent use of extralegal devices, such as the stricken without leave (SOL) policy, which entails a dismissal of current charges. The prosecution, however, is permitted to refile within 120 days, but investigation and counseling can occur. This disposition has been found to be particularly successful in burglary and theft cases, in which the defendant frequently offers restitution. Another extralegal device is that of "good behavior," which means that conviction is deferred and the defendant is released with a general admonition. Finally, there is a policy of court supervision without a conviction. This generally extends for a period of one year. Such informal dispositions have been employed by the Boys Court for more than twenty years.

Nimmer differentiates between referral and supervision in his discussion of diversion, with referral meaning pretrial diversion and supervision meaning post-conviction supervision in other than the traditional and

---

[10] *Manpower Administration* (Washington, D.C.: United States Department of Labor, 1972).

official probation status.[11] The three patterns of pretrial intervention, then, are *traditional processing, informal referral without trial,* and *post-conviction informal supervision* in a kind of deferred sentencing pattern.

PROBATION WITHOUT ADJUDICATION AND DEFERRED PROSECUTION PROGRAMS

There are several types of pretrial intervention for adult offenders, both alleged misdemeanants and felons. *Accelerated rehabilitative disposition* (ARD) is the term preferred in Pennsylvania. This type of intervention bypasses the trial procedure; the judge, defendant, district attorney, and defense lawyer meet around a small conference table. There is no interest in punishment nor even in determining guilt. Rather, the concern is to save the defendant from the criminal justice system. In 1971 and 1972, the total offenses for which ARD were used were as follows:

Offense	Percentage
Narcotic Drug Laws	28.0%
All Other Offenses	21.9
Minor Assault	13.7
Burglary	9.6
Larceny (except auto)	8.3
Auto Larceny	7.6
Driving While Intoxicated	6.0
Weapons Offenses	4.9

The program has been so successful that the Supreme Court of Pennsylvania on May 24, 1972, adopted Criminal Procedure Rules 175 to 185, which provide the procedures for an accelerated rehabilitative disposition within the court system.

Florida uses the concept of *probation without adjudication,* which uses some of the same procedures. The number of alleged felons on probation without adjudication in Florida in 1973 was around 1,200— these individuals had faced felony and misdemeanor charges, generally driving while intoxicated.

The United States Courts and several others (such as Genesee County, Michigan) use the concept of *deferred prosecution.* The federal courts

---

[11] Raymond T. Nimmer, *Diversion: The Search for Alternative Forms of Prosecution* (Chicago: American Bar Foundation, 1974), p. 33.

have been using it since 1946 for handling youthful offenders through the United States District Attorney's Offices. Genesee County began it as a function of the prosecuting attorney's office in November 1965, utilizing volunteer citizens of social work and related professional backgrounds for purposes of supervision.[12]

Deferred prosecution plans provide alternatives to prosecution in criminal courts and limit the accused citizen's involvement in the criminal justice system. They thereby improve the process of rehabilitation and reduce the caseload of the prosecutor and the court. Supporting prosecution and defenders' services programs (1) improve management of prosecutors' offices, (2) improve training of prosecutors and assistants, (3) provide assistance to prosecutors' offices in high crime areas with heavy caseloads, (4) provide centralized appellate services, and (5) provide both adult and juvenile indigent criminal defendants with full and adequate legal services.[13]

In Boston, the pretrial diversion project has been diverting people from the criminal justice system since 1971.[14] The Court Resource Project (TCRP) was originally funded by the Office of Manpower Administration, but is now funded by LEAA (Law Enforcement Assistance Administration). It operates thirteen district courts in three counties. TCRP screeners review daily arraignments for defendants between 17 and 22 years of age who have committed misdemeanors or felonies such as breaking and entering. If the decision is to divert, a fourteen-day continuance is requested, during which time the prospective client meets his or her counselor and career developer to plan school and job placement. If it is approved, a ninety-day continuance is requested. During a three-year period, 1,800 clients were screened, 1,000 were accepted into the program, and the re-arrest rate was only 8 percent. The average cost of TCRP supervision is $1,000 as compared with an incarceration cost in Massachusetts of $12,000 per year.

Diversion of some offenders from the criminal justice system appears to be predicated on the increasing recognition of deficiencies in the criminal justice system that aggravate problems rather than ameliorating

---

12 Robert F. Leonard, "Deferred Prosecution Program," *Source Book in Pretrial Criminal Justice Intervention Techniques and Action Programs* (Washington, D.C.: National Pretrial Intervention Service Center of the American Bar Association Commission on Correctional Facilities and Services, May 1974), pp. 43–45. Originally published in *The Prosecutor: Journal of the National District Attorneys Association,* July–August 1973 issue.

13 Robert C. Trojanowicz, John M. Trojanowicz, and Forrest M. Moss, *Community Based Crime Prevention* (Pacific Palisades, Cal.: Goodyear, 1975), pp. 110–11.

14 "Boston Closely Guides Diverted Offenders," *Target* (newsletter of innovative projects funded by the Law Enforcement Assistance Administration), 4, No. 5 (May 1975), 6.

them; an awareness that many offenders are products of their environment in the community; and a greater sophistication concerning social
and political factors in the citizenry.[15]

Consideration for pretrial intervention generally involves a series of
considerations for eligibility. Most frequently, misdemeanors or less serious felonies are considered. Pretrial intervention has to be voluntary on
the part of the alleged offender with the consent of the judge and prosecutor. The offender must waive his right to speedy trial. Generally, no
prior adult criminal record, except minor traffic offenses, and no significant juvenile record are allowed. The alleged offender must agree to meet
the mimimum residence requirements for the pretrial intervention program, which may range from three to twelve months. The alleged offender must be willing to obey conditions and actively participate in
treatment programs. The consent of the victim is important.

Reasons for rejection include inability to contact the alleged offender
or his or her declining to be a part of the program. Serious prior behavior
or other charges pending might also reduce the possibility for participation in the program. If the police object strongly or if there are objections
from the victim, the judge, or the prosecutor, pretrial intervention is not
feasible. If a serious offense is involved, the pretrial intervention program
is probably not appropriate. Sources of referral of offenders generally
come from the jail, the court docket, defense counsel, and sometimes the
police, security officers, prosecutor, judge, and other well-intentioned citizens. Table 3-1 provides a summary of guidelines for pretrial intervention.

The procedure generally follows this order: (1) referral, (2) personal
interview, (3) investigation, (4) approval of the judge, (5) prosecuting
attorney's consent, (6) determination of period of participation, (7) first
recommendation to prosecuting attorney, (8) exit interview for successful
termination, and (9) complete follow-up.

EVALUATION OF PRETRIAL DIVERSION

Diversion has been viewed as an outgrowth of a fragmented justice
system that has been neither completely just nor efficient, increasing demands of the citizenry in the affairs of government, and recognition that
the community is an appropriate base for many justice operations. Continued use of diversion will result in changes in the justice system that

15 Robert M. Carter, "The Diversion of Offenders," in Gary R. Perlstein and Thomas
R. Phelps, eds., *Alternatives to Prison: Community-Based Corrections* (Pacific Palisades,
Cal.: Goodyear, 1975), pp. 16–25. Originally published in *Federal Probation*, 36, No. 4
(December 1972), 31–36.

Table 3-1

Sample Guidelines for Pretrial Intervention

A. TO BE ELIGIBLE FOR CONSIDERATION
1. Select third degree felony(ies) or a misdemeanor.
2. Eighteen years or older.
3. Consent of judge of initial appearance hearing.
4. Voluntary.
5. Waive right to speedy trial.
6. Agreeable to meet residence requirement of program for six months.
7. No prior adult criminal record (excluding minor traffic offenses).
8. No significant juvenile record.
9. Willing to obey conditions and actively participate in treatment programs.
10. Consent of any victim(s) (no contact by defendant).
11. Consent of state attorney.
12. Consent of pretrial intervention administrator.

B. REASONS FOR REJECTION
1. Unable to contact.
2. Declines program.
3. Other charges (prior record, retainer).
4. Significant emotional/behavioral problems.
5. Strong police objections.
6. Victim objects.
7. Program administrator objects.
8. Judge rejects.
9. State attorney rejects.
10. Defendent pleaded guilty.
11. Bench warrant outstanding.
12. Defendant's charges dismissed.
13. Another program.
14. Type of offense.
15. Unwilling to stay in area.
16. Not able to stay in area long enough to complete program.
17. Co-defendant is not acceptable.

C. SOURCE OF REFERRAL
1. Commitment sheet (jail).
2. Court docket.
3. Attorney (private or public defender).
4. Police.

5. Security (store, school, etc.).
6. Self.
7. Other well-intentioned citizens.
8. Judge.
9. State's attorney.

D. SUGGESTED PROCEDURE
   1. Referral, consider attorney contact.
   2. Personal interview:
      a. explanation of program
      b. brochure
   3. Investigation.
   4. Approval of judge.
   5. SAO (state attorney's office) consent with use of contract:
      a. PTI consent
      b. defendant consent
      c. effective date of entry
   6. Period of participation.
   7. First recommendation to SAO:
      a. return to trial
      b. successful termination
      c. continue for 90 days
   8. Second recommendation to SAO:
      a. successful termination
      b. unsuccessful termination
   9. Exit interview for successful terminations.
   10. Complete follow-up questionnaire.

E. TYPE OF SERVICES EACH CLIENT COULD RECEIVE
   1. Client orientation.
   2. Vocational guidance/testing.
   3. House placement.
   4. Individual counseling.
   5. Group counseling.
   6. Educational counseling.
   7. Educational placement.
   8. Drug counseling.
   9. Alcohol counseling.
   10. Medical referral.
   11. Psychological evaluation.
   12. Psychotherapy.

This is a standard outline used in several jurisdictions—provided for the purpose by the Florida Parole and Probation Commission.

may range from administrative reorganization and modifications in policy and procedure to major changes in the populations served by various components of the justice system. New bureaus or divisions of community service would require new roles for some personnel and realignment of the focus of correctional agencies.

As has been mentioned, the deferred prosecution diversion program in Genesee County, Michigan, has been in existence since 1965. Called the Citizens Probation Authority, it came about as a response to the desire to prevent stigmatization of nonviolent first offenders not yet committed to criminal careers.

In 1975, the Department of Justice announced plans to expand pretrial diversion projects.[16] Pretrial diversion supported by the Department of Labor keeps people working or in vocational training, rather than incarceration. Pretrial diversion in the Northern District of Illinois has resulted in significant savings, with no increase in federal crime in that district. The positive results convinced the Department of Justice to allocate $165,000 for six months in 1975 to expand pretrial diversion to eight additional United States Judicial Circuits, including Minnesota, Northern Texas, Washington, D.C., the southern and eastern districts of New York, North Dakota, Western Tennessee, and Oregon. It was stipulated that offenders would be diverted from the court system before trial and put on probation for a maximum of twelve months, after which the prosecutor would formally drop the charges and the alleged crime would be stricken from the record. After an undecided period of time, the record of participation in the diversion program would also be stricken. Prosecutors would have the option in picking defendants eligible for the program. Those ineligible would be narcotics addicts, offenders with two or more past felony convictions, public officials who had violated trusts, and persons charged with offenses relating to national security. The supervision had to be by federal probation offices, metropolitan correctional centers operated by the United States Bureau of Prisons, local social service agencies, and church groups. If the offender failed to complete the program, the prosecutor had the option of proceeding with prosecution.

The success of diversion projects is dependent upon coordination between social service and criminal justice agencies.[17] Lack of understanding of objectives and complementary services and their coordination leaves the agencies confused and the diverted offender unserved.

---

16 *Criminal Justice Newsletter,* 6, No. 9 (April 1975), 6.

17 S. Anthony McCann, *Local Alternatives to Arrest, Incarceration, and Adjudication* (Washington, D.C.: National Associations of Counties, Criminal Justice Project, 1975).

In the last few years diversionary programs have begun to gain acceptance in the criminal justice system.[18] Criminal offenders who do not display a "continuing pattern of antisocial behavior" are not prosecuted if they successfully complete a period of probation and counseling. Like juveniles who receive informal dispositions, adult offenders who submit to pretrial probation lose many of the protections they have traditionally enjoyed under our present system of criminal justice, such as the constitutional guarantees of the right to trial before a jury, together with confrontation, cross-examination, and other "due process" rights. These rights are waived with the admission of guilt and acceptance of pretrial diversion. The potential for abuse by placing a person under supervision without determining legal guilt is hidden beneath the "rehabilitative jargon" used to describe diversionary programs.

Some have viewed deferred prosecution as coercion in disguise.[19] The Citizens Probation Authority takes the position that participation involves a totally voluntary compliance on the part of the client in a mutually agreed-upon cooperative effort.[20] On the other hand, the National Advisory Commission on Criminal Justice Standards and Goals fears that sometimes diversionary projects use the threat or possibility of conviction to encourage an accused person to agree to supervision.

Many experts in the field of criminal justice and law believe that pretrial diversion programs should be applauded.[21] At any rate, problems of speedy trial, due process, and equal protection are all involved in pretrial intervention. Certainly, the procedural safeguards surrounding termination of unsuccessful participants and the requirements of a plea of guilty for participation and the right of counsel are all important.

As plea bargaining and trials become displaced by less formal diversionary procedures, the dollar cost of the criminal justice system may decrease. On the other hand, some writers ask the system and the taxpayers alike to consider whether, in the long run, pretrial diversion is really a bargain.[22]

---

[18] R. W. Balch, "Deferred Prosecution: The Juvenilization of the Criminal Justice System," *Federal Probation*, 38, No. 2 (June 1974), 46–50.

[19] *A Prosecutor's Manual on Screening and Diversionary Programs* (Chicago: National District Attorneys Association, undated), p. 129.

[20] *Working Paper on "Courts,"* National Conference on Criminal Justice, January 23–26, 1973, p. 19.

[21] Daniel L. Skoler, "Protecting the Rights of Defendants in Pretrial Intervention Programs," *Criminal Law Bulletin*, 10, No. 6 (1974), 473–92.

[22] Nancy E. Goldberg, *Pre-Trial Diversion: Bilk or Bargain?* (Chicago: World Correctional Services Center, reprinted from the *National Legal Aid and Defender Association Briefcase*, 1973).

The dangers of diversion have been pointed out by some writers.[23] Movements to reduce the reach of the criminal law sometimes really extend that reach. For example, if a juvenile is diverted from the court, and the parents resent the intrusion of the supervisory probation agent into the family and vigorously object, the court could conceivably remove all the children from an "unsuitable family situation." And where diversion programs are available, there is the danger that more offenders will be reached by the law because the diversionary procedures appear to be innocuous, in that it is less troublesome and sometimes less dangerous to accept supervision informally than to go through a trial and risk conviction.

CONCLUSIONS

It is difficult to arrive at definite conclusions regarding the outcome of community-based corrections programs. It is obvious that fewer people who have gone through pretrial and pre-hearing diversion procedures come into conflict with the law again, compared with those who have gone into the criminal justice system. Whether that is a function of selection, rehabilitation, or both is as yet unclear; it is left to the judgment of the courts, the prosecutors, and the supervisors who operate the programs. Until an adequate data base is developed for comparison between experimental and control groups on an adequate basis, the success of pretrial diversion will remain conjectural.

The John Howard Society of Ontario held a series of thirteen seminars on diversion programs in 1974. The consistent conclusion among all the seminars was that the diversion program is beneficial at both the pre- and post-trial stages. The rationale seen behind pretrial diversion was determined to be that it

1. Avoids in the adult the stigma of a criminal record, if successful.
2. Keeps the individual out of a system that is failing and may mark him for failure once he is officially in it.
3. Maintains him in his community.
4. Makes more flexible resources available to him to meet his needs than would be available if institutions were used.
5. Has a potential, not yet proven, for greater success than institutional programs.
6. Is more economical.
7. Still holds him accountable.[24]

---

[23] Norval Morris, *The Future of Imprisonment* (Chicago and London: University of Chicago Press, 1974), pp. 9–12.

[24] *Newsletter* (Toronto: John Howard Society of Ontario, December 1974), p. 2.

With the exception of the first two points, stigma and the chance of repeating, post-trial diversion methods offer the same benefits.

The American Bar Association's national pretrial intervention centers [25] have examined the results of their efforts and have compiled a report. It recommends the expansion of pretrial intervention and the provision of community correction service to pre-adjudicated offenders instead of criminal prosecution.[26]

Diversion at the pretrial stage can be developed as a formalized option.[27] There is responsibility at each stage of the criminal justice process to justify further use of the criminal procedure. Useless processing of people through the criminal justice system or any part of it can be damaging to the person and to society. Diversion is a matter of restraint. It includes such things as decisions by victims or bystanders not to call police, exercise of discretion on the part of police and the prosecutor, and similar decisions for diversion and dealing with trouble in low key. These can be more productive than escalating a conflict into a full-blown trial. The advantages of pretrial diversion or a settlement mechanism affect the offender, the victim, and the society, alike; this warrants encouragement and development of legislation to formalize this type of procedure. The criminal law and its processes are the last and limited resort in dealing with social conflict. It should be used with restraint.

[25] Headquartered in Suite 701, 1705 DeSales Street, NW, Washington, D.C. 20036, this group is supported by Staff Assistant under subcontract with the National District Attorney's Association (NDAA), 2118 East Chicago Avenue, Chicago, Illinois 60601.

[26] *Source Book in Pretrial Criminal Justice Intervention Techniques and Action Program* (Washington, D.C.: American Bar Association's National Pretrial Intervention Service Center, May 1974), p. 189.

[27] Law Reform Commission of Canada, "Diversion—Working Paper 7," *Canadian Journal of Criminology and Corrections*, 17, No. 3 (July 1975), 277–308 (25).

Chapter 4

Diversion
from Jail and Bail

There have been increased attempts in recent years to divert the alleged offender from the courts and from the criminal justice system in a way that is commensurate with the public safety. Many official, quasi-official, and professional bodies and organizations have supported this diversion. The President's Commission on Law Enforcement and Administration of Justice did so in its report published in 1967.[1] The National Advisory Commission on Criminal Justice Standards and Goals established as correction standard 3.1 the use of diversion.[2] The American Bar Association similarly supported diversion practices,[3] as has the American Bar Foundation.[4]

On the other hand, resistance to and resentment about diversion techniques have been voiced by police and law enforcement officers, who sometimes object to seeing the alleged offender on the street soon after he or she was arrested. Many police officers have remarked indignantly after picking up a juvenile that "the kid beat me home!" At the adult level, many cases are dismissed by judges for a variety of reasons, which many

---

[1] *Task Force Report: Corrections* (Washington, D.C.: The President's Commission on Law Enforcement and Administration of Justice, 1967), p. 22.

[2] *Corrections* (Washington, D.C.: National Advisory Commission on Criminal Justice Standards and Goals, 1973), pp. 95–97.

[3] National Pretrial Intervention Service Center; *Source Book in Pretrial Criminal Justice Intervention Techniques and Action Programs* (Washington, D.C.: American Bar Association Commission on Correctional Facilities and Services, 1974).

[4] Raymond T. Nimmer, *Diversion: The Search for Alternative Forms of Prosecution* (Chicago: American Bar Foundation, 1974).

44

law enforcement officers do not understand. In Los Angeles County, for example, 53 percent of the cases made by police in 1973 were dismissed because judges thought that there may have been illegal search and seizure, failure to read the Miranda warnings, violations of the Escobedo decision on confessions, entrapment, due process, and other considerations. Further, many conservative newspapers have editorialized that diversion has violated the concept of "blind" justice because some are convicted while others are not even tried for similar offenses.

Nevertheless, society is moving toward diversion from the criminal justice system when such a procedure appears to be best for the individual and does not endanger the public safety. In recent years, the practice has increased.

A kind of compromise has developed for some offenders who are not to be diverted from the criminal justice system, but can be diverted from jail detention and bail. These people do not need to be detained awaiting trial. Further, sentences can be deferred and modified after conviction. Many offenders can be diverted from local detention, although this is not a diversion from the criminal justice system.

REASONS FOR DIVERSION

The reasons for diversion involve the entire criminal justice system, including police, courts, and correctional programs. And it is generally in the interests of the individual, when it is appropriate, to be diverted from the criminal justice system.

Although much of the criminal justice process rests on the assumption that criminal cases initiated by police will be decided by trial, this assumption is not justified and is contrary to fact.[5] Most cases are decided outside the traditional trial process by police, by prosecutor, or by the judge.

The courts are traditionally overburdened. In fact, they have been referred to as "the bottleneck" in the criminal justice system. When the riots occurred in the houses of detention in New York City in 1970, some accused persons had been awaiting trial from eighteen months to two years. Diversion procedures assist to lighten the burden of the courts.

The police themselves make more decisions in this area than any other segment of the criminal justice system. An excellent discussion of this appears in Skolnick's *Justice Without Trial*.[6] While police determine

---

5 *Task Force Report: The Courts* (Washington, D.C.: The President's Commission on Law Enforcement and Administration of Justice, 1967), p. 4.

6 Jerome H. Skolnick, *Justice Without Trial: Law Enforcement in Democratic Society* (New York: Wiley & Sons, 1966), p. 279.

whether or not to arrest and then whether or not to "make a case" and charge an offense at the adult level, probably more diversion is made by them in the juvenile area. Many police departments have juvenile divisions or youth aid bureaus that supervise more juveniles than are referred to juvenile court.

The prosecutor frequently does not follow a case because of lack of admissible evidence. Many cases are eliminated because of legal contamination of evidence or procedure. Further, many busy prosecutors fail to prosecute (nolle prosse) lesser cases and concentrate on the more serious ones.

There is considerable precedence, then, for diversion programs, both from the criminal justice system and from local detention. Though police and prosecutors have used such programs for a long time, recently developed formalized diversion programs have brought the problem and the activity into public view.

One of the most important reasons for diversion is to avoid placing younger persons into the criminal justice system. The earlier a person gets into the system, the longer he stays in it. Though some have considered that early entry into the criminal justice system causes labeling and initiates a "self-fulfilling prophecy," [7] practitioners in that system consider that early attraction of social authority to an individual means the existence of problems. While there may be interaction between these two viewpoints, the fact remains that the younger a person is when he or she enters the criminal justice system, the more time that person will

TABLE 4-1   Percent of Repeaters by Age Group

(Persons Released in 1963 and Re-Arrested within Four Years)

Age	Percentage of Repeaters
Under 20	70
20–24	67
25–29	65
30–39	61
Total of all ages	60
40–49	51
50 and over	38

Crime in the United States—Uniform Crime Reports, 1967 (Washington, D.C.: Federal Bureau of Investigation, released August 27, 1968), p. 38.

---

[7] Robert K. Merton, Social Theory and Social Structure, rev. ed. (New York: Free Press, 1957), pp. 421–36.

stay in it. Persons released in 1963 and rearrested within four years according to age group can be shown in Table 4-1.

These and other data suggest that persons who come in contact with the law before age 15 come in contact with the law again in between 85 and 90 percent of the cases. At least the conclusion can be made that if the cause of this repetition is the "self-fulfilling prophecy," then diversion is even more important. On the other hand, if the cause is early identification of problem people, then early diversion would mean that the damaging effects of institutionalization and the risk of perpetuating delinquent and criminal patterns of behavior might be avoided.

There are several other related reasons why it is important to avoid jail confinement if possible. Among them is the problem of homosexuality.[8] Patterson and Conrad point out that homosexuality is a problem in all penal institutions, and many young girls and boys are introduced to homosexuality by force in these places of confinement. After a period of years in this setting, it sometimes becomes a way of life. Diversion from jail is important not only to save money for the taxpayer, but to spare individuals the problems that come along with imprisonment.

The formalizing of diversion programs has brought opposition and resentment from other components of the criminal justice system in some places. Providing counsel for indigents, release of indigents on their own recognizance, and other attendant facets of diversionary programs will take time for adjustment. In *Gideon* v. *Wainwright* (1963), the United States Supreme Court ruled that indigent defendants in criminal trials were entitled to counsel. The public defender movement accelerated to provide broader coverage than had previously been available through legal aid societies and the "duty rosters" of the local bar associations. This changing procedure in the courts has aroused intense feelings in some places. For example, when Paul Bradley became public defender in Cairo, Illinois, his office was sprayed with bullets by unknown persons, a judge sentenced one of his associates to thirty days in jail for advising a client not to answer questions in a welfare fraud case, and another judge refused to permit a different associate to represent indigents in his courtroom.[9] Similar problems have occurred elsewhere. It is apparent that jurists resent the new system because it takes longer and is more formal, while cases used to be handled expeditiously in a kind of informal type of negotiation.

---

[8] Haywood Patterson and Earl Conrad, *Scottsboro Boy* (New York: Bantam Books, 1962), p. 68.

[9] Wayne E. Green, "Weak Defense? Right to Free Lawyer Often Proves Shaky for Indigent Suspects," *The Wall Street Journal*, 185, June 9, 1975, p. 1.

BAIL PROJECTS—RELEASE ON OWN
RECOGNIZANCE (ROR)

In 1969, Justice William O. Douglas, in *Bandy* v. *United States* (81 S.Ct. 197, 198, 1960), asked whether an indigent man could legitimately be denied his freedom in cases in which a wealthy man would not, simply because he does not have the property to pledge for his freedom. The following year, in *Bandy* v. *Chambers* (82 S.Ct. 11, 13, 1961), Justice Douglas said that no man should be denied release because of indigence and that persons should be released on their own "personal recognizance" where other factors suggest that they will comply.

In 1961, the Vera Foundation (reorganized into the Vera Institute of Justice in 1966) launched the Manhattan Bail Project in cooperation with the New York University Law School. This project demonstrated that judges released more defendants on their own recognizance when they were presented with verified information about family ties, residence, and employment. Further, dependents with community ties could usually be depended upon to return to court, whether or not bail was posted. As a result of these findings and experiences elsewhere in federal jurisdictions, the attorney general's committee on poverty and the administration of federal criminal justice recommended the policy of release on recognizance in the United States courts system; this was implemented in March 1963. The Manhattan Bail Project also led to permanent pretrial release operations in New York City, District of Columbia, and nearly 100 other communities in over half the states in the country.

Stationhouse release also reflected the growing use of procedures by which persons are released while awaiting trial. In 1964, the New York City Police Department initiated the experimental Manhattan Summons Project with the assistance of the Vera Foundation to prevent detention on minor criminal charges such as simple assault, petty larceny, malicious mischief, and disorderly conduct. Use of stationhouse release avoids unnecessary loss of liberty for the accused and leaves the police free to devote more time to patrolling streets and less to transporting and guarding prisoners. Court appearances can be set in a more orderly manner and it substantially cuts down the setting of bail for defendants who have already proved their reliability by appearing in response to a summons or citation.

In the period 1964 to 1966, legislation encouraging the use of release without bail or nominal or cash bail has been passed in many states, including Alabama, Alaska, Delaware, Florida, Illinois, Kansas, Maryland, Michigan, Missouri, New Jersey, Ohio, Oklahoma, Oregon, Texas, and

Virginia. Administrative rules made during that same period affected bail practices in Connecticut, Pennsylvania, Minnesota, and New Jersey.

In the federal system, changes in pretrial release procedures and resources were reflected in (1) the Bail Reform Act of 1966 (Public Law 89-465), (2) the District of Columbia Bail Agency Act (Public Law 89-519), and (3) amendments to Rule 46 of the Federal Rules of Criminal Procedure adopted by the Supreme Court and transmitted to Congress to be effective July 1, 1966. Rule 46, entitled "Release on Bail," strengthened the policy against unnecessary detention of defendants pending trial.

None of these projects eliminates the procedure of arrest or trial. Rather, they are designed to reduce unnecessary confinement awaiting trial, which permits the arrested person to live at home and keep his job and helps the criminal justice system by reducing significantly the jail population of unconvicted persons awaiting trial.

National conferences were held on bail in 1964 [10] and in 1965.[11] Several questions were addressed, including eligibility for release on own recognizance (ROR), reason for refusing bail, circumstances in which the police oppose bail, the problem of unnecessary obstacles in the bail-bond business, facilities for appeal, and whether the power to impose short sentences when the offense does not warrant it might be a manipulation of bail discretion.

The initial appearance in court occurs after the law enforcement officer making arrest brings the individual before a judge. This happens within a short period of time. At this appearance, several steps are taken: (1) the defendant is informed of the charges against him, generally by a reading of the complaint; (2) he is informed of his rights, including constitutional privilege against self-incrimination; (3) mechanical process of assigning an attorney may begin if the individual requests one and cannot pay for one; (4) arrangements may be made concerning release before further proceedings. Release may take several forms; the traditional one is for the defendant himself or a professional bondsman to set bail. Pretrial release in some jurisdictions takes the form of release on one's own recognizance. Still other forms have been used, such as referral to counseling services. In minor cases, the individual may plead guilty, sometimes almost informally, but serious charges are brought to court. At a later time, a full preliminary hearing may be held, at which the prosecutor introduces evidence to establish probable cause to believe the defendant guilty. Subsequently, the filing of a formal charge through

---

[10] Daniel J. Freed and Patricia Wald, *Bail in the United States: 1964* (Washington, D.C.: Office of the United States Attorney General, 1964).

[11] *Bail and Summons: 1965* (New York and Washington, D.C.: Vera Foundation, Inc., and United States Department of Justice, 1965).

an indictment by the grand jury or information by the prosecutor sets up the arraignment, where the charges are read in open court to the defendant and his counsel—here the defendant is required to make his first formal appearance before the court and plead to the charge. Unless the defendant enters a guilty plea, the full adversary process is put into motion for a trial. The National Advisory Commission on Criminal Justice Standards and Goals recommended in 1973 that pretrial release is desirable. The pretrial release (Standard 4.6) wording is as follows:

> Adequate investigation of defendants' characteristics and circumstances should be undertaken to identify those defendants who can be released prior to trial solely on their own promise to appear for trial. Release on this basis should be made wherever appropriate. If a defendant cannot appropriately be released on this basis, consideration should be given to releasing him under certain conditions, such as the deposit of a sum of money to be forfeited in the event of nonappearance, or assumption of the obligation to pay a certain sum of money in the event of nonappearance, or the agreement of a third person to maintain contact with the defendant and to assure his appearance.
>
> Participation by private bail bond agencies in the pretrial process should be eliminated.
>
> In certain limited cases, it may be appropriate to deny pre-trial release completely.[12]

A third person may vouch for the individual's appearance in court. In fact, the person may become a private jailer in his role as the individual who guarantees the appearance of the defendant in court.

Several steps can be taken in case of nonappearance at the trial. First, of course, any bail or surety property is forfeited. A possible approach is also to continue the trial in the absence of the defendant, which is an extreme measure; but there is some indication that trials in absentia could be conducted within the existing constitutional framework.[13]

The Vera Institute of Justice has supported several programs in the area of diversion from jail and bail. The Manhattan Bail Project began in the early spring of 1961, after a study between 1954 and 1957 showed that of those jailed in Philadelphia because they could not afford bail, only 18 percent were eventually acquitted, as opposed to 48 percent of those free on bail. Jail defendants received prison sentences two and one-half times as often as did bailed defendants, and, in New York City,

12 "Standard 4.6—Pre-trial Release," in *Courts* (Washington, D.C.: National Advisory Commission on Criminal Justice Standards and Goals, 1973), p. 83.

13 *State* v. *Tacon*, 107, Ariz. 353, 1971, cert. granted, 407 US 909, 1972. Also covered in "Standard 4.7—Nonappearance after Pre-Trial Release," in *Courts*, p. 86.

bailed defendants received suspended sentences four times as often as jailed defendants.[14] The Manhattan Summons Project began with a request by Mobilization for Youth to study the feasibility of a legal services unit to serve MFY clients. Though Vera recommended establishment of such a unit, MFY did not, so Vera set up the project on its own. The Manhattan Bowery Project was an alternative for the drunkenness offender; it was begun in 1967 when there were 10 to 15 thousand derelicts in New York City, with 4 to 5 thousand in the Bowery area alone.[15]

These pretrial diversion programs involving ROR and bail reform have been evaluated and have resulted in pleas for law reform.[16] Many people are caught up in the criminal justice system in manners that are counterproductive and damaging, rather than helpful. There is a sufficient number of programs for diversion from jail and bail that more adequate evaluation could be done.

SUBSTITUTES FOR JAIL—THE DES MOINES PROJECT

Substitution of other facilities for jails is more rare than bail reform and ROR. Jails have increasingly been called upon to develop correctional programs in terms of (1) developing job skills in the unskilled, (2) improving educational achievement in the uneducated, and (3) treating personal problems, such as alcoholism, personality deficiencies, marital and financial difficulties, and other types of personal problems.[17] Determination of programs, program objectives, maximum use of existing community and jail resources, and implementation of these programs become matters of first priority.

Most jails are small, with three-quarters of them holding twenty or fewer inmates. Texas has the largest number of jails (318), followed by Georgia (239) and Florida (164); and the South, including the District of Columbia, had the largest number of jail inmates of any region (55,461).[18] Combined with California, New York, and Pennsylvania, this

---

[14] *Programs in Criminal Justice Reform—Ten-Year Report 1961–1971* (New York: Vera Institute of Justice, 1972).

[15] Ibid., p. 59.

[16] F. E. Zimring, "Measuring the Impact of Pretrial Diversion from the Criminal Justice System," *University of Chicago Law Review*, 41, No. 2 (1974), 224–41.

[17] Alice Howard Blumer, *Jail Management: A Course for Jail Administrators, Book 3: Jail and Community Corrections* (Washington, D.C.: United States Bureau of Prisons, 1970), p. 1.

[18] *Survey of Inmates of Local Jails: Advance Report* (Washington, D.C.: National Criminal Justice Information and Statistics Service, U.S. Department of Justice, 1974), pp. 6–7.

Since the Polk County Jail was condemned in 1970, Fort Des Moines has been used in place of the jail. The Des Moines Project, founded by LEAA, was part of an old cavalry fort, and its security derives from relationships with the staff.

Courtesy of the Des Moines Project.

group included nearly half the jail inmates in the United States in 1972 (70,961).[19] This means that the problem in any specific locality is generally relatively small and could be manipulated.

When the Polk County Jail in Des Moines, Iowa, was declared unsuitable in 1970, some action had to be taken. Funds were simply unavailable and other approaches had to be taken. During the 1970–71 session, the Iowa State Legislature enacted Senate File 190, which authorized county boards of supervisors to establish alternative county institutions not under the direction of the sheriff.[20] The Des Moines project developed to become an example of what could occur when community facilities and services replaced the county jail in some cases. Several other cities are now replicating the plan.

The Des Moines Pre-Trial Release Project began in 1964 as a private agency sponsored by the Halley Foundation, but it has since been incorporated in the Department of Court Services created in 1971 to serve as an administrative framework for coordination and development of

19 Ibid.

20 Harry Woods, Jr., *Fort Des Moines Residential Corrections Facilities* (Des Moines: Fifth Judicial District, mimeographed, 1971), p. 1.

several projects providing alternatives to the traditional institutions in the criminal justice system. As the offender goes through various stages of the criminal justice system, he is transferred without interruption from one component to the other. The goals of this program are to release the maximum number of persons consonant with public safety and to assist them in becoming qualified for probation as a final disposition. The probation unit handles both pre-sentence investigation and probation supervision.[21]

The Des Moines Community Corrections Project was initiated in 1970 to meet the needs that the Pre-Trial Release Project could not handle.[22] All persons who are admitted are interviewed earlier by the Pre-Trial Release staff, as are those referred by attorneys, judges, agencies, and others. A person released from jail to the project must report to his counselor every day. Staff members counsel in the areas of personal, family, and other needs, and are not concerned with guilt or innocence, which is to be determined by the trial. A person may be required to spend some evenings at the project office for classes or films, on, for example, alcoholism, use of legal counsel, use of welfare services, effects of marijuana, planned parenthood, medical insurance, vocational rehabilitation services, and remedial education. During its first two years of operations, almost 98 percent of the project's clients appeared for trial. About 17.5 percent of the project defendants and those released on bail had further offense allegations during the release period, and it was determined that the project's staff selection decisions were quite accurate, because defendants rejected by the project as poor release risks who were released on bail had the highest rate of pretrial new-offense allegations (39 percent).

The Fort Des Moines residential program in Iowa was evaluated in 1973.[23] Of the 246 clients seen in the first eighteen months, 188 were sentenced on felony charges and 58 on nonfelony charges. A study of 42 individuals revealed that the program's clients appear to have had relatively unstable family relationships, poor employment history, low educational background, fairly high drug usage, and some criminal background. New offenses during the commitment period were charged against only 13 percent of the program's clients and only 3 percent of all clients were charged with offenses against persons, property, morals,

---

21 *A Description of the Functions and Procedures of the Polk County Department of Court Services* (Des Moines: Polk County Court Services Department, 1972).

22 *The Des Moines Community Corrections Project: An Alternative to Jailing* (Hackensack, N.J.: National Council on Crime and Delinquency, 1972).

23 *Residential Corrections: Alternative to Incarceration* (Davis, Cal.: National Council on Crime and Delinquency Research Center, 1973).

A counselor working with an inmate at Fort Des Moines.

Courtesy of the Des Moines Project.

or drug offenses. The program appears to be quite effective. Compared with existing state correctional programs, it is an extremely low-cost correctional effort. Lack of comparative recidivism information makes it difficult to assess effectiveness, but new charges subsequent to release from the program were made against 35.7 percent of all released program clients, and 25.6 percent have been convicted on new charges. Factors related to recidivism were narcotics, employment status, primary source of income, job stability, and number of prior arrests.

The Model Neighborhood Corrections Project in Des Moines, Iowa, exemplifies how pretrial release can be built into a correctional program. The purpose of the project is to permit offenders to show their reliability during the pretrial release period so that their chances for probation will be increased. After screening, those selected for release are supervised by staff, who link the releasees with social agencies and other existing community resources. Evaluation indicates that those released on the project are as good risks as those released on money bail. Further, they are less likely to be convicted if tried, less likely to be imprisoned if convicted, and likely to receive shorter sentences if imprisoned than those not in the project.

The conclusions are that this community-based program has provided an effective alternative to the traditional forms of incarceration.[24] Since its inception in 1971, it has reduced the jail population by nearly one-half. The National Institute of Law Enforcement and Criminal Justice has allocated $1,250,000 for replication of the project in five communities—Baton Rouge, Louisiana; Duluth, Minnesota; Orlando, Florida; Salt Lake City, Utah; and San Mateo, California. (Vancouver, Washington, later joined this group.)

The Ford Foundation has assisted in similar research projects in the field of criminal justice, concentrated in five criminal justice centers at Chicago, Georgetown, and Harvard Universities and the University of California's Berkeley and Davis Units.[25] Activities include design and evaluation of experiments to reform the criminal justice system and public education functions. The Probation Case Aid Project in Chicago, the Offender Rehabilitation Project in the District of Columbia, the Sacramento 601 Diversion Project for Juveniles, and the deinstitutionalization of Massachusett's Juvenile Corrections were all part of this project.

SHORT-TERM TREATMENT AND RELEASE

Short-term incarceration followed by probation has been used since the 1950s. In fact, Michigan had a probation recovery camp in the law for this purpose as early as 1937, but its Camp Pugsley was not opened until the late 1950s. The United States Bureau of Prisons has a thirty- to ninety-day observation and evaluation sentence that federal judges can use to determine whether or not certain individuals should be placed on probation. In July 1965, the Ohio General Assembly enacted a statute providing for early release of incarcerated felons by the court for a similar purpose (sections 2951.03 and 2951.09 of the revised code). Subsequent studies have indicated that it has not been applied evenly and uniformly.[26] The federal "split-sentence" act (18 U.S.C. sec 3651, 1969) was first passed in 1958 and has been viewed as an advance in sentencing procedure.[27]

---

24 "National Institute to Promote Adoption of Innovative Projects," *Research Information Letter,* No. 8, April 30, 1974, p. 3, National Institute of Law Enforcement and Criminal Justice.

25 *Law and Justice* (New York: Ford Foundation, Office of Reports, 1974), p. 47.

26 David M. Peterson and Paul C. Friday, "Early Release from Incarceration: Race as a Factor in the Use of 'Shock Probation,'" *The Journal of Criminal Law and Criminology,* 66, No. 1 (1975), 79–87.

27 Judge Richard Hartshorne, "The 1958 Federal 'Split-Sentence' Law," *Federal Probation,* 23 (1959), 9.

Several countries in Europe have made extensive use of short-term treatment of adult offenders, particularly the Netherlands and Denmark.[28] During the short institutionalization, wide use of other alternatives are also used, such as weekend detention, semi-detention (evenings, weekends, holidays), semi-liberty as a transition period for release, open work centers, provisional release, and other types of leaves from the institution.

Operation de Novo (New Start) is a sentence modification type of program in Minneapolis that maintains (1) an educational unit, (2) a survival skill unit for females, (3) a job developer and placement unit, (4) a restitution unit, and (5) a teacher corps unit. Those in the educational unit go to school if they are under 16, or work for the G.E.D. high school equivalency diploma if they are older. The survival skill unit for females provides assistance to young women whose lifestyles make them susceptible to pimps and dope pushers and also helps them learn how to survive in street life. The job developer and placement unit is the employment phase of the program. The restitution unit assists in providing restitution to victims of property crimes. The teacher corps unit is an experimental unit developed by the University Without Walls in the University College of the University of Minnesota to (1) assist clients in meeting special educational needs and (2) upgrade educational alternatives within the site of each component.

In summary, short-term treatment is generally associated with probation status and is an alternative sentence after conviction, usually on a guilty plea. Although it does not save a citizen-offender from the formal conviction, it does either avoid or shorten a period of incarceration before supervision.

DEFERRED SENTENCING

There are several programs of deferred sentencing in cases in which conviction is obtained, generally on a guilty plea, and the sentencing is deferred on several conditions. The most frequent condition is good behavior. Another is restitution, in cases of property offenders. *Service sentencing* is sometimes imposed; this means that the convicted offender must perform civic and public duties for a specific length of time (jobs such as mowing or cleaning public parks, tutoring retarded students in various subjects, or any of a wide variety of other tasks).

The Bronx Sentencing Project was begun in 1968 to provide diversion from the criminal justice system after conviction. The purpose was to

---

[28] *Short-Term Treatment of Adult Offenders* (Strasbourg: Council of Europe, European Committee on Crime Problems, 1975), p. 19.

provide alternatives to prison. During the first year of operation, non-prison recommendations were followed by some type of nonprison disposition in 83 percent of the cases. On the other hand, FIO (For Information Only) reports were made without such recommendations and 87 percent of these were followed by prison sentences. It soon became obvious that a sharply increased number of adult misdemeanants could receive alternative dispositions if the information were made available.

Restitution is a frequent condition of deferred sentencing. Equity in restitution prevents the offender from being "exploited." Restitution to a corporation or a large concern is much less effective than restitution to an individual or a family. Face-to-face contact between the offender and his victim helps make the victim a real person to the offender, rather than just a faceless entity. This type of contact can expiate guilt on the part of the offender and perhaps even change his attitude about committing further property crime.

Minnesota has diversion programs at the police level: pretrial diversion, post-conviction diversion, and the parole board level diversion.[29] The White Bear Lake Youth Resource Bureau has been providing diversion services since 1972 with six salaried staff and thirty volunteers. Operation de Novo, in Minneapolis, diverts both adult and juvenile defendants from felony and misdemeanor courts. The post-conviction diversion is to the Probation Offenders Rehabilitation and Training (PORT) Project of Olmsted County (Rochester, Minnesota); this is a community-based residential program for convicted felons and adjudicated delinquents. Parole-level diversion includes adult male property offenders who are diverted from the Minnesota State Prison to the Minnesota Restitution Center in the fourth month following admission to the prison. These programs have not been adequately evaluated, but they certainly cost less and are as effective as the conventional alternatives.

Oklahoma has a deferred-sentencing program in which an offender, found guilty in court (on a plea of guilty), can be returned to the community without sentencing. Mandatory supervision is provided by the Department of Corrections. The deferred-sentence period may be from one month to two years. If the offender gets into trouble during the deferred-sentence period, the probation officer asks the court for acceleration to a suspended sentence or a sentence. From the practical standpoint, lack of communication between jurisdictions may result in an offender having several deferred sentences in different jurisdictional areas, but this is an extreme situation seldom encountered.

In California, Alameda County's Court Referral Program handles

---

29 Joel Hudson, Burt Galaway, William Henschel, Jay Lindgren, Jon Penton, "Diversion Programming in Criminal Justice: The Case of Minnesota," *Federal Probation*, 39, No. 1 (March 1975), 11–19.

minor offenses—such as less serious traffic offenses, welfare fraud, possession of marijuana, petty theft, and malicious mischief—in a diversionary manner.[30] Generally, offenders must serve their time as volunteers for worthwhile community health and welfare organizations.

In August 1974, the Home Secretary in England gave authority to probation departments to introduce community service sentencing,[31] beginning on a national basis in April 1975. The pioneer project in Nottinghamshire had begun in 1972 and had been joined by six pilot areas to test community service as an alternative to longer sentencing. Early results indicated that many offenders responded enthusiastically and with initiative to the responsibilities placed upon them. Similar service sentencing has been recommended for the Netherlands.[32]

CONCLUSIONS

The recent emphasis on diversion is due to (1) the increasing recognition of the deficiencies in our system of justice, (2) the rediscovery of the ancient truth that the community itself has a significant impact upon behavior, and (3) a growing desire of the citizenry to be more active in the affairs of government.[33] The problems in diversion include the absence of guidelines for diversion, fiscal complexities, political and social issues, inadequate and uneven community resources, lack of assessment or evaluation of diversion programs, and the need to redefine traditional roles in dealing with offenders.

The Saginaw Project, the California Probation Subsidy Program, the Sacramento and Stockton Community Treatment Project, and the Pretrial Intervention Program have demonstrated that community-based corrections programs are more effective than imprisonment.[34] The Saginaw Project was a three-year experiment conducted between 1957 and 1960 in Michigan. Probation staffs and facilities were strengthened to a more adequate level of services through small caseloads and intensive supervision. The proportion of convicted felons was raised from 59.5

---

30 S. Sullivan, "Convicted Offenders Become Community Helpers," *Judicature*, 56, No. 8 (1973), 333–35.

31 J. Harding, "The Offender and the Community: Some Change Aspects of an Old Relationship," *Social Work Today*, 5, No. 16 (1974), 478–81.

32 H. Singer-Dekker, "Work Rather than Imprisonment: Here and Overseas," *Process*, 53, No. 4 (1974), 79–85.

33 Robert M. Carter, "The Diversion of Offenders," *Federal Probation*, 36, No. 4 (December 1972), 31–36.

34 *Marshaling Citizen Power to Modernize Corrections* (Washington, D.C.: Chamber of Commerce of the United States, 1972), p. 9.

to 67.1 percent, while the proportion of probation failures decreased from 32.2 to 17.4 percent. Estimated savings to the taxpayers was about a half-million dollars. This was possible because of reductions in costs of institutional care, welfare for prisoners' families, and parole expenditures. The California Probation Subsidy Program was supportive of traditional probation services and beyond the scope of the narrow definition of community-based corrections, but nevertheless, the savings to the state were substantial with a decrease in recidivism. The Sacramento and Stockton Community Treatment Project assigned eligible people at random to the project and to the regular traditional procedures. After the first two years, studies showed that 41 percent of the experimental group had had their paroles revoked, as opposed to 61 percent of the control group.[35]

There are hundreds of new diversion projects being undertaken in the United States.[36] Diversion techniques have been used by police and by the courts. Particularly in the juvenile area, police have traditionally diverted cases from the juvenile court in voluntary police supervision. Diversion programs attempt to give the offender a set of social controls other than the criminal justice system. They have nothing to do with "leniency" or "toughness"—the assumption that many who violate criminal laws will always violate criminal laws and thus need to be caged is simply not true.

[35] Ibid., p. 11.

[36] Elizabeth W. Vorenberg and James Vorenberg, "Early Diversion from the Criminal Justice System: Practice in Search of a Theory," in Lloyd E. Ohlin, ed., *Prisoners in America* (Englewood Cliffs, N.J.: Prentice-Hall, 1973), p. 155.

Chapter 5

Halfway Houses

Halfway houses, community correctional centers (CCC), community treatment centers (CTC), and similar designations have been used to identify the small, local facilities designed to work with offenders in the community. They use community resources and keep the citizen-offender in the community. They serve offenders who do not need to be in maximum custody prisons for the public safety, but do need some control.

Halfway houses are relatively small facilities, either residential or nonresidential, and are usually located in or near a city or town.[1] The residents, inmates, or wards of the halfway houses participate in the daily life of the open community by working, going to school, and participating in other community programs. The halfway house may be part of the criminal justice system supported by tax funds or it can be privately funded, administered, and operated. The name of this type of facility is derived from the fact that it is halfway between the community and the prison or other large institution. It may serve persons who are released from prison or those received directly from the court. The populations of halfway houses generally range between twenty and fifty residents, but there are some larger and some smaller. Halfway houses for juveniles generally hold ten to fifteen boys or girls.

The rationale for halfway houses is the same as the rationale for all community-based programs. First, deviant and criminal activity originates in the community, so the community has some responsibility, if it is

---

[1] Oliver J. Keller, Jr. and Benedict S. Alper, *Halfway Houses: Community-Centered Correction and Treatment* (Lexington, Mass.: D. C. Heath, 1970), p. 10.

only the failure to take adequate measures in school or child guidance programs to forestall serious deviant behavior. Second, the subculture in which many delinquents and offenders live tends to make their lifestyle resistant to the middle-class, authoritarian agents of social control. Moreover, sending a person who has exhibited deviant behavior because he has been in "bad company" to a prison would only intensify and aggravate the problem. The best place for treatment is in the community; this prevents the breaking of all constructive social ties.

Halfway houses are widely varied in physical plant, staff, and program. There is no unitary definition of a "halfway house," except that it is a small facility in or near a community, and it uses the services and resources of the community. There are halfway houses for delinquent children, adult public offenders, persons with special problems like alcohol and drug addiction, neglected children, psychiatric patients, and many other people whose problems are too serious to be handled at home but not serious enough to merit institutionalization. Halfway houses have developed in this manner because of the varying needs for different target populations in the communities—when they began, there were no guidelines to follow.[2] Halfway houses may be in private houses, converted motels, YMCAs, remodeled schools, former lodge halls, beach clubs, nursing homes, or any other existing facilities. Even the names vary, there are residential treatment centers, rehabilitation residences, restitution shelters, and so forth. As in the rest of community-based corrections, halfway house programs tend to follow the personality of the administrator. Where people are working with other people, standardization may be undesirable.

DEVELOPMENT OF HALFWAY HOUSES

The first countries to settle persons with mental disturbances and problems within homes in the community were the Netherlands, Belgium, Luxembourg, Switzerland, and England as early as 1870.[3] The Japanese developed the idea in 1880. By 1910 it was accepted procedure in many European countries. Around 1850, one of the English pioneers in starting "halfway houses" was a Dr. Bernardo,[4] who opened 112 homes for children who had made their living by begging and stealing; his work was carried by the Philanthropic Society of London.

---

2 John M. McCartt and Thomas J. Mangogna, *Guidelines and Standards for Halfway Houses and Community Treatment Centers* (Washington, D.C.: Law Enforcement Assistance Administration Technical Assistance Division, 1973), p. 7.

3 Keller and Alper, *Halfway Houses*, p. 6.

4 Erving Goffman, *Asylums* (Garden City, N.Y.: Anchor Books, Doubleday, 1961), p. 14.

In the United States, Massachusetts, New York, and Pennsylvania pioneered in the development of halfway houses, as they had in the development of prisons and probation.[5] In the 1820s a Massachusetts commission urged the establishment of what would now be called halfway houses.[6] A halfway house for women released from institutions opened in Boston in 1864 and operated for about twenty years. A similar establishment was opened by a group of Quakers in New York City in 1845; it survives today as the Isaac T. Hopper Home for Women.[7] The House of Industry opened in 1889 in Philadelphia to receive parolees from prisons in Pennsylvania. The Volunteers of America opened a halfway house in the Washington Heights section of Manhattan in 1896.[8] In 1903, a second Hope Hall opened in Chicago, and other halfway houses under the auspices of the Volunteers of America were established in San Francisco; New Orleans; Fort Dodge, Iowa; Columbus, Ohio; Waco, Texas; and Hampton, Virginia. (The activity by the Volunteers of America was initiated by Mrs. Maud Booth in September 1896, the Volunteers of America having seceded from The Salvation Army.) There was little activity in the halfway house area through the 1920s. In 1932, a mission-type home known as "The Parting of the Ways" provided shelter for ex-offenders in Pittsburgh.[9] It was not until the 1950s when Dismas House in St. Louis, St. Leonard's House in Chicago, and 308 West Residence in Wilmington, Delaware, became the beginnings of today's halfway house movement.[10]

The term "halfway house" had been used informally for some time before its first appearance in the literature in 1953.[11] The first use of the term was in the mental health field. Since that time, the idea has been modified to fit the needs of other groups, such as narcotics addicts, for which Synanon was opened in 1958. Social workers in the mental health field have suggested two other concepts that have been used, but not necessarily so labeled, in the field of corrections in recent years. One is the "quarter-way house," which cares for people who need close super-

---

[5] Ibid., p. 7.

[6] John Conrad, *Crime and Its Correction* (Berkeley: University of California Press, 1965), p. 275.

[7] Edwin Powers, "Halfway Houses: An Historical Perspective," *American Journal of Correction,* 21 (July–August 1959), 35.

[8] Susan F. Welty, *Look Up and Hope* (New York: Thomas Nelson and Sons, 1961), p. 141.

[9] Negley K. Teeters and John Otto Reinemann, *The Challenge of Delinquency* (Englewood Cliffs, N.J.: Prentice-Hall, 1950), p. 78.

[10] Keller and Alper, *Halfway Houses,* p. 8.

[11] Lewis E. Reik, "The Halfway House: The Role of Laymen's Organizations in the Rehabilitation of the Mentally Ill," *Mental Hygiene,* 37, 4 (October 1953), 615–18.

vision on a near-permanent basis. The "three-quarter-way house" is designed to care for persons in acute, temporary crises, needing short-term residential care and little supervision. Halfway houses in the correctional field throughout the country span this spectrum.[12]

HALFWAY "IN" HOUSES—DIVERSION

Many halfway houses are for people who have problems too serious to allow them to remain at home but are not sufficiently serious to require them to be institutionalized. One of the tasks of corrections is to build or rebuild an individual's ties with the community, thereby integrating or reintegrating him or her into community life. His (or her) removal from the community would be a type of "social surgery," cutting *all* ties, both positive and negative. Some of these types of centers have been called (1) halfway houses, (2) reintegration centers, (3) community corrections centers, (4) alcohol detoxification units, (5) drug abuse centers, and (6) restitution houses.[13] These are all halfway "in" houses, the use of which have diverted the offender from the major institutions in the criminal justice system.

There is no empirical evidence to suggest that prison deters crimes of any sort, including crimes of passion, crimes of those who have no stake in conformity, or crimes of the obviously deranged. Any deterrent value is lost after incarceration because of the lowering of self-concept, immersion in prison values, increase of dependency needs, loss of a sense of responsibility, deprivation of family contacts, and many other facets of the maximum custody prison. Recidivism rates indicate that large institutions do not provide protection for society, and the financial cost of institutional operation is almost staggering. A child could be sent through Harvard University for less than it takes to send him through the maximum security prison system.

It seems to be paradoxical to remove an individual from the community because his deviant behavior has been caused by "bad company," only to place him in a prison. In association with other prisoners, values that were previously undesirable become normal—abnormal values in an abnormal environment become normal. When the person is returned to society he is apt to be more deviant than when he was taken out of it. This is the reason the halfway "in" house is a contribution to the criminal justice system.

12 "Halfway Houses," in Robert Morris, Bess Dana, Paul Glasser, Rachel Marks, Martin Rein, and Paul Schreiber, eds., *An Encyclopedia of Social Work*, 16th Issue, Vol. I (Washington, D.C.: National Association of Social Workers, 1973), pp. 481–86.

13 Paul H. Hahn, *Community Based Corrections and the Criminal Justice System* (Santa Cruz, Cal.: Davis Publishing Co., 1975), p. 156.

A unit of Talbert House in Cincinnati.
Courtesy of Talbert House. Photo by Richard L. Shenk.

Halfway houses handle many problem groups, including juvenile and adult offenders. They represent a realization that if satisfactory adjustment to society is a goal, then the individual should not be isolated from society. Alper points out that "while there are almost as many definitions as there are halfway houses, and these must total into [*sic*] the thousands today, they all have several basic features in common. In the first place, they are community based, and located in the neighborhoods which provide a wide range of resources. . . ." [14]

The Highfields Experiment was a first: in it a program of guided group interaction or group counseling was combined with living and working in a residential center that was completely open. [15] It was housed at the estate in rural New Jersey formerly occupied by Charles Lindbergh. Highfields became the prototype for many other such programs. It cared for a population of about twenty boys for a period of four months,

[14] Benedict S. Alper, *Prisons Inside-Out: Alternatives in Correctional Reform* (Cambridge, Mass.: Ballinger, 1974), pp. 103–104.

[15] Lloyd W. McCorkle, Alber Elias, and F. Lovell Bixby, *The Highfield Story* (New York: Henry Holt, 1958).

with work activity during the day and guided group interaction sessions during the evening. Similar programs were established at Essexfields,[16] located at Newark, New Jersey; at Southfields in Louisville, Kentucky; and at the Minnesota State Training School at Red Wing.

Saint Leonard's House in Chicago is a center for work in corrections sponsored by the Episcopal Diocese. It offers the services of a halfway house to ex-offenders and is also a community treatment center for offenders.[17] It houses twenty-one men and serves two meals a day. Ninety percent of the men are under supervision; only 15 percent are serving time for

Clarification of procedure is made by program coordinator during staffing session.

Courtesy of St. Leonard's House.

their first felony. Intake is voluntary and application is made directly by mail by the inmate while he is still in an institution. In 1961, this agency was one of four visited by a team from the United States Bureau

---

[16] Albert Elias and Saul Pilnick, "The Essexfields Group Rehabilitation Project for Youthful Offenders," in *Correction in the Community* (Sacramento: Youth and Corrections Agency, June 1964), pp. 51–57.

[17] Keller and Alper, *Halfway Houses*, p. 8.

of Prisons, out of which developed the Pre-Release Guidance Center
Program of the Bureau of Prisons. In 1967, the Illinois legislature ap-
propriated funds to establish work release and halfway house programs
at the state level; consequently, Saint Leonard's House modified its approach so as not to duplicate any state service.[18] Specialized programs
were initiated, the first involving narcotics addiction. Women offenders
began to be served by Saint Leonard's House in 1965. When it was found
that 25 percent of the men and 75 percent of the women were also ex-
addicts, this institution was funded by a grant from the Office of Economic
Opportunity to develop a comprehensive narcotics rehabilitation project.
Another project involves training ex-offenders in new careers in human
service. The basic principle of this approach is that persons in trouble
can be helped by others who have "been the route" more effectively than
by those who have not had the experience. Saint Leonard's shows how
the private correctional agency located in the community can be an excellent laboratory for the correctional field.

The Probational Offender Rehabilitation and Training (PORT) project was developed in Rochester, Minnesota, as a community-based and
community-supported treatment project for adult offenders and juvenile
delinquents. Serving three counties in southeastern Minnesota, PORT
provides a live-in facility on the grounds of the Rochester State Hospital.
There have been eight to twelve male resident counselors, mostly college
students, who live in the building and room with the offenders. There
is an average of twenty male offenders in the house at any given time.
The average length of stay is eight months. One out of three juvenile
offenders has gone on to more institutional commitments, while only
one out of nine adult offenders has gone back to an institution. The
program is a combination of group treatment and behavior modification.
PORT wants to provide an effective correctional service and develop a
model program that can be transferred to other communities.[19]

The PORT program starts newcomers at the bottom level of a group-
evolved classification system with categories ranging from 1, or minimum
freedom, to 5, or freedom comparable to that of an individual of the
same age in the community. Working from minimum freedom to community freedom is accomplished through a combination of earned points
and group evaluation. The program provides real-life experiences, places

---

18 Robert P. Taylor, "The Evolving Program of a Privately Operated Halfway
House," in *National Conference on Pre-Release: A Symposium on Adult Offender Pro-
grams—"Halfway Houses, Pre-Release, Work Release"* (Huntsville, Tex.: Sam Houston
State College and Texas Department of Corrections, 1967), pp. 23–30.

19 David Wettergren, Margaret Thompson, O. Russell Olson, *PORT Handbook: A
Manual for Effective Community Action with the Criminal Offender* (Rochester, Minn.:
PORT of Olmsted County, 1972).

a premium on dollar savings, and makes heavy use of existing community resources. It is designed to house males who are on probation but who require a greater change in their life-style than probation could accomplish; these are individuals who would otherwise have been incarcerated in a prison or a training school. A facility like PORT will not eliminate all correctional institutions, but such programs can reduce the size of prisons and provide greater effectiveness in rehabilitation and treatment.[20]

In England, halfway houses are generally called "hostels," and the National Association for the Care and Resettlement of Offenders (NACRO) has used hostels as alternatives to imprisonment of men and juveniles referred by the courts.[21] The family model is based on the assumption that a simulated family situation can repair damage created by deprivation and unsatisfactory early relationships. The supportive boardinghouse model is similar to commercial boardinghouses where the residents pay for their board and lodging. In the democratic community model, the residents pay a major part of running the hostel, and they participate in the decisions so that they can reach their full potential as citizens. NACRO also uses apartments as short-term accommodations for persons for whom some kind of confinement might be the only possible alternative solution.

In Holland, the Corridor is a combination of the Outward Bound Program and guided group interaction. Designed for young men 17 to 23 years of age, the Corridor is for first offenders who stay from six to twelve weeks. It provides a situation in which harmfully unrealistic masks or images of the residents can be removed voluntarily.

HALFWAY "OUT" HOUSES—PRE-RELEASE

The vast majority of halfway houses are halfway "out" houses or pre-release houses. The United States Bureau of Prisons began these in 1961; now more than half the states have initiated their use.

In September and October 1961, the United States Bureau of Prisons sanctioned pre-release guidance centers in Los Angeles, Chicago, and New York. The center in New York City was operated on a contract basis by Springfield College in Massachusetts. The rationale was that the six months immediately following release from an institution were most critical in terms of success or failure on parole. Pre-release guidance centers were designed to provide orderly reintroduction of youth and juvenile

---

[20] Kenneth F. Schoen, "PORT: A New Concept of Community-Based Correction," *Federal Probation*, 36, No. 3 (1973), 35–40.

[21] Alper, *Prisons Inside-Out*, pp. 137–38.

offenders to the community in the sixty or ninety days immediately preceding their release on parole. This involved persons from 18 to 25.
Specifically, the people were committed under the Federal Juvenile Delinquency Act and the Youth Correction Act. The Youth Correction Act
involved a six-year sentence with parole possible any time after the first
day. Parole was mandatory no later than four years from the date of
commitment.

Most halfway "out" houses are located in metropolitan areas. Some
are located in semi-rural areas. Halfway houses located in the intercity
area are closer to schools, work, and community resources. There is no
way to the "duck responsibility" by the "out of sight, out of mind" concept in community-based corrections.[22]

Three correctional models have been identified by O'Leary.[23] The
reform model emphasizes compliance; people are required to adopt new
behaviors so that they will learn congruent attitudes. The *rehabilitation*
or *client-centered model* assumes that people are motivated by growth
needs and will gravitate toward the social values of "mature" persons
once they are free to do so. Authority is antithetical to such a free choice
and trust and appreciation are vital. The *reintegration and credibility
model* uses the need for compliance and personal goal expression inte-
grated into a "make-sense" approach in which behaviors that produce
rewarding living become foremost and reality testing is a major theme.
These models can be applied throughout the entire criminal justice system, including pre-release and halfway house concepts.

The general purpose of a halfway "out" house or a pre-release center
is to return a person to the community in which he intends to live, help
him or her to obtain a job, and let him or her get acclimated gradually
to the community again. When offenders are released, they simply move
from the halfway house back to their homes, keeping their jobs and their
social contacts.

Blackburn House is a private, nonprofit halfway facility in San Antonio, Texas, which is under contract to the United States Bureau of
Prisons. Its purpose is to offer services to inmates who are to be released
into the San Antonio area. Counselors help find jobs, provide needed
guidance and support, help with family problems and other difficulties,
including drug addiction and alcoholism, and give other services to the
ex-offenders being returned to the community. Group sessions and individual counseling are mandatory as long as a person is at Blackburn

---

[22] O. J. Keller, Jr., "Halfway House Programs—A National Overview," in *National
Conference on Pre-Release*, p. 9.

[23] Vincent O'Leary, "Correctional Assumptions and Their Program Implications,"
National Conference on Pre-Release, pp. 41–48.

A unit of Talbert House in Cincinnati.

Courtesy of Talbert House. Photo by Richard L. Shenk.

House. The four phases through which the residents usually pass during a 90- to 120-day stay are (1) the observer phase, in which the new resident becomes oriented to the program; (2) the involvement phase, during which job hunting and home visits are begun and the real problems of readjustment have begun; (3) the period in which the person comes to terms with individual problems and anxieties and makes use of counseling and group sessions; and (4) a two- to three-week planning period for return home.[24]

Brooke House is a halfway house for men released from Massachusetts correctional institutions; it was opened in Boston in 1965. By 1974, its service included two residences for parolees, a drop-in center, the first credit union in the country for offenders in a halfway house, a drug treatment program, a nonresidential walk-in center for releasees from county houses of correction and a facility that provides a thirty-day housing service, and a program for training personnel in the community correc-

---

[24] Paul F. Cromwell, Jr., "Release from Prison: Transition and Re-Assimilation," in George G. Killinger and Paul F. Cromwell, Jr., eds., *Corrections in the Community: Alternatives to Imprisonment—Selected Readings* (St. Paul, Minn.: West Publishing Co., 1974), pp. 492–99.

tional field.[25] (It is interesting that the bad-debt rate in the credit union amounted to 5.6 percent of total loans made, as compared with a bad-debt rate of 7 percent on federally granted student loans.[26])

Blitz House is Louisville, Kentucky's, newest and its only halfway house for female ex-offenders. The parent organization, Mission House, Inc., does not like its projects to be labeled halfway houses because this term denotes an institution. The only rule at Blitz House is that the women must be home by 10:30 at night. Opened in 1974, it accommodates seven women, each of whom stays as long as necessary. When a resident feels as though she is financially ready to become independent, she gets permission from her parole officer and is free to go. Another program established by Mission House, Inc., is Augusta House, which is a rehabilitative home for alcoholic women. Emmaeus House is a facility for transient, homeless women.[27]

THE INTERNATIONAL HALFWAY HOUSE ASSOCIATION

A small group of people operating halfway houses for ex-offenders met in Chicago in 1964 to discuss the establishment of an organization that would meet their needs. This organization became known as the International Halfway House Association. The first edition of the IHHA Directory was published in mimeographed form in 1966 with approximately forty halfway houses listed for the United States and Canada. The 1971–72 edition listed over 250 halfway houses and community-based centers. They included facilities for ex-offenders, alcoholics, drug addicts, juveniles, probationers, parolees, and the mentally ill. The 1974 Directory listed about 1,300 programs.[28]

In 1973, the first *Guidelines and Standards for Halfway Houses and Community Treatment Centers* was published under the leadership of John M. McCartt.[29] Because of the heterogeneity of halfway houses, the guidelines had to be general in nature and still provide direction for the operation of the programs. *Guidelines and Standards* discusses the his-

25 Benedict S. Alper, *Prisons Inside-Out*, p. 21.

26 Massachusetts Halfway House, Inc., *Annual Report* (Boston), MHH, 3, No. 3 (January–February 1973), 8.

27 See "Blitz House: 'A House Built on Truth and Love,'" *The Kentucky Inter-Prison Press*, 3, No. 4 (March 1975), 1, 8.

28 *International Halfway House Association Directory—United States—Canada* (Cincinnati: International Halfway House Association, 1974).

29 See McCartt and Mangogna, *Guidelines and Standards for Halfway Houses and Community Treatment Centers*, p. 160.

tory of halfway houses in the United States and presents an orientation to the role and function of this type of institution in the criminal justice system. Standards are presented regarding planning and implementing, training of personnel, financing, and some recommended program standards for administration, program, and personnel. The information is based on 94 questionnaires returned from the 160 that were sent to directors of halfway houses and community-based treatment programs. The questionnaire itself involved seventy questions about specific programs, and the second part included fifty-three questions asking for values that were considered to be essential. The resulting standards developed by McCartt and Mangogna appear to be the best currently available in the field because they are based on the responses of people working directly in the field.

RESTITUTION SHELTERS

Restitution shelter programs are community-based facilities in which the offender resides in a halfway house, but keeps a job or obtains one, using his earnings to pay board and room and repay his victim through established administrative procedure. On funding by LEAA, several states have established restitution shelters or houses. Minnesota was one of the first. Georgia has established six such shelters in major urban areas.

Many countries, including Argentina, Colombia, Norway, and Sweden, use restitution as part of a sentence. Sweden has developed a "day-fine" system in which the fine is based on earnings per day. For example, if the individual were fined one or two days, then it would be computed on the basis of his take-home pay each day, regardless of the amount. One person might have to pay $10 while another would have to pay $100, depending upon income. This type of sentence can be effected without moving an individual to a restitution house; but sometimes it is advisable to move the offender to a community-based facility in order to control his leisure-time activities, particularly if he has a drinking or drug problem. In any case, restitution has become an important part of community-based corrections. Group therapy or counseling in some form can help the offender understand the reasons for his or her particular sentence.

A typical restitution center is located at the YMCA in Minneapolis. Supported by a grant from LEAA, the program has four phases: (1) admission, (2) planning of employment and restitution procedures, (3) preparation for release, and (4) supervision under parole on the street.

An innovative approach to compensation is the 4-A Program (Arbitration as an Alternative to the Criminal Warrant) of the American Arbitration Association's National Center for Dispute Settlement. This program has been operating in Philadelphia and Hartford. It handles every kind of criminal warrant arising from neighborhood altercations (except murder), as well as property offenses.[30] Significant reductions in workload have been experienced in courts where such programs are used.[31]

PROGRAMS IN HALFWAY HOUSES

Programs in halfway houses generally involve work release or study release and group sessions for therapy and counseling. Again, the programs vary widely, frequently in response to the personality of the administrator, but the general purpose of reintegration of an offender into the community is always present. Because work release and study release are discussed more extensively in Chapter 6, further discussion of them here would be redundant. Suffice it to say that contact with the outside that involves alcohol, drugs, and the opposite sex always presents hazards in a correctional setting, even in the halfway house. Programs have to be developed to accommodate or ameliorate these problems.

Rehabilitation of offenders requires modification of behavior, but it also involves modification of social environment. When treatment is limited to an isolated setting of the traditional prison, the environment is not conducive to normal adaptation, and the environment the offender will return to in the community remains unchanged. A program of treatment in or near the offender's home community can include efforts to deal with social relationships and groups with which he or she will be involved after release. With these principles in mind, a prototype program was designed by Stoneman in Vermont for resident population of eighty male offenders 16 years of age or older; about forty of these were in a detention center in the community and about forty had been sentenced to more secure institutions.[32] The prototype center will provide for three types of program services—specialized social and psychological services, general services for the mental well-being of inmates, and services for physical well-being. Offenders will be furloughed to the community to the extent that they appear capable of accepting such freedom without further violation of the law. Second-felony adult offenders can be retained there and treated in the community at no greater risk to public safety than first offenders and with considerable

30 Hahn, *Community Based Corrections in the Criminal Justice System*, p. 104.

31 Janet Kole, "Arbitration as an Alternative to the Criminal Warrant," *Judicature* (American Judicature Society), 56, No. 7 (February 1973), 294.

32 Kent Stoneman, *A Prototype for a Community Correctional Center in Burlington, Vermont*, 1971 (mimeographed).

savings in financial and manpower resources.[33] The Community Treatment for Recidivist Offenders Project in Oakland County, Michigan, is one such program. It is an integral unit of the probation department in Pontiac. The special service for recidivists provides casework services and group methods with caseloads not exceeding thirty-five cases per officer. Volunteers are also used.

As mentioned earlier, there are three systems generally applied to programs in the correctional process: (1) change by compliance, (2) client-centered change, and (3) change by credibility in that it "makes sense." [34] The compliance model is designed to instill good habits, particularly work habits. The client-centered model assumes that the offender is a sick person and needs diagnosis and treatment that result in insight and understanding. The credibility model emphasizes inmate participation in shaping their program, making decisions, sharing information, and reintegration into the community as a desirable goal. This system emphasizes community treatment and avoids institutions as much as possible.

Community treatment centers have been constructed in several states. They are generally around urban areas where industry and commerce afford jobs and where treatment resources are available in the community. It appears generally not feasible to place a community treatment center in an area of less than 20,000 population because of the lack of support services. The size of the community treatment centers usually ranges between 30 to 100 residents.

The staff of a large center appropriately includes a superintendent with a program director and operations director reporting to him or her. The program director supervises counseling, group treatment, employment counseling, and mobilizes whatever treatment resources there are in the community. The operations director is responsible for the kitchen and food services, maintenance, transportation, and correctional workers. The correctional worker is primarily concerned with security and orderly regimen in the center. (Although community-based corrections is and should be less concerned with security and discipline than major institutions, it would be naive to ignore it completely.) The correctional worker grants passes, furloughs, and extended visitation hours. When problems arise because of residents coming in so late that their functioning on the job the following morning might be impaired, or when they come in drunk or under the influence of drugs, the correctional worker

---

[33] Mack E. Bradford, *A Study of the Community Treatment for Recidivist Offenders Project of Oakland County Circuit Court Probation Department* (NCCD, Pontiac, Michigan, Project) (East Lansing, Mich.: School of Criminal Justice, Michigan State University, 1972).

[34] Vincent O'Leary, "Correctional Assumptions and Their Program Implications," *National Conference on Pre-Release,* pp. 41–48.

Encounter group in drug treatment at Talbert House in Cincinnati.
Courtesy of Talbert House. Photo by Richard L. Shenk.

has to take appropriate action. This action can range from verbal counseling, perhaps reprimand, to a transfer to a more secure institution if the resident cannot handle the responsibility required to allow him to remain in the community treatment center. A small center could be supervised by the superintendent and a program director or counselor, with the superintendent taking over the functions of a program director and operations director. Programs in such facilities should include placement and assistance in making out job applications, budget management, constructive use of leisure time, passes and furloughs, religious activities, medical and dental services, counseling, driver licensing, educational placement and training, legal assistance, and parole orientation. Some halfway houses and community treatment centers, particularly for youth, have begun to use their in-house schools, rather than those in the community, because Title I of the Higher Education Act provides funds for education of delinquent children. Most of these centers, however, use community facilities.

Problems among the residents of halfway houses sometimes involve the intrusion of "street ethics." But such dicta as "keep your mouth shut" and "do your own time" cannot be allowed in a therapeutic community. In a halfway house the offender is his brother's keeper—mutual responsibility is foremost. Sometimes, residents can make decisions to a point decided by authority, which delimits their responsibility. It is desirable for them to make as many decisions as possible in the house. Regarding the use of decision-making authority, the question has to be the extent to which residents are permitted to take responsibility. Some programs permit only a token responsibility on the part of the residents; this is counterproductive to the idea of the halfway house. (This is one of the reasons that transfer of personnel from maximum security prisons to a community correctional center should be done sparingly and carefully.)

PROBLEMS IN HALFWAY HOUSES

Problems in halfway houses include alcohol, drugs, and sex. Further, community acceptance of the halfway house is always a problem. It has been suggested that Antabus (sometimes popularly referred to as "anta-buse") and community-based corrections go together, since it makes a person ill after drinking alcohol. The rules in some facilities permit visitors of the opposite sex and limited amounts of alcohol. In any case, many rules have to be explained adequately and loosely enforced. In an autocratically structured society, information is passed from the staff down, with little up-and-down communication. In a halfway house, however, success of the therapeutic community is dependent upon free up-and-down communication between the staff and residents without unnecessary display of authority.

Two basic errors have been committed in setting up some halfway houses.[35] First, there is a tendency simply to move institutional practice programs into smaller, community-based units. Some of this results from using personnel from the existing prison system to staff halfway houses operated by statewide correctional departments or divisions. Second, the mere placement of offenders in an open system does not mean they can handle this freedom without assistance and support. Beautiful buildings, new neighbors, and freedom do not automatically result in successful adjustment. As indicated previously, adjustment refers to social inter-action with other people and really has little to do with surroundings and demographic factors other than other people. Assistance, counseling, and group sessions are needed to avoid problems and to work out those that arise.

Good relationships with the press result in good relationships with the public, because many ideas and attitudes develop from information received in the mass media.[36] Like everyone else, newsmen are products

35 See Hahn, *Community Based Corrections in the Criminal Justice System*, p. 157.
36 Kuyk Logan, *The News Media and Work Release*, in *National Conference on Pre-Release*, pp. 82–91.

of their environment and can hardly be expected to report thoroughly or accurately on something to which they may never have been exposed. Consequently, correctional programs, particularly community-based programs, must involve the press and newsmen as well as police, the courts, and other correctional services. The news media can be used constructively and without "propagandizing" in order to inform the public of the objectives and problems in the correctional field.

CONCLUSIONS

Among convicted felons in America, approximately 56 percent are in maximum security institutions. Approximately 30 percent are in medium security institutions and about 14 percent in minimum security institutions. This means that a very small percentage are in community-based correctional facilities, although more are in halfways houses on probation or ex-offender status. It has been pointed out that total reliance upon community-based programming would be naive, because it would leave administrators "with a one-stringed banjo" while they were trying to deliver a "well orchestrated, diversified set of services." [37] Some offenders have demonstrated sufficient uncontrollable behavior to indicate removal from the community to varying degrees of institutional security. Offenders and ex-offenders in community-based programs must be selected in the interest of public safety, balanced against the knowledge that, in most cases, the sentence will terminate; public safety demands that offenders be released through the least dangerous procedure at the least dangerous time.

Every attempt at adjustment should be made before residential placement. All sorts of private resources should be used before using official facilities. For those requiring official facilities, small community-based settings, including halfway houses, specialized facilities such as residential treatment centers, detoxification units, reintegration centers, restitution shelters, and other facilities should be used. Maximum security institutions should be used only for dangerous offenders.

Halfway houses could become a viable alternative to prisons, according to a General Accounting Report to Congress, but more federal standards and state planning are needed.[38] GAO is the investigative arm of Congress over and above its own committees. A review of fifteen halfway

---

37 Milton Luger and Joseph S. Lobenthal, Jr., "Cushioning Future Shock in Correlations," *Federal Probation,* 38 (June 1974), 19.

38 "A New, Coordinated Effort Needed to Make Halfway Houses a Viable Alternative to Prisons—GAO Report Concludes," *Corrections Digest,* 6, No. 12 (June 11, 1975), 1.

houses operated by state and local government in Florida, Missouri, Pennsylvania, and Texas between September 1973 and June 1974 indicated that halfway houses could reduce the need to place many persons in outdated and overcrowded prisons commensurate with the public safety. Halfway houses are at a crucial stage in development, offering promise of a viable alternative to traditional corrections, but are still tenuous because of lack of funds and public support. The lack of efficiently organized, planned, and operated systems is partially because no single agency has been responsible for coordinating any statewide system. In the fifteen halfway houses subjected to review, there were about 3,000 offenders, of whom 2,600 had gone through the programs. Of those who failed to complete the program successfully, about 27 percent had absconded and 46 percent were returned to prison. The other 27 percent were discharged or their status was not determined. In comparison with the traditional prison program, it is obvious that the effects of residence in halfway houses are not any worse than probation, prison, and parole—and they appear in some cases to be better.

Chapter 6

Work Release, Study Release, and Furloughs

Work release, study release, and furloughs have been the most recent programs designed to maintain the contact of an institutionalized offender with the community. These projects permit a person confined in a prison or other correctional institution to go into the community to work, study, or visit family and friends. At first, such programs (then called day paroles) were applicable only to misdemeanants. Their purpose was to permit constructive contact with the community during the daytime while keeping the individual under control in the institution nights and weekends and most leisure time. The programs appeared to have both economic and rehabilitative value.

DEVELOPMENT OF WORK RELEASE PROGRAMS

On September 10, 1965 President Lyndon B. Johnson signed into law the Prisoners Rehabilitation Act of 1965, which authorized work release for adult felons in the United States Bureau of Prisons. Since that time, work release in the federal system has been quite extensive. By 1973, thirty-six states had authorization for such programs in state institutions and twenty-six states had authorization in county or municipal institutions; twenty-four of those also had programs in state institutions.[1] At present, other states are also using work release programs at the misdemeanant and felony level.[2]

---

[1] Sol Rubin, *The Law of Criminal Correction*, 2nd ed. (St. Paul, Minn.: West Publishing Co., 1973), p. 329.

[2] Stanley E. Grupp, "Work Release—Statutory Patterns, Implementation, and Prob-

When the Prisoners Rehabilitation Act was passed by Congress in 1965, community-based corrections, including work release, had achieved recognition and acceptance. But even when the law permitted work release plans, they were used sparingly. Martin Myrick, representing the Wisconsin's Sheriffs Association, for example, points out that even though the day parole plan originated in Wisconsin and was given the best trial there, it is still viewed with mixed emotions, with some counties using it and others ignoring it.[3] The same observation was made by Sanger Powers, Director of the Wisconsin Division of Corrections.[4] An official survey done by the Wisconsin Division of Corrections of the State Department of Public Welfare repeated the observation.[5] By November 1966, eight states, the District of Columbia, and the United States Bureau of Prisons had work release programs actually in operation.[6] It becomes obvious, then, that while the *idea* of work release was accepted, its actual implementation was quite slow. There were only 136 inmates on work release in Wisconsin between July 1, 1959, and June 30, 1961.[7] By December 31, 1965, 7,166 inmates had been approved for work release in North Carolina and, as of December 31, 1965, there were 406 felons and 601 misdemeanants on work release programs.[8]

Work release programs began with misdemeanants; it was not until

---

lems," *The Prison Journal,* 44, No. 1 (Spring 1964), 4–6. Also Sol Rubin, "Developments in Correctional Law," *Crime and Delinquency* (Vol. II, 1965: 196; Vol. 12, 1966: 187; Vol. 13, 1967: 362). Also Sol Rubin, "Developments in Correctional Law," *Crime and Delinquency,* 11 (1965), 196. Also Sol Rubin, "Developments in Correctional Law," *Crime and Delinquency,* 12 (1966), 187. Also Sol Rubin, "Developments in Correctional Law," *Crime and Delinquency,* 13 (1967), 362.

[3] Martin E. Myrick, "The Area of American Correction that Stood Still," *American Journal of Correction,* 20, No. 3 (May–June 1958), 7.

[4] "Day-Parole for Misdemeanants," *Federal Probation,* 22, No. 4 (December 1958), 42–46. John R. Gagnon repeated and emphasized the same problem—see "Jail Work Release Under the Huber Law," Proceedings of the 88th Annual Congress of Correction of the American Correctional Association (New York: American Correctional Association, 1958), pp. 391–98.

[5] Dean V. Babst, *Day Parole and Employment of County Jail Inmates, 1960 Survey of Wisconsin's Huber Law* (Madison, Wis.: State Department of Public Welfare, Bureau of Research, Research Bulletin C-6, February 1962).

[6] David D. Bachman, *Work-Release Programs for Adult Felons in the United States: A Descriptive Study,* Florida State University, unpublished master's thesis, June 1968, and Research Monograph No. 3, published by the Florida Division of Corrections, 1968.

[7] Martin R. Peterson, "Work Release Program," *Proceeding of the 22nd Meeting of the Southern States Prison Association* (New Orleans: Southern States Prison Association (1964), p. 25.

[8] Allen Ashman, "Work Release in North Carolina," *Popular Government,* 12, No. 9 (June 1966), 4.

1959 that North Carolina included felons from the state institutions in the programs. There are probably two reasons for North Carolina's leadership in this field of work release. First, all prisoners are sentenced to the State Department of Correction, whether they are misdemeanants or felons; this made simple the expansion of the 1957 law covering misdemeanants into the 1959 law that included felons sentenced to five years or less. George Randall, Director of Corrections at that time, indicated that both Wisconsin's Huber Law and North Carolina's version of it had been too restrictive, because they authorized the courts to recommend "work release privileges"—but almost half those recommended were denied these privileges because they lacked suitable employment.[9] And, too, North Carolina was having budget problems and had to find some way to reduce expenditures. By letting offenders go out on work release, the state could approach a balanced budget.

By 1966, work release was well enough established in several jurisdictions that a survey of state-operated programs in the United States appeared in the *Correctional Management Memo*.[10] In this publication, the state programs developed well enough to be included were those in California, Maryland, Massachusetts, North and South Dakota, Oregon, and Wisconsin. In addition, of course, the United States Bureau of Prisons had developed a program as a result of the Prisoners Rehabilitation Act of 1965.

The introduction of work release in North Carolina rested on economic factors favoring a creation of consensus among state agencies that the approach was desirable.[11] The State Highway and Public Works Commission experienced increased costs for highway construction at a time when greater mechanization of maintenance tasks reduced the feasibility of employing inmates. Simultaneously, North Carolina authorities were trying to improve the quality of rehabilitation programs. Employment of prisoners for highway maintenance required the dispersion of prisoners in relatively small units throughout the state, which would require a little capital investment. As a result, the program gained acceptance.

Economic and rehabilitative advantages of work release programs began to be recognized, and other states slowly began to adopt the program. Michigan authorized work release for misdemeanants in 1958,

9 George W. Randall, "North Carolina's Work Release Law," *Proceedings of the 93rd Annual Congress of Correction of the American Correctional Association* (Washington, D.C.: American Correctional Association, 1963), p. 98.

10 Walter Dunbar, "State Operated Work Furlough Programs in the United States," *Correctional Management Memo* (July–August 1966), pp. 1–15.

11 Elmer H. Johnson, "Work Release—A Study of Correctional Reform," *Crime and Delinquency*, 13 (October 1967), 521–30.

extended it to felons in 1962, but did not actually implement the program until 1968. Minnesota began a work release program in 1957 for misdemeanants, but it was not until 1964 that an reporting available to the public appeared,[12] and in 1965, it was learned that only twenty-one of the state's sixty-two counties had utilized the program at all.[13] California adopted its first work release legislation in 1957; it was patterned after Wisconsin's Huber Law and referred to the "work furlough." By March 1967, nineteen counties had passed enabling ordinances and eighteen counties had work furlough programs in effect.

In California, work furloughs for felons began in 1965. By 1971, an estimated 1,500 prisoners had passed through work furlough programs to parole. Work furlough is seen to be one of the most beneficial reforms of recent years, because it permits inmates to accumulate savings, money is sent home to support families, and moreover, long-term incarceration is avoided.[14] The short-term return, in which parolees experiencing problems may be returned to the institution for short periods of time in preference to formal revocation of parole, has also been successful.[15] The application of work release in California has been well delineated and functions uniformly throughout the state.[16]

The Ohio constitution prohibits private employment of felons. Consequently, work release and furlough programs have been limited in Ohio to misdemeanants and study release. Nevertheless, of 9,000 prisoners in 1972, there were about 2,000 who were eligible for this type of furlough.[17] Here, before any furlough can occur, the resident must have served one-third of his minimum sentence.

The Minnesota Department of Corrections work release program included 178 felony offenders from January 1, 1969 to December 31, 1969.[18] The work releasees were similar to the general population of the institutions with respect to race, marital status, and criminal record. There was, however, a higher proportion of women and older participants, a lower

---

[12] Elmer R. Anderson, "Work Release Sentencing," *Federal Probation*, 28, No. 4 (December 1964), 7–11.

[13] James F. Hulburt and Nathan G. Mandel, *Work Release in Minnesota* (St. Paul, Minn.: Minnesota Department of Corrections, 1966), pp. 1–14.

[14] *Pattern of Change* (Sacramento: California Department of Corrections, 1972), p. 13.

[15] Ibid., p. 10.

[16] *State Work Furlough Program Information Kit* (Sacramento: California Department of Corrections, 1967), p. 2.

[17] George J. Denton and N. Gatz, "Ohio's Work Furlough: College for Felons," *American Journal of Corrections*, 35, No. 3 (1973), 44–45.

[18] Carole L. Bartholomew, James J. Ryan, and Nathan G. Mandel, *Analysis of Work Release for Felons in Minnesota* (St. Paul, Minn.: Minnesota Department of Corrections, 1970).

Work release in South Carolina.

Courtesy of the South Carolina Department of Corrections, Columbia, South Carolina.

proportion of crimes against persons, and a higher proportion of theft and related crimes. Further, the work releasees had a higher level of skills than did the general inmate population. On the average, the participants had spent 23.85 months in an institution, but the average length of stay in the work release program was only four months. Of the 140 terminations during 1969, 79 were defined as successes and 61 as failures. No one was returned for a new offense, and about half of the failures were violations of work release rules; the other half of the "failures" absconded.

The work release program in Madison, Wisconsin, is extensive. Nearly all inmates serving jail sentences were released from confinement one or more times during the four-week study period—this included persons convicted of serious offenses who could have been incarcerated in state prisons. No elaborate screening guidelines or procedures were used, and there was no effort to screen out participants on the basis of seriousness of crime or presumed dangerousness. During the four-week study period, only one of forty-nine persons engaged in work release failed to return to jail at the prescribed time, and he turned himself in after a few days. This supports opinions that most offenders sentenced to jail can safely be permitted to participate in work release.[19]

---

[19] Richard K. Brautigam, "Work Release: A Case Study and Comment," *Prison Journal*, 52, No. 2 (1973), 20–35.

The number of prisoners on work release in each state in 1971 is shown in Table 6-1.

TABLE 6-1   Inmates on Work Release—1971

State	Number of Men on Work Release	Total Adult Male Population	Percentage of Men on Work Release
Alabama	0	4,000	—
Alaska	47	400	11.8
Arizona	12	1,350	0.9
Arkansas	0	1,324	—
California	300	17,900	1.7
Colorado	36	1,943	1.9
Connecticut	14	1,500	0.9
Delaware	120	600	20.0
District of Columbia	326	1,700	19.2
Florida	650	9,000	7.2
Georgia	85	6,215	1.4
Hawaii	25	256	9.8
Idaho	12	391	3.1
Illinois	100	7,086	1.4
Indiana	150	4,500	3.3
Iowa	115	1,600	7.2
Kansas	No estimate available	660	—
Kentucky	0	3,010	—
Louisiana	125	4,100	3.0
Maine	0	350	—
Maryland	300	5,000	6.0
Massachusetts	15	2,300	0.7
Michigan	104	9,210	1.1
Minnesota	36	1,651	2.2
Mississippi	0	1,850	—
Missouri	No estimate available	3,449	—
Montana	10	272	3.7
Nebraska	40	1,000	4.0
Nevada	0	705	—
New Hampshire	10	217	4.6
New Jersey	125	5,500	2.3
New Mexico	7	742	0.9
New York	No estimate available	12,208	—
North Carolina	1,075	10,076	10.7
North Dakota	3	137	2.2
Ohio	0	9,145	—
Oklahoma	35	3,112	1.1
Oregon	133	1,831	7.3
Pennsylvania	0	5,328	—
Rhode Island	35	550	6.4
South Carolina	575	3,267	17.6
South Dakota	17	389	4.4

TABLE 6-1 (Continued)

State	Number of Men on Work Release	Total Adult Male Population	Percentage of Men on Work Release
Tennessee	146	3,300	4.4
Texas	36	14,640	0.2
Utah	40	540	7.4
Vermont	0	142	19.0
Virginia	150	6,000	2.5
Washington	125	2,437	5.1
West Virginia	0	1,046	—
Wisconsin	450	2,600	17.3
Wyoming	0	257	—

Kenneth J. Lenihan, "The Financial Condition of Released Prisoners," *Crime and Delinquency,* 21, No. 3 (July 1975), 275. Reprinted with permission of the National Council on Crime and Delinquency.

A directory of work release programs was produced by the American Justice Institute in Sacramento in 1972.[20] Such a directory was also produced at the Southern Illinois University at Carbondale in 1972.[21] With the introduction of new programs periodically and modifications of other programs for various reasons, it is difficult to keep a directory in any phase of community-based corrections current. Nevertheless, those available provide information concerning the well-established programs.

Legislation for work release had been enacted in forty-three states by 1973 (this includes the District of Columbia and the United States Bureau of Prisons). A survey of these programs has been presented in a series of six technical reports developed by the Center for the Study of Crime, Delinquency, and Corrections at Southern Illinois University at Carbondale.[22] Similarities were found between eligibility for work release, exclusion of certain types of offenders, the collection and disbursement of wages, conditions of employment, revocation of work release privileges, and the status of the releasee. A most significant finding was that 3.17 percent of the felon population of the United States is in work release. General optimism was found among supervisors and offenders on work

---

[20] W. H. Busher, *Work Release—A Directory of Programs and Personnel—Work Release Resource Document No. 2* (Sacramento: American Justice Institute, 1972).

[21] R. J. Scott, *Work Release—Toward an Understanding of the Law, Policy and Operation of Community-Based State Corrections—National Directory—State Work Release Centers* (Carbondale, Ill.: Southern Illinois University, 1972).

[22] Richard M. Swanson, *Work Release: Toward an Understanding of the Law, Policy and Operation of Community-Based State Corrections* (Carbondale, Ill.: Southern Illinois University, Center for the Study of Crime, Delinquency, and Corrections, 1973).

release regarding the success of community-based correctional programs. Variables considered to be superior in work release were attitudes toward the work release program itself, attitudes toward earning a living, expectations of attaining life goals, and atttitudes toward law and justice.

There has, however, been some public resistance and concern in many areas about work release programs. As such programs began to be implemented in the mid-1960s practitioners and researchers working together on the problem expressed a need for caution.[23] The entire Spring 1964 issue of *The Prison Journal* was devoted to work release programs in Europe and in the United States.[24] Grupp noted that in Illinois, such programs were not active and that the sheriffs in Illinois had mixed viewpoints about them.[25] A subsequent survey of sheriffs on a nationwide basis indicated that the majority were in favor of these programs, but had neither the personnel nor the physical facilities to handle them.[26] Grupp's survey of work release in the United States indicated that by 1965, there were twenty-four states and eleven foreign countries that had some type of work release program.[27]

PRACTICES AND PROBLEMS IN WORK RELEASE PROGRAMS

The overall objectives of work release programs can be listed as follows. They exist to

1. Ease the transition from the prison to the community.
2. Place the offender on a job he can retain.
3. Enable the inmate to support himself by reimbursing the state for his maintenance.
4. Enable the inmate to support dependents.
5. Help determine readiness for parole.
6. Preserve family and community ties.[28]

---

[23] John J. Galvin, ed., *Treating Youth Offenders in the Community* (Washington, D.C.: Correctional Research Associates, 1966), p. 20.

[24] *The Prison Journal*, 44, No. 1 (Spring 1964), 4–25.

[25] Stanley E. Grupp, "Work Release as Viewed by Illinois Sheriffs," *Police*, 9, No. 6 (July–August 1965), 19–25.

[26] Stanley E. Grupp, "Work Release—the Sheriffs' Viewpoint," *Crime and Delinquency*, 13 (July 1967), 513–20.

[27] Stanley E. Grupp, "Work Release and the Misdemeanant," *Federal Probation*, 29, No. 2 (June 1965), 7–8.

[28] Bachman, *Work-Release Programs for Adult Felons*, p. 46.

Some administrators have suggested that any candidate who could be trusted on work release should be a suitable candidate for probation.[29] Others believe that work release is a good mid-point between probation and institutionalization, in which the individual can remain in his community but have his evenings and weekends controlled to avoid "leisure-time problems." The most recent *Manual of Correctional Standards* has only one paragraph and two other brief references to work release and does not provide any "standards."[30] The American Law Institute suggested a model law covering work release in 1962.[31] It recommended that discretion for work release programs be left with the institution, rather than the court. It also suggested collection of an inmate's wages with distributions to his or her dependents, and suggested extra time allowances for successful performance on work release programs. The National Council on Crime and Delinquency presented a Model Sentencing Act in 1963 that did not mention work release during sentencing, but did recommend its use for misdemeanants.[32] A similar reference was made in the 1966 version of the Model Sentencing Act.[33]

Certainly, work release programs can eliminate or reduce the "social surgery" that occurs when ties are cut with family and community. Many work release programs are designed to be retained after parole. This is effected by placing the offender on a program in the city in which he intends to reside after release. This permits him (or her) to go from the community correctional center to his home, and he can keep his job. As has been mentioned before, most programs of this type require that the inmate pay the state a stipulated amount for board and room and another amount for transportation. In addition, there is frequently a requirement for a savings of 10 percent of take-home wages, which are generally turned over to the community correctional center counselor or bookkeeper for deposits in a savings account and allowance for incidental expenses. The rest is sent home for support of dependents. Successful completion of a work release program, of course, is a demonstration of a person's ability to get along in the community and to hold a job.

The purposes for which work release may be granted are as follows:[34]

1. Participation in education, training, or on-the-job training programs.
2. Working at regular gainful employment.

---

29 Mark S. Richmond, "The Jail Blight," *Crime and Delinquency*, 2 (1965), 137.

30 *Manual of Correctional Standards*, 3rd ed. (New York: American Correctional Association, 1966), pp. 17–135, 147.

31 *Model Penal Code* (Philadelphia: American Law Institute, 1962), pp. 264–66.

32 *Model Sentencing Act* (New York: NCCD, 1963), p. 26.

33 *Standard Act for State Correctional Services* (New York: NCCD, 1966), p. 29.

34 Ibid., p. 47.

3. Seeking employment.

4. Conducting own business or profession.

5. Receiving treatment (medical, psychiatric, alcoholics anonymous, etc.)

6. Rendering free service to nonprofit organizations.

Work release programs, of course, emphasize employment.

Eligibility for work release includes many factors. Generally, it is made possible at the end of the person's sentence, so that he or she may have six months to a year in work release programs. Practice in various programs has been to eliminate certain types of offenders from consideration (e.g., those convicted of assaultive or violent and/or aggressive crimes, or crimes of sex deviation, child molestation; also eliminated are narcotics addicts, professional criminals, mental defectives, serious alcoholics, and recidivists with extensive criminal records). (See Table 6-2.)

It has been discovered that a broad knowledge of the work release programs needs to be provided to law enforcement agencies, courts, labor unions, and other interested persons, and agencies. If police do not know a person is involved in such a program, they may pick him up for investigation of possible escape. Support from these agencies of the criminal justice system is needed for a successful program.

Some employers are hesitant to hire offenders on work release programs. Suggestions as to how to overcome this hesitancy have been presented in an informative article on work release by Mason Sacks. These include

1. Placing emphasis on the careful screening of offenders in the work release program.

2. Providing testimonials from other satisfied employers.

3. Encouraging employer-inmate face-to-face contact before employment.

4. Stressing how much the inmate has at stake.

5. Demonstrating proven record of success during the past few years.

6. Assuring the employer that he does not have to "babysit" the offender.

7. Suggesting hiring on trial basis.

8. Assuring the employer that the prison staff is available 24 hours a day in case of emergency.[35]

Other resistance to work release programs sometimes comes from citizens who think that they should have had first priority for jobs, particularly during times of high unemployment.

---

[35] Mason J. Sacks, "Making Work Release Work: Convincing the Employer," *Crime and Delinquency*, 21, No. 3 (July 1975), 255–65.

TABLE 6-2 Criteria for Exclusion from Work Release Programs
by Offense or Background

	Violence	Sexual Crimes	Narcotics Sale	Narcotics Use	Notoriety	Organized Crime
California	X	X	X	—	—	—
Connecticut	X	X	X	X	X	X
Florida	—	X	X	—	—	X
Georgia	X	—	—	—	X	X
Illinois	X	X	X	X	X	X
Indiana	X	X	X	X	X	—
Louisiana	X	—	X	X	—	—
Massachusetts	X	X	—	—	—	—
Maryland	X	X	X	X	X	—
Michigan	X	X	X	—	—	X
Minnesota	X	X	X	X	—	—
Montana	X	—	—	—	X	—
Nebraska	X	—	—	—	X	X
New Jersey	X	X	X	—	X	X
New Mexico	X	—	—	—	—	X
New York	X	X	X	X	—	—
New York City	X	X	X	X	X	X
North Carolina	—	X	X	X	X	—
South Carolina	—	X	X	X	X	—
South Dakota	X	X	—	—	—	—
Texas	X	X	X	X	—	X
Virginia	—	X	X	X	—	—
Washington	X	—	—	—	X	—
Wisconsin	X	X	—	—	—	—
TOTALS	20	18	16	12	12	10

Lawrence S. Root, "State Work Release Programs: An Analysis of Operational Policies,"
Federal Probation, 37, No. 4 (December 1973), 53.

Rule violations in work release status are more a product of accommodation to the half-free status of the participants than a threat to the
internal security of the prison or safety of the community. If a prisoner's infractions of rules intended to maintain the prison's internal security
have been of low frequency, but there is unorthodox behavior at the
place of employment (drunkenness, traffic violations, difficulties with
employers or fellow employees, attempting to withhold the paycheck,
and similar offenses), this means that the violations *per se* are simply
the function of the new status rather than violations of the social order.
Remedies appear to be limited to more stringent and cautious selection
of people to go on work release and better counseling, since stronger custody would not be appropriate in a work release program. Some of-

fenders have been temporarily withdrawn from the program as a reprimand and then reinstated successfully.

Absconding is one of the primary problems in work release programs.
A study was done of the District of Columbia misdemeanor work release
program.[36] Except for the incidence of drug offenses, the absconders (36
out of 294 participants) were similar to those who did not abscond in
terms of offense, age, and other recorded factors. A sizable proportion of
them were skilled workers with weekly income of at least $60.

Some work release programs take extensive measures to avoid abuse.
The Spokane, Washington, work release unit attempts to protect society
while resocializing adult offenders and assisting in their re-entry into
society. The resident's time away from the facility and his work attendance are closely controlled. Further, polygraph tests and urinalysis are
used for control purposes. Any use of alcohol or drugs can be found
immediately, and questionable activities are investigated by interrogation
with the use of the polygraph.

A correctional client's attitudes toward placement in a community as
compared with a jail work release setting usually depends upon the
attitudes of the community.[37] In general, most individuals prefer to be
placed in the community. Jail personnel who work with offenders all the
time tend to develop negative attitudes to a greater extent than people
in the community.

Work releasees respond to the expectations of counselors and job supervisors. Not surprisingly, if they are treated favorably, they tend to have
better self-esteem, and negative self-esteem results from negative treatment. Reaction to treatment is higher at the beginning of the work release period, but it usually stabilizes after three to six months. The more
mature a work releasee is, the less he or she is affected by treatment by
counselors and job supervisors. Younger offenders seem to be more negative toward authority.

Waldo, Chiricos, and Dobrin compared a group of control inmates
with work release inmates with similar backgrounds and demographic
characteristics in a study of attitudes.[38] They found that there was no
significant change in attitudes that could be attributed to work release in

[36] L. E. Morrison and J. P. Hefferan, "A Carefully Administered Work Release
Program Does Work," *Washington Law Enforcement Journal*, 4, No. 2 (1974), 17.

[37] B. S. Brown and J. D. Spevacek, "Work Release in Community and Institutional
Settings," *Corrective Psychiatry and Journal of Social Therapy*, 17, No. 2 (1971), 35–42.

[38] Gordon P. Waldo, Theodore G. Chiricos, and Leonard E. Dobrin, *Community
Contact and Inmate Attitudes: An Experimental Assessment of Work Release*, Southeastern Correctional and Criminological Research Center, Florida State University, 1972
(mimeographed).

the factors they measured. In attitudes relating to perception of legitimate opportunity, there was no difference. For achievement motivation attitudes, there was a slight tendency in favor of work releasees, but it was not statistically significant. Both groups were pessimistic in terms of legal self-concept and chances of further conflict with the law. In self-esteem, there was improvement among the work releases. Both groups emphasized that nothing works out right without some luck, felt that a person should never back down from a fight, and that the tough guy has it made. Self-esteem holds up for six months or so, but tends to diminish after then.

Work release has been viewed in some quarters as sometimes lacking in beneficial effects. One study of dysfunctional factors observed by the research staff in the Manpower Administration in 1971 and 1972 found some factors (such as overcontrol in some areas) that, despite positive value or potential, degenerated into a source of anger and frustration on the part of the work releasees.[39] This, of course, would be counterproductive to the work release objectives.

Other studies have found that the work releasees in some places did not define themselves as criminals, but the staff of the jail did.[40] Also, in this 1968 to 1970 study of 2,360 minimum security inmates of the Santa Clara County Jail in California, specialized vocational rehabilitation service was found to be a high-cost, low-yield venture. Work furlough inmates were found to have made a far better adjustment in the post-release period than did nonfurlough inmates.

Work release programs are not meeting the promises of their rhetoric, apparently because of the need for traditional correctional administrators to maintain control beyond that which is necessary.[41] Work release is for those who are not considered to be threats to the community but nevertheless need closer supervision and more support than is possible under probation or parole. A positive public relations effort is clearly needed. Otherwise the public will react only to those persons who have failed on the program and thus get into the newspapers. Until implementation reflects a consideration of the needs of the offender and a realistic view of the safety of society, the work release program will be only a transitory thing, ornamenting the traditional correctional structure.

On the other hand, cost benefit analyses of work furlough programs

39 R. Pooley, "Work Release Programs and Corrections: Goals and Deficits," *Criminal Justice Behavior*, 1, No. 1 (1974), 62–72.

40 Alvin Rudoff and T. C. Esselstyn, "Evaluating Work Furlough: A Followup," *Federal Probation*, 37, No. 2 (1973), 48–53.

41 Lawrence S. Root, "State Work Release Programs: An Analysis of Operational Policies," *Federal Probation*, 37, No. 4 (December 1973), 52–58.

have shown conclusively that the taxpayer saves money while simultaneously achieving better results from community-based corrections.[42]

STUDY RELEASE

A study release program permits a resident of a prison or correctional institution to leave the institution and go to school. One of the early programs of this type was at the United States Penitentiary at Marion, Illinois, which permitted inmates and officers to go together to the Southern Illinois University at Carbondale, twelve miles west, for study. In that situation, officers and inmates were in the same classes, left the institution together, and returned together. For the institutions that do not have vocational training and other educational programs, the community may be able to provide these. Many states use study release programs for technical training and junior college study. Computer programs and the conventional trades have been the most popular areas of study.

Study release at the TEC Center (technical school).

Courtesy of the South Carolina Department of Corrections, Columbia, South Carolina.

---

[42] Alvin Rudoff and T. C. Esselstyn, *Jail Inmates at Work* (San Jose, Cal.: San Jose State College Foundation, 1971), esp. Chapter X, Fiscal Analysis, pp. 74–75.

Many states and the United States Bureau of Prisons have made arrangements with local colleges, universities, junior colleges, vocational schools, and other educational institutions and training institutes to enable inmates to learn trades, get a high school diploma, or earn a degree. From federal institutions alone, 3,000 inmates were in college in 1973 [43] and there were many more than that from various state systems around the country.

In Ohio, where the constitution prohibits state prisoners from working for private persons or firms (thus eliminating work release programs), study release is available. After one-third of the sentence has been served, state prisoners become eligible for such programs. One problem involved is finding an educational institution that is willing to house furloughees below the maximum cost allowable by the state.[44] This daily cost is based on the cost of imprisonment. Tuition, books, and materials must be acquired through other resources if the costs exceed the daily allowable cost.

THE NEWGATE PROGRAM

The NewGate Program brings the university into the prison to instruct inmates who will be released. As they are released, they are moved to a halfway house or other facility on the university campus and live like other students. Originated in 1967 in Oregon by Thomas Gaddis (author of *Birdman of Alcatraz*), the program was funded by the Office of Economic Opportunity, and the NewGate Program is now in six states, and is being promoted by the National Council on Crime and Delinquency (NCCD). The NewGate Program was evaluated by the NCCD in 1971 and 1972 and optimistic results were reported.[45] In some of the later programs (such as in New Mexico), the halfway house on campus has been eliminated and the student-offender is allowed to live in a university dormitory, reporting once a week to a counselor as part of the supervision.

FURLOUGHS

Furloughs have always been permitted for prisoners for family illness and death. Traditionally, an officer accompanied a prisoner on

---

[43] Harry E. Allen and Clifford E. Simonsen, *Corrections in America: An Introduction* (Beverly Hills: Glencoe Press, 1975), p. 461.

[44] George J. Denton and N. Gatz, "Ohio's Work Furlough: College for Felons," *American Journal of Corrections*, 35, No. 3 (1973), 44–45.

[45] Rex Herron, *Project NewGate—Past, Present, and Future* (Albany: State University of New York, 1973).

furlough. Recently, however, the program has been extended so that some individuals can be checked out by family or friends. Many people consider the furlough to be one of the best means of preserving and strengthening the inmate's family ties, provided it is supplemented by the preservation and creation of other linkages with the community.[46]

The furlough is one of the most widespread newer methods of providing people in custody with an opportunity to prepare themselves for release by letting them leave the institution and visit their families and interview employers. Pennsylvania has had a furlough program since October 1971; 4,250 prisoners were released the first year, with only 37 not returning at the appointed time. Many other countries also grant furloughs, including the U.S.S.R., Denmark, Germany, and England.

The furlough has been viewed as superior to the conjugal visit in maintaining family heterosexual relations.[47] Its focus is not on sex—it is considered primarily a social and family event. In some jurisdictions, nonmarried mates have been permitted to check men and women out of the institution for up to eight hours.

Of fifty-two correctional agencies surveyed regarding furlough practices, forty-four states and the United States Bureau of Prisons had furlough programs in 1971, five did not (Delaware, Maryland, Nevada, New Mexico, and Wyoming), and two did not respond (Hawaii and Missouri).[48] Twenty-five agencies reported unsupervised home furloughs. Only Arkansas and Mississippi have been conducting home furloughs on a formal basis for more than fifteen years. The maximum time a person can be gone on furlough ranges from one day to thirty days. The number of absconders from furlough ranged from none (in nine agencies) to a high of 8 per 100.[49] The jurisdictions with furlough programs and their authorization are shown in Table 6-3; absconding rates are shown in Table 6-4. Table 6-5 depicts the 1974 data on furloughs in the United States.

Prison furloughs were first authorized by Congress for the District of Columbia prisons and the United States Bureau of Prisons in 1967. By August 1971, almost 2,000 "evaluative furloughs" had been granted. Primarily because of police resistance, the program was temporarily halted for a while in late 1971; but it was reinstated, and during 1973, 500 in-

---

[46] Norval Morris and Gordon Hawkins, *The Honest Politician's Guide to Crime Control* (Chicago: University of Chicago Press, 1970), pp. 128–29.

[47] Carson W. Markley, "Furlough Programs and Conjugal Visiting in Adult Correctional Institutions," *Federal Probation*, 37 (March 1973), 19–25.

[48] Robert R. Smith and Michael A. Milan, *A Survey of the Home Furlough Policies of American Correctional Agencies* (Montgomery, Ala.: Experimental Manpower Laboratory for Corrections, Rehabilitation Research Foundation, 1972), p. 3.

[49] Ibid., p. 4.

TABLE 6-3   Jurisdictions with Furlough Programs and Their Authorizations

		Authorization	
		Legislative Provisions	Departmental Regulations
	Alaska	X	X
	Arkansas		
	California	X	
	Colorado	X	
	Connecticut	X	
	District of Columbia	X	
	Federal Bureau	X	
	Florida	X	
Agencies reporting home	Hawaii	X	
furlough programs in opera-	Idaho	X	
tion as of January 1, 1971	Iowa	X	
	Louisiana		X
	Maine	X	
	Maryland	X	
	Michigan		X
	Minnesota	X	
	Mississippi		X
	Nebraska	X	
	New Mexico	X	
	North Carolina	X	
	North Dakota	X	
	Oregon	X	
	South Carolina	X	
	Utah	X	
	Vermont	X	

Robert R. Smith and Michael A. Milan, *A Survey of the Home Furlough Policies of American Correctional Agencies* (Montgomery, Ala.: Experimental Manpower Laboratory for Corrections, Rehabilitation Research Foundation, 1972), p. 10.

mates were granted a total of 20,000 furloughs.[50] U.S. Attorney General Saxbe halted them again in 1974, but they were reinstated in 1975.

Unfortunately, evaluations of furlough programs by law enforcement officers and some representatives of the courts, such as in the District of Columbia, have been generally negative. To mitigate these negative attitudes and enhance the success of the furlough program, it is advisable to consult with the police, the judiciary, the prosecution, and other interested people so they will support the program or not attack it and not

[50] "Furloughs in D.C.—A Tense Issue," *Corrections Magazine,* 1, No. 4 (March/April 1975), 55–58.

TABLE 6-4 Abscondence Rates in Furlough Programs

		Agencies Reporting Home Furlough Program in Operation	Agencies Reporting Abscondence Rates	Weighted Mean Abscondence Rates
	1	2	2	.000
	2	8	4	.008
Maximum number of days of	3	4	4	.008
release permissible under provi-	4	1	1	.000
sions of home furlough program	5	2	1	.004
	10	4	4	.018
	30	4	2	.012

Robert R. Smith and Michael A. Milan, *A Survey of the Home Furlough Policies of American Correctional Agencies* (Montgomery, Ala.: Experimental Manpower Laboratory for Corrections, Rehabilitation Research Foundation, 1972), p. 12.

be surprised when they see a person on the street whom they had arrested only a few months before! The positive results of continued family and community contacts have been evaluated less extensively and based on interviews and observation. But it seems apparent that the continuing ties have made it easier for prisoners to be reintegrated into the community.[51]

CONCLUSIONS

Work release, study release, and furlough programs are designed to preserve contacts with the family and the community so that a prisoner's reintegration into society will be easier. Work release has been said to have begun in Vermont in 1906,[52] but the first authorization for it in state law was the Huber Law in Wisconsin in 1913. In 1959 North Carolina was the first state to use it for felons as well as misdemeanants. Since that time, the majority of jurisdictions in the United States and many foreign countries have used it in the criminal justice system. Study

[51] An excellent bibliography of the field of furloughs and work release was developed in 1973 at the University of California. See Dorothy Campbell Tompkins and Walter H. Busher, *Furlough from Prison* (Berkeley: University of California Institute of Governmental Studies, Public Policy Bibliographies No. 5, 1973).

[52] Walter H. Busher, *Ordering Time to Serve Prisoners: A Manual for the Planning and Administering of Work Release* (Washington, D.C.: United States Department of Justice, Law Enforcement Assistance Administration, 1973), p. ix.

TABLE 6-5   National Survey on Prison Furlough Programs

This chart reflects the results of a national survey of furlough programs conducted by *Corrections Magazine*. Most of the statistics were solicited by letter. Many state correctional agencies had no statistics available on their furlough programs. In some cases, they were able only to estimate the number of furloughs granted in a typical month and in all of fiscal 1974. In some cases, the annual total was divided by twelve to provide an approximate monthly figure. In general, rounded-off figures are estimates. In all cases, these figures represent the number of furloughs granted, not the number of individuals involved. Most agencies could not supply the latter figure. Many inmates receive multiple furloughs.

	NUMBER OF FURLOUGHS			
	Adults		Juveniles	
	Per Month	Fiscal 1974	Per Month	Fiscal 1974
Alabama	90	1,805	NA[1]	NA
Alaska	NA	NA	NA	NA
Arizona	NA	77[2]	NA	NA
Arkansas	14[3]	170[3]	NA	NA
California	93[3]	1,121[3]	25	960
Colorado	190	2,300	150	1,800
Connecticut	550	6,600	235	2,800
Delaware	25	450	75-80	800-1,000
D.C.	3,000[4]	38,000[4]	NA	NA
Florida	4,388[5]	53,000	84	1,011
Georgia	230	2,800	137	1,643
Hawaii	Not permitted		27	499
Idaho	21	200	43	300
Illinois	375[3]	4,500[3]	1,400	16,300
Indiana	38	425[6]	110	1,300
Iowa	186	2,238	NA	NA
Kansas	25	302	122	1,346
Kentucky	45	500	7	78
Louisiana	NA	1,671	NA	NA
Maine	78	935	64	767
Maryland	500-700	5,000	210	2,100
Massachusetts	651[5]	8,115	No juvenile institutions	
Michigan	400-500	5,282	45	500
Minnesota	33	393	NA	600
Mississippi	40	490	60-75	800-900
Missouri	NA	934	Not permitted	
Montana	Not permitted		34	402
Nebraska	194	2,322	Included in adult figures	
Nevada	Furlough program just approved		1-2	8-10
New Hampshire	Furlough program just approved		100	1,200
New Jersey	8,352	696	NA	NA
New Mexico	NA	135	Included in adult figures	
New York	1,352	16,226	188	2,250
North Carolina	2,918	35,020	130[7]	1,560

	NUMBER OF FURLOUGHS			
	Adults		Juveniles	
	Per Month	Fiscal 1974	Per Month	Fiscal 1974
North Dakota	6	29	7	168
Ohio	Furlough program just approved		200-300	3,160
Oklahoma	Not permitted		106	1,282
Oregon	3,716	27,000	NA	NA
Pennsylvania	350	1,506	1,500	18,000
Rhode Island	Furlough program just approved		150	1,800
South Carolina	753	9,877	Not permitted	
South Dakota	1	10	Included in adult figures	
Tennessee	105	1,300	459	5,508
Texas	Not permitted		200	2,400
Utah	45	540	25–40	350-400
Vermont	778	9,340	50	700
Virginia	NA	4,500	127[8]	2,000
Washington	239	2,865	86	1,040
West Virginia	Not permitted		Not permitted	
Wisconsin	Not permitted		NA	NA
Wyoming	Not permitted		Not permitted	
Federal System	1,450	17,400	No juvenile institutions	

Michael S. Serrill, "Prison Furlough in America," Corrections Magazine, 1, No. 6 (July/August 1975), 5. Copyright © 1975 by Corrections Magazine/CIS, Inc., 801 Second Avenue, New York, N.Y. 10017; reprinted by permission.

[1] NA = Figures not available.
[2] From December 1974 through April 1975.
[3] Excludes furloughs from work release centers.
[4] Includes some work- and study-release. Program recently cut back sharply.
[5] For April 1975.
[6] From July 1974 through May 1975.
[7] From January 1975 through May 1975.
[8] For May 1975.

release is a modification of the work release program; it permits offenders in prison to go to school and college in the community. Study release is of much more recent origin (1960s). Home furloughs have been used by Arkansas and Mississippi for over fifteen years and became part of the criminal justice system in a formal way after Congress authorized their use in the federal system in 1967.

Evaluation of work release, study release, and furlough programs remains mixed. Researchers using experimental and control groups tend to indicate that there are no real results, either negative or positive; thus many groups who want to "keep the criminal off the streets" accept that as an indication that the programs are not working. Others have held that evaluating success and failure on the basis of race, sex, age, annual income, and other factors easily collected is an oversimplification. Rather, there are social, emotional, personality, and other factors that are not easily measured or accounted for in evaluating success and failure. Practitioners in these programs evaluate them in a judgmental way and are optimistic about their success. Some researchers have shown that in terms of cost benefit analysis, the programs are effective and cost the taxpayer less money than is the case for traditional incarceration.

Chapter 7

Community Services Management

Community services management is central to community-based corrections. It requires intimate knowledge of community resources and close contact with the offenders and ex-offenders it serves so that they can be counseled and guided into using community resources to the extent of their needs. This function can be served by a community services officer in the police department, as suggested by the President's Commission on Law Enforcement and Administration of Justice in 1967;[1] a community services coordinator, as established in Atlanta and other larger cities in 1967 by the United States Bureau of Prisons; a community-based correctional administrator or practitioner; or by persons specially assigned from the traditional correctional agencies in probation, institutions, and parole.

The President's Commission on Law Enforcement and Administration of Justice recommended using a "community service officer" to handle the mobilization of community resources to assist offenders and ex-offenders. This person assists the police, probation and parole agents, and other persons and agencies concerned with the criminal justice system.

> Basic police functions, especially in large and medium sized urban departments, should be divided among three kinds of officers, here termed the community service officer, the police officer, and the police agent.[2]

---

[1] *The Challenge of Crime in a Free Society* (Washington, D.C.: The President's Commission on Law Enforcement and Administration of Justice, 1967), pp. 68, 98, 108–109, 118.

[2] Ibid., p. 98.

Contact and communication with the police is a basic function of the community services officer, because police are generally the first to encounter trouble in the community. Furthermore, no agency knows the community better than the police. Good contacts with the police are necessary for effective communication of the problems and objectives of the corrections component.

Community services management is designed to mobilize community resources so that the probation and parole agent or officer is free to perform the assistance, counseling, and casework services he was originally hired to provide. A community services manager provides links between various agencies comprising the criminal justice system and all agencies in the community. His is not a supervisory function; rather, he has a complementary role. His activities may include mobilizing activities involving education, brokerage, help, enablement, guidance, mediation, advocation, innovation, coordination, and any other services that help resolve problems of offenders and therefore increase the probability of their successful adjustment in society.[3] He makes contacts with business and industry for employment, welfare agencies for income maintenance when necessary, mental health and child guidance agencies, legal aid and public defender agencies. He may solicit volunteer assistance from professionals and lay persons, making contacts with churches and religious groups. He provides assistance in all sorts of crises. In short, the community services agent is a resource person for the probation and parole agents, the police, the courts, and all segments of the community.

As in other phases of community-based corrections, there is no single type of organization or delivery of services that could clearly identify a single pattern of community services. There are community service coordinators, representatives, directors, and divisions. A division of community services was established in the United States Bureau of Prisons in 1967 and later divided into community treatment centers and regional managers for community programs. The regional managers are described as having "primary responsibility for developing and coordinating community services to offenders within their respective regions" and "coordinate technical assistance to state and local organizations for the broad purpose of upgrading correctional practices."[4] At the federal level, there are regional offices headed by community programs managers in Baltimore, Atlanta, Chicago, Dallas, Denver, and San Francisco. These offices

---

3 H. Thomas Tubbs, "Community Services for Adults," in *Proceedings of the Thirteenth Annual Southern Conference on Corrections, February 29–March 1, 1968,* Florida State University, pp. 112–17.

4 *1973 Directory—Juvenile and Adult Correctional Institutions and Agencies* (College Park, Maryland: American Correctional Association, 1973), p. 122.

supervise and promote community services in their respective regions. Several states also have community services programs.

Minor crises that would not bother most people throw many offenders and ex-offenders into a state of frustration, confusion, and panic. Without help and proper guidance, they may resort to the only solution they know and commit further crime as an anxiety-reducing procedure. In fact, this is central to the recidivism cycle.[5] This is why community service management needs to provide personal assistance and guidance in some of the simplest social and economic problems.

EMPLOYMENT

Employment is one of the most difficult and crucial functions in the adjustment of offenders and ex-offenders. Before the establishment of community services, many probation and parole agents spent a great deal of their time finding jobs for offenders. Some institutions and correctional departments maintained a permanent job placement officer. Now the community services agent, wherever he functions, has taken that heavy burden from the workload of probation and parole agents.

The United States Employment Service, operating under the Department of Labor, maintains employment services throughout the United States. Community services agents work closely with these offices. In addition, they can work with the many private employment agencies, some of which may specialize in certain areas of interest to the offender or ex-offender. (Because of the high fees of private agencies, however, the private employment agency is generally used as a last resort.) Personal contacts with local businesses and industries are also helpful. There are some large, well-known corporations that view the hiring of offenders and ex-offenders favorably because of the extra supervision provided by parole and probation functions and the crisis intervention available from the community services agent.

Attitudes of employers vary quite widely regarding hiring offenders and ex-offenders. Some firms are truly altruistic—there is one middle-sized Midwestern corporation that hires *only* offenders and ex-offenders, because the president of the firm went through the prison experience when he was a younger man. There are some businesses, however, that hire people with prison records mainly for exploitation. Some firms refuse flatly to hire offenders and ex-offenders. Some of these rejections are motivated by fear, while others are based on the "moral" grounds that

---

5 Vernon Fox, "Analysis of Prison Disciplinary Problems," *Journal of Criminal Law, Criminology and Police Science*, 49, No. 4 (November–December 1958), 321–26.

the company does not want a deviant or "criminal" in the organization. Any agent must be wary and protect his clients from such companies. Some state and federal regulatory and licensing boards and agencies exclude prisoners and ex-prisoners from their professions and trades. Many states and, until recently, the federal civil service commissions include a question, "Have you ever been convicted of a felony?" on their applications. If the answer is affirmative, the applicant is automatically disqualified. In recent years, these barriers have been reduced, but they still exist in many jurisdictions and occupations.

The majority of jobs obtained by community services agents for offenders and ex-offenders are in the areas of labor and service occupations, but the best jobs require licensing and bonding, so are seldom available, because insurance companies selling fidelity bonds exclude those with prison records. For example, a former inmate may work as a taxi driver and save enough money to buy the company—but he cannot do this because of insurance regulations and policies regarding bonding. There have been some private agencies that have supported bonding for ex-offenders. And there has been movement recently by some organizations to relax the bonding problem. Bonabond, an ex-offender organization in Washington, D.C., has succeeded in bonding many ex-offenders. The United States Bureau of Prisons now has ex-offenders working in its central office and elsewhere. Many states are now using ex-offenders in correctional facilities. Some jobs in the Federal Prison Industries, Inc., provide inmates of the United States Bureau of Prisons with Social Security coverage. But although the restrictions are being relaxed, they are still sufficiently strong that employment remains a major problem for the offender and ex-offender.

Offenders and ex-offenders as a group are not well known for good work habits. Many have never been on a schedule. Consequently, a primary task of the community services agent—and the probation and parole agent, as well—is to impress upon the individual the importance of getting to bed early before work days and reporting consistently and diligently to work. Another important function of the community services officer is to arrange to teach offenders and ex-offenders how to write résumés. Additionally, practice in filling out job applications is most helpful.

LEGAL AID

Legal problems face the offender and ex-offender quite frequently. Restoration of civil rights is only one problem. In some countries, such as Japan, civil rights are automatically restored upon release from prison. In some jurisdictions in the United States, including six states (Michigan,

Pennsylvania, Arizona, New Hampshire, Vermont, and Alaska) civil rights are not lost.

With the increase of community-based corrections and minimum security programs, contacts with legal agencies have increased in the community. When people under the jurisdiction of diversion facilities get into trouble, they frequently are lodged in jail by the local law enforcement agency and charged with something. When the halfway house or community correctional center staff discovers what has happened, the simplest procedure is to contact the community services agent, who finds out what has happened and arranges for help. In many cases, when the relationship between the community services agent and the police and the prosecutor's office is good, an informal adjustment can frequently be made.

The Sixth Amendment of the Constitution provides that "in all criminal prosecutions, the accused shall enjoy the right . . . to have the assistance of counsel for his defense." This was interpreted in 1938 by the United States Supreme Court as meaning that the federal courts must provide an attorney for a person accused of a serious crime if he cannot employ one himself (*Johnson* v. *Serpst,* 304 U.S. 458, 1938). In 1963, the same requirement was applied to the state courts (*Gideon* v. *Wainwright,* 372 U.S. 335, 1963). Consequently, court-appointed attorneys are required in federal and state courts.

Legal service is available for offenders and poor people from several sources, including public defenders and court-appointed attorneys. There are many legal aid societies sponsored by private funds, sometimes including the United Fund, Community Chest, or whatever it is called in individual communities. Almost all local bar associations have a "duty roster" to provide legal services to courts and poor people upon request. Many of the organizations concerned with defense of alleged offenders are joined together in a mutual legal aid and public defender association. The Office of Economic Opportunity's Legal Service Program (OEO/LSP) was established under the Economic Opportunity Act in 1967. By June 1960, there were 209 legal service offices, 132 of which had a paid legal staff.[6] By 1969, there were 646 offices, 599 of which had a paid legal staff. An amendment to the Economic Opportunity Act in 1968, however, prohibited these offices from handling "criminal" cases, which has resulted in an increased load and increased staff in public defender offices. These OEO offices can still be used in delinquency cases and in noncriminal cases, however.

The American Civil Liberties Union has, since World War I, taken

---

[6] Emory A. Brownell, *Legal Aid in the United States* (Supplement) (Rochester, N.Y.: Lawyers Cooperative Publishing Company, 1961).

cases of minorities and offenders to protect the rights of citizens and to defend the citizen's "right to be different." Consequently, they have accepted many criminal cases, particularly "victimless" offenses such as homosexuality, prostitution, and other cases in which civil rights may have been violated under the law.

Traditional legal aid programs remain free, and eligibility is based upon income. Generally, eligibility for free legal service is based on poverty-level or marginal income. Some free legal services do not handle criminal matters nor fee-generating cases. The kinds of legal problems that need attention in this situation are found in Table 7-1.

Defender offices, both public and private, have increased in recent years. In 1960, for example, there were 96 defender offices in the United States; in 1970, there were 323, 270 of which received all their support

TABLE 7-1   Total and Lawyer Outside Resource Responses to Concrete Problems

| | | Outside Resource Response | |
Concrete Problems **	Frequency N	Total N	Lawyer N
Real Estate Purchase	52	—*	24
Divorce	38	—*	30
Separation	36	—*	4
Cash Fraud	25	3	0
Installment Fraud	25	2	1
Collection of Benefits	23	6	5
Delinquent Credit/Loan	21	5	5
Delinquent Rent	20	6	0
Welfare Problems	20	0	0
Support Arrangements	19	10	6
Arrest	16	3	2
Collecting Support	14	9	7
Juvenile Delinquency	13	6	1
Child-School (Truancy)	13	11	0
Bankruptcy	12	10	10
Delinquent Home Payments	11	1	1
Bad Debt	8	3	2
Trick Sale	6	2	2
Estate Matters	5	4	4
Overcharge Loan	4	0	0
Overcharge Purchases	4	1	1

Felice J. Levine and Elizabeth Preston, "Community Resource Orientation among Low Income Groups," *Wisconsin Law Review*, 1970, No. 1 (1970), 100. Copyright 1970 by the University of Wisconsin.

* Subjects were asked only about lawyer resource, not about other outside resources.

** Table does not include concrete problems for which there was no affirmative response.

from public funds. The defender office has been the most frequent resource for community service agents in criminal cases involving ex-offenders or walk-aways from halfway houses and community correctional centers. The free legal services and legal aid societies are used most frequently in other types of legal difficulties, such as property settlements, divorce and family settlements, small claims court actions on bad debts, and other noncriminally related activities. These services are also used in many cases simply as sources of information and guidance.

PERSONAL AFFAIRS

"Personal affairs" in this context refers to the kind of assistance that may be needed to fill the legal requirements of society that do not require a lawyer, such as those services sometimes rendered by a personal affairs officer in a major prison. These include such things as obtaining birth certificates and Social Security numbers; the signing of property settlements or adoption papers; divorce; the handling of unpaid debts and obligations through negotiation; and similar matters. On occasion, naturalization procedures are involved.

Social Security numbers are required for everyone. The community services agent can send any person he serves to the nearest Social Security Office, where he can fill out an application for a Social Security number.[7] These forms can be obtained at Social Security offices, Internal Revenue offices, and most post offices.

Birth certificates legally establish an individual's identity and status for such purposes as the right to vote, right of passport, rights to inheritance, obligations to enter school under compulsory education laws, obligation to register for Selective Service or military service, pension and retirement plans, and other uses. Although many offenders do not possess a birth certificate, a community services agent can help secure one by writing the county clerk in the courthouse of the county in which the individual was born or to the State Department of Health, Division of Vital Statistics.

Some offenders and ex-offenders encounter problems as a result of unwanted pregnancy. If the potential father and mother want to be married, the "legitimacy" of the child can be protected. Judges in civil ceremonies and most clergymen will consent to leaving the marriage date off the marriage certificate. They will not, of course, participate in what they consider to be dishonesty by registering an erroneous date. By leaving the date off the marriage certificate, however, the couple can enter

---

7 *Your Social Security Rights and Responsibilities: Retirement and Survivors Benefits* (Baltimore: Social Security Administration, 1975), p. 19.

or have entered whatever date they want, generally preserving their anniversary date, but entering it as having occurred a year earlier.

On occasion, an unwed mother with a child already born will have delayed registration of the birth. She may want help in this area—here again, the community services agent can be of help. In some circumstances, an abortion may have to be arranged; or the services of child placement and adoption agencies may be needed. In all such cases, the community agent can be helpful.

The marital status of an offender or ex-offender is a factor that is often vital to the well-being and success of the ex-offender who is trying to reintegrate into the community. A stable wife or husband who is loyal to her or his spouse can provide a significant social tie that contributes to the adjustment of a former prisoner. On the other hand, the divorce rate among offenders and ex-offenders tends to be higher than the average. In most states, conviction of a felony and sentence to prison become automatic grounds for divorce if the offender's spouse wants it.

Common-law marriages, recognized in most states, tend to be more frequent among those who have been imprisoned. Rights involving property and children are generally involved. Consequently, it is sometimes necessary for a community services agent to determine the legal status of a common-law marriage.

Divorce and annulment are frequent among offenders and ex-offenders. Guidance is sometimes needed from the community services agent as to how to respond to charges, how to negotiate child support and alimony, and how to arrive at an equitable distribution of property and custody of children.

The community services agent must also be acquainted with law and procedure regarding property. Transfer of property by purchase and sale and by foreclosure on mortgages involves legal services generally by the bank, savings and loan association, and/or the abstract and title company. To properly assist his clients, the community services agent should know the landlord-tenant law and/or the direction the courts tend to follow in disputes between landlords and tenants.

Eviction is often a problem among ex-prisoners, because many of them are unable to manage their money. Consequently, eviction is a problem that has to be faced. The eviction process begins when the landlord obtains three forms from the Clerk of Court, generally under the title, "Notice to Tenant." It notifies the tenant that he is behind in his rent by a specific amount and demands payment of the rent for, or possession of, the premises within three to five days. One copy is presented to the tenant or nailed to the front door of the property, a second copy is filed with the Clerk of Court for a fee generally around ten dollars, and the third copy is filed with the Sheriff's Office for a fee fre-

Eviction Notice

NOTICE TO TENANT—ORIGINAL
RENT UNPAID
C. G. L. 5399 (3535)

______________________, Fla., ______________________, 19____

TO______________________________________

____

You are hereby notified that you are indebted to me in the sum of ______________________

______________________________ Dollars, for the rent and use of the premises

____

______________________ County, State of Florida, now occupied by you, and that I demand the payment of the said rent or the possession of said premises within three days from the date of this notice, to-wit: on or before the __________ day of ______________________, A.D. 19____

____

____

____
Phone #

Form 59

Figure 7-1. Eviction Notice

quently around $7.50. Although eviction laws differ from jurisdiction to jurisdiction, the tenant may be evicted by the sheriff in 30 to 60 days after the filing of the notice. An example of an eviction notice is shown in Figure 7-1.

PERSONAL BUDGET COUNSELING

One of the most crucial areas in the counseling of offenders and ex-offenders in the community is that of personal finances. The areas of greatest risk in social adjustment and, conversely, of greatest importance in successful adjustment to work are those involved in personal finances. In financial counseling, appropriate use of credit is critical. If a person uses no credit at all, then he is not making full use of his economic power at whatever level it is. On the other hand, many persons overspend and overuse credit to the extent that they cannot keep up payments or, if marginal, must rely on a stable economic level in the community and job security.

The community services agent can be of great value in this respect. He can benefit both the society and the ex-prisoner by helping his clients learn how to save, how to use credit, how to plan and use a budget, and how to handle the monetary responsibilities that come with being a wage-earner and provider—and thus a responsible member of the community. He can help his client learn how to see where his money is going and determine whether he really wants it to go that way. A suggested listing of assets and expenses can be seen in the following tables.[8] Table 7-2 is a

TABLE 7-2   Your Income

Source	Amount
Annuities	$_____
Social Security	_____
Pensions, veterans' benefits, etc.	_____
Dividends	_____
Interest	_____
Rents from real estate	_____
Salary, wages, commissions	_____
Other:	_____
	_____
Total income	$_____

Lucille F. Mork, *A Guide to Budgeting for the Retired Couple* (Washington, D.C.: United States Department of Agriculture, 1972), p. 12.

suggested listing of income. Table 7-3 concerns holdings—such as a house, automobile, etc.—together with liabilities—such as a mortgage, car and other loans, and other debts. Table 7-4 is a listing of expenditures. These three lists can be used in budget counseling by the community services officer.

Credit ratings are developed by local credit bureaus. These bureaus are regulated by state regulatory agencies and by the Federal Credit Reporting Act of 1971. Local business and professional persons and companies sign membership contracts, pay dues, and pay for each report. Only members can obtain credit ratings. Credit ratings range from 0 and 1 to 9, ranging from the best to the worst credit ratings. An adverse report is limited to seven years from the date of the report, while bankruptcy can remain on the record for fourteen years. Because credit has

[8] Lucille F. Mork, *A Guide to Budgeting for the Retired Couple* (Washington, D.C.: United States Department of Agriculture, Home and Garden Bulletin Number 194, 1972), pp. 8, 10.

TABLE 7-3 Your Holdings

Assets and Liabilities	Amount
Assets:	
House	$_____
Other real estate	_____
Life insurance	_____
U.S. savings bonds	_____
Stocks and other bonds	_____
Net cash value of business	_____
Automobile	_____
Checking accounts	_____
Savings accounts	_____
Other:	_____
Total assets	$_____
Liaibilities:	
Mortgage	$_____
Personal loans	_____
Installment contracts	_____
Notes	_____
Charge accounts	_____
Other:	_____
Total liabilities	$_____

Lucille F. Mork, *A Guide to Budgeting for the Retired Couple* (Washington, D.C.: United States Department of Agriculture, 1972), p. 10.

traditionally involved heads of households as viewed by the Internal Revenue Service, the recent influx of women with their own credit ratings has been viewed by some credit bureaus as a problem, since the household becomes "split" into two credit ratings, rather than one. Credit bureaus also have a collection department that sends out notices of bills past due upon request. Experience has been that most collections are made for hospitals and physicians. The majority of credit reports, of course, generally go to business members, particularly retail stores. In summary, the credit rating is probably the best single index of a person's dependability and capability of managing his own affairs. Table 7-5 shows a usual credit rating sheet; Table 7-6 shows the codes of consumer credit information—specifically what is bought that relates to the "Type Account" in Table 7-5.

Income tax problems are also within the realm of assistance provided by the community services agent. Many ex-prisoners forget to file their

TABLE 7-4   Your Expenses

Fixed Items	Amount per Month	
Rent or mortgage payment	$_____	
Taxes	_____	
Insurance	_____	
Savings	_____	
Debt payment	_____	
Other:	_____	
Total fixed	_____	$_____
Variable items		
Food and beverages	_____	
Household operation and maintenance	_____	
Furnishings and equipment	_____	
Clothing	_____	
Personal	_____	
Transportation	_____	
Medical care	_____	
Recreation and education	_____	
Gifts and contributions	_____	
Other:	_____	
Total variable	_____	$_____
Total expenses		$_____

Lucille F. Mork, *A Guide to Budgeting for the Retired Couple* (Washington, D.C.: United States Department of Agriculture, 1972), p. 8.

income tax forms or do not know how to do it. Information regarding income tax law can be found in forms provided at the post office and in many private publications.[9]

Stability in all areas—employment, domestic, geographic, and others— provides a base for adequate adjustment to the community. Consequently, if an offender or ex-offender shows any capacity for stability, the purchase of a permanent residence within his means might well be encouraged as contributing to stability. Living in rooming houses and low-rent apartments does not provide the "anchorage" conducive to long-term successful adjustment. The community agent again has an area in which he can be of great help to ex-prisoners.

Stability and dependability are best shown in credit ratings and home ownership. The community services agent can assist the offender and

---

[9] For example, see J. K. Lasser Tax Institute, *J. K. Lasser's Your Income Tax* (New York: Simon and Schuster, 1975).

TABLE 7-5

- Terms of Sale—To show what sort of a payment agreement a consumer had with a credit grantor, the Common Language groups the terms of sale into three classifications:
    1. Open or "O" account—This includes:
       An account to be paid after one billing
       An account expected to be paid in one payment, such as a 30-day account
       An account in which the entire amount is to be paid within certain limits, such as 60 or 90 days with no interest or service charge.
    2. Revolving or "R" account—This describes:
       An account with regular monthly payments which may vary in amount, based on the amount of the balance due.
    3. Installment or "I" account—This describes:
       An account with a fixed number of specified payments—specified as to amounts and time and including interest charges.
- Usual Manner of Payment—When a credit grantor furnishes his ledger experience to the credit bureau, he classifies the consumer's usual manner of payment in the following way:

Usual Manner of Payment	Type Account		
	O	R	I
Too new to rate; approved but not used	0	0	0
Pays (or paid) within 30 days of billing; pays accounts as agreed	1	1	1
Pays (or paid) in more than 30 days, but not more than 60 days, or not more than one payment past due	2	2	2
Pays (or paid) in more than 60 days, but not more than 90 days, or two payments past due	3	3	3
Pays (or paid) in more than 90 days, but not more than 120 days, or three or more payments past due	4	4	4
Account is at least 120 days overdue but is not yet rated "9"	5	5	5
Making regular payments under Wage Earner Plan or similar arrangement	7	7	7
Repossession (Indicate if it is a voluntary return of merchandise by the customer)	8	8	8
Bad debt; placed for collection skip	9	9	9
If Account Is Disputed, Indicate DISP.			

Extending Credit Profitably: A Training Aid for Credit Department Personnel (Houston, Tex.: Associated Credit Bureaus, Inc., 1974), p. 9.

TABLE 7-6   The Common Language

- The Common Language serves two purposes:
  1. It makes consumer credit information more precise for credit grantors while also making it easier for the credit bureau to report.
  2. It insures that all credit grantors use the same objective terms to describe the same kind of paying habits.
- By using a combination of letters and numerals, the Common Language is able to describe three things:
  1. Kind of Business—the type of firm the consumer did business with
  2. Terms of Sale—the kind of payment arrangements the consumer had with a firm
  3. Manner of Payment—the manner in which the consumer paid his bill to a firm
- Kind of Business—To represent different types of businesses, the Common Language uses different code letters. In most cases, the first letter of the kind of business being classified and the code letter are the same. For example, clothing stores are represented by the letter "C" and banks by the letter "B."

Code	Kind of Business
A	Automotive
B	Banks
C	Clothing
D	Department and Variety
F	Finance
G	Groceries
H	Home Furnishings
I	Insurance
J	Jewelry and Cameras
K	Contractors
L	Lumber, Building Material, Hardware
M	Medical and Related Health
N	National Credit Card Companies and Air Lines
O	Oil Companies
P	Personal Services Other than Medical
Q	Mail Order Houses
R	Real Estate and Public Accommodations
S	Sporting Goods

TABLE 7-6 (Continued)

Code	Kind of Business
T	Farm and Garden Supplies
U	Utilities and Fuel
V	Government
W	Wholesale
X	Advertising
Y	Collection Services
Z	Miscellaneous

Extending Credit Profitably: A Training Aid for Credit Department Personnel (Houston, Tex.: Associated Credit Bureaus, Inc., 1974), p. 8.

ex-offender in personal budgeting and management of his personal affairs. In fact, it is quite probable that some of his most productive effort can be in personal budgeting counseling.

WELFARE PROBLEMS

The primary effort to assist offenders and ex-offenders in income maintenance is generally directed toward personal budget *counseling*. Prisoner aid societies have learned that financial help alone simply creates dependency. The most effective method has been personal budget counseling with a minimum of emergency financial aid. This kind of counseling involves convincing the individual to keep records about all of his or her income and expenditures. Sometimes, flaws in spending habits become obvious. Recording income and tailoring expenditures to match it takes more effort and persuasion than most clients have been accustomed to exerting. Even after personal budget counseling, the needs of individuals sometimes still exceed their income, and some have no income for varying periods of time—so welfare resources are needed.

Welfare programs generally fit into five categories in federal, state, and local programs: (1) Old Age Assistance (OAA), (2) Aid to the Blind (AB), (3) Aid to Families with Dependent Children (AFDC), (4) Aid to the Permanently and Totally Disabled (APTD), and (5) General Assistance (GA). All except the last category receive federal funds—"General Assistance" is simply a convenient term applied to all public assistance programs conducted by state and local governments without federal financial participation. It is generally administered by the same agency that handles federally funded welfare programs, most frequently called "Department of Public Welfare." The federally funded programs began in 1936 when the public assistance titles of the Social Security Act became effective. Welfare programs before that were generally at the county level or sponsored by private charitable organizations, with the exception of the Federal Emergency Relief Administration (FERA), created by Congress in 1933. The public assistance titles of the original Social Security Act included OAA, AB, and ADC (Aid to Dependent Children). ADC became AFDC under 1962 amendments. The 1962 amendments also included the new program for APTD.

The two categories used mostly by offenders and ex-offenders are AFDC and GA. Female offenders and ex-offenders most frequently use AFDC, as do the wives of offenders while they are in prison. Most male offenders and ex-offenders who need welfare payments use General Assistance. Total recipients of all programs probably represent about 8.5 percent of the total population.

For persons receiving income below the poverty level, food stamps can be purchased to provide greater purchasing power than cash would provide. Food stamps are generally distributed by the Food Stamp Office of the same state agency that distributes other welfare funds, frequently the Department of Public Welfare. The food stamp program is federally financed by the United States Department of Agriculture.

The children of people who have been in jail sometimes do not have enough money for school lunches. The School Lunch Program, also funded by the United States Department of Agriculture, is available to people at the poverty level.

In addition, some emergency welfare funds are available from private charitable organizations. The Salvation Army has been especially helpful in emergencies.

HEALTH PROBLEMS

Historically, health services for the poor have been provided by private local organizations and clinics. The first ambulatory medical care program in the United States began with the founding of the Boston Dispensary in 1796, followed by the establishment of similar dispensaries in Philadelphia and New York City. Today, the primary health-delivery system is still at the local level, generally in the form of a county health clinic headed by a public health officer. By 1936, a study of 174 local health departments by the Public Health Service indicated that the cost per visit was $.81, with a range of $.75 to $1.46; patients' fees paid about 40 percent of the costs, tax funds about 11 percent, gifts around 12 percent, with a deficit of 40 percent to be picked up by the hospital. The county health unit and the outpatient unit of charitable hospitals have become the primary source of health care for the poor. The community services agent must be acquainted with available health services and, in addition, with volunteer physicians, dentists, and other professionals.

Governmental funding came into the health field in the 1960s. The Educational Assistance Act of 1963, with 1965 amendments, was designed to increase the supply of health professionals, expecially physicians. The Nurse Training Act of 1964 and Allied Health Professions Act, together with the Manpower Development and Training Act, were aimed at increasing the supply of other auxiliary personnel. The Child Health Act of 1967 was really the old Title V of the Social Security Act without child welfare services; it provided 366,400 expectant mothers in 1967 with maternity clinic services and cared for 73,000 in-patient hospital cases. The Medicaid Program was initiated by Title XIX of the Social Security amendments of 1965 to extend assistance to the medically indigent and to children under state plans. This should be implemented by 1977. Government involvement was expanded by the enactment of the Medicare Program as Title VIII of the Social Security amendments of 1965, instituting a system of health insurance for the aged.

Because of its size, the Blue Cross and Blue Shield insurance systems, which are nonprofit, coordinate most of the health services and are aware of most health services in the area. The community services agent can learn much from this group about his local area and the health services available. There are seventy-five Blue Cross plans, with a membership of about 68 million concerned with hospitalization insurance; Blue Shield has about seventy-three systems with a membership of 60 million to provide insurance against physicians' services. Among the group of nonprofit providers associated with these plans are the voluntary hospitals, which numbered 3,440 in 1966.

Probably the most complete study of the functions and responsibilities of health departments in the middle of the century was Haven Emerson's *Local Health Units for the Nation,* which was published in 1945. It listed six basic programs as (1) vital statistics, (2) sanitation, (3) communicable disease control, (4) public health laboratories, (5) maternal and child health, and (6) public health education. The role of health departments, health units, and all public health delivery systems incorporate these functions.[10] Offenders and ex-offenders who are veterans with honorable discharges can be served by Veterans Administration hospitals and other medical services.

---

[10] Haven Emerson and Martha Luginbuhl, *Local Health Units for the Nation* (New York: Commonwealth Fund, 1945).

OTHER HELPING SERVICES

There are many other helping services in the community, such as the mental health and child guidance clinics, Family Service Association, Travelers Aid Society, marriage counseling units, alcohol detoxification units, residential drug programs, crisis intervention hotlines, and many others. Services of almost every type are available in communities of 100,000 population and more and many are available in smaller communities. In fact, a reasonably good supply of services would be available in an area of 30,000 population within commuting distance of population centers of at least 10,000.[11] In communities smaller than that, the community services agent must rely on local persons as volunteers to provide services.

Most cities of 50,000 or more population have directories of social service agencies. Entries in most directories might include the following agencies:

1. Action Line (generally with a local newspaper)
2. Alcohol and Drug Abuse Program
3. American Cancer Society
4. American Civil Liberties Union
5. American National Red Cross
6. Community Mental Health Services
7. Behavior Analysis and Research Associates, Inc.
8. Associated Charities
9. Epilepsy Foundation
10. Biracial Committee
11. Learning Center Preschool Project
12. Black Cultural Center
13. Blood Bank
14. Boy Scouts of America
15. Bureau of Blind Services
16. Bureau of Housing Assistance
17. Crisis Alternatives Information and Referral (CAIR)
18. Medical Society
19. Curricular Career Information Services (CCIS)

---

[11] *Rural Youth in Crisis* (Washington, D.C.: United States Bureau of the Census, 1964), p. 5.

20. Chamber of Commerce
21. Children's Home Society
22. Children's Medical Services
23. Children's Services
24. Children's Visual Aid Society
25. Community Action Program
26. Communication Gap, Inc. (provides services for the deaf)
27. Community Coordinated Child Care
28. Comprehensive Planning Health Council
29. Comptroller's Consumer Information Office
30. Continuing Consumer Education Program
31. Counseling and Guidance Clinic
32. Credit Bureau
33. Drug Information Service Center
34. Division of Consumer Services
35. Division of Family Services
36. Division of Retardation
37. Division of Vocational Rehabilitation
38. Feminist Women's Health Center
39. Council for the Blind
40. Lung Association
41. Research Foundation for Dyslexic and Hyperkinetic Children
42. State Employment Service
43. Food Stamp Office
44. Friends of the Retarded
45. Gay, Rap, Peer Counseling Group (to serve the homosexual community)
46. Girl Scout Council
47. Goodwill Industries
48. Grassroots Free School (alternative to public school to provide noncompulsive and nongraded education)
49. Head Start Program (educational program for economically deprived preschoolers)
50. Home Care Department of the Hospital
51. Information Resources Center
52. La Leche League (for any mother interested in breast feeding)
53. Lawyer Referral Service

54. Legal Aid Foundation
55. Association for Retarded Citizens
56. Alcoholism Center Halfway House
57. Alcoholism Center Sobering-Up Station
58. Association for Mental Health
59. Diabetes Association
60. County Food Cooperative (reduced prices for food)
61. County Health Department
62. County Public Library
63. County Schools Adult General Education Program
64. County Schools Cross-Age Tutoring
65. County Schools Early Childhood Education
66. County Schools Exploring Childhood Program
67. County Schools Failsafe: Reading Skills Management System
68. County Schools Guidance Services
69. County Schools Hearing Impaired Program
70. County Schools Occupational Specialist Program
71. County Schools Placement and Follow-Up Services
72. County Schools Planning Instructional Program for Hospitalized and Homebound Students
73. County Schools Poets in the School Program
74. County Schools Psychological Services
75. County Schools Reading Program
76. County Schools Right to Read Program
77. County Schools Volunteers Program
78. County Schools Special Education Programs (educable mentally retarded, emotionally disturbed, gifted, hearing problems, job training, multiple handicapped, physically handicapped, socially maladjusted, specific learning disabilities, speech- and language-impaired programs, trainable mentally retarded program, and visually handicapped program)
79. County Schools Student Record Center
80. County Schools Teenage Parent Program
81. County Schools Visiting Teacher and Social Work Services
82. County Schools Youth Services Center
83. Handicapped Club
84. Interfaith Child Care
85. Manpower Development and Training

86. March of Dimes (birth defects)
87. Meals on Wheels (nutritious meals delivered to persons 60 and over unable to shop or cook)
88. Medical Family Practice Residency Program
89. National Council of Negro Women
90. National Organization for Women
91. Office of Consumer Information
92. Operation Peace of Mind
93. Parent Helpers Association
94. Parents Without Partners, Inc.
95. Poison Control Center
96. Pre-marriage and Marriage Counseling
97. Project Upward Bound—Special Services
98. Protective Services
99. Salvation Army
100. Senior Community Services Aids
101. Senior Society Planning Council
102. Small Change Foundation (help low-income housing programs)
103. Social Security Administration
104. Speech and Hearing Center
105. State Attorney's Office
106. Literacy Council, Inc. (teaching reading)
107. Physical Therapy Services
108. Rape Crisis Service
109. Recreation Department
110. Urban League, Inc.
111. Tax-Aide Program (assistance in income tax)
112. Telephone Counseling Service
113. Unicorn Club (for single or divorced people)
114. United Cerebral Palsy Association
115. United Ministries Center
116. Ministerial Alliance
117. Veterans Administration
118. Voluntary Action Center
119. Walk-In Counseling Center (alcohol and drug abuse)
120. Women's Educational and Cultural Center
121. YMCA

122. YWCA
123. Comprehensive Health Planning Council
124. Family Life Services
125. Family Service Association
126. Private Counseling Services
127. Drug and Crisis Center
128. Institute for Transactional Analysis, Inc.
129. Homemakers (home- and health-care services)
130. Human Resources Clearinghouse
131. National Runaway Switchboard
132. Neighborhood Clinic (health services)
133. Pastoral Counseling Service
134. Drug "Rap" House
135. Institute for Family Unity, Inc. (marriage and family counseling)
136. Problem Pregnancy Service
137. Animal Shelter
138. Youth Employment Service
139. Epilepsy Foundation
140. Mental Health Clinic
141. Legal Services Clinic
142. Community Welfare Councils (organization of social welfare agencies)

These agencies are basic. The New York City directory describes more than 7,000 agencies, offices, and organizations available to the community services manager.[12]

These are only a few of the entries that appear in most local directories of social services. In the larger cities, the listings are voluminous. In all the larger and middle-sized cities, there is also a Social Service Clearinghouse or Social Service Index, to which member social agencies report contacts with families. The contacts are recorded in the central clearinghouse and when a new contact is reported, a card is automatically sent back to the reporting agencies to indicate previous contacts, together with dates. This permits agencies with new contacts with families to obtain information from agencies with older contacts; it also helps to prevent duplication of service. The community services agent should be

[12] *Directory of Social and Health Agencies of New York City 1975–1976* (New York: Columbia University Press, 1975). Published for the Community Council of Greater New York, Inc.

a member of the central clearinghouse. In this way, he can better coordinate community resources for the assistance of the people he serves.

AGENCY COORDINATION

The proper coordination of various agencies with differing immediate objectives, even though they have similar overall goals, provides a problem. Although the primary goal in criminal justice is the protection of society, law enforcement personnel focus on getting the criminal off the street; courts want to remain aloof so that they can provide a fair and impartial trial; and correctional service people are interested in successful release. These immediate objectives could be viewed as mutually exclusive and in conflict. Consequently, the community services agent must be able to interpret to all phases of the criminal justice system the functions and duties of all others aimed at protecting society.

TECHNICAL ASSISTANCE

Technical assistance is the provision of professional guidance to criminal justice agencies in planning, implementing, and evaluating programs. It may take the form of assistance in preparing a comprehensive criminal justice manpower plan for the governor or legislature, providing resources for the evaluation of institutional and community programs, and any other service in the area of technical assistance.

CONCLUSIONS

The community services agent has a broad variety of potential areas in which he can work. His primary function is the mobilization of community resources to assist the offender and ex-offender in successful adjustment commensurate with the public interest and safety. In practice, personalities vary, and therefore the manner in which community services agents may function also varies. It is ideal to have several different types of personalities on the community services team; this can occur in the large metropolitan areas. The community services agent can be considered to be a "free-wheeler" who "does his own thing," with his effectiveness dependent upon his personality, his competence, and his willingness to work with people to bring community resources to bear upon the problems of the offenders and ex-offenders he serves.

One problem this individual has is related to referral to agencies. Frequently, when he refers a client to an agency, the client never shows.

Consequently, "linkage" is more effective than "referral." Linkage occurs when the community services agent takes the individual to the other agency for the first interview. In that way, the client can visualize a connection and a meaningful relationship.

Knowledge of the needs of offenders and ex-offenders is most important for the community services agent. A study in Massachusetts in 1971 explored the needs of men after they had been released from correctional institutions to provide guidance to planners responsible for developing community-based correctional programs.[13] Clinical interviews with four groups of men about to be paroled—some within the previous three months, some a year previously, and some returned for parole revocations—provided the information that was substantiated by contacts with agencies and groups serving offenders just before and after release. The findings presented a profile of men with multiple needs. Needs in occupational training and placement, educational areas, financial management, social-recreational needs, family relationships, living arrangements, alcohol and drug control, medical services, counseling services, and legal services were prominent in the group. Alcohol was more of a problem than drugs. Over half of the pre-parole group was seen as highly unlikely to make use of services because of ignorance of their need and a subcultural lifestyle, rather than hostility to the institution. The unmet needs were generally discovered after release. It was found that the delivery of pre- and post-release services could best be organized around a "case manager" who could provide personal support and continuity during the period of transition back into the community by making effective use of existing community resources.

Community workers need to know the roles of other people and agencies in the community. Not only will they confront workers from other agencies playing different roles in relation to the treatment of offenders and with different objectives, but they may have to play some of these roles on occasion. A community worker identifies problems, intervenes constructively when some segment of the community relates to the offender, serves as an advocate, is an organizer, and is a developer.[14] Community work is necessary because the offender and the community that developed him or her are both the targets of community services.

13 John O. Boone, *A Study of Community-Based Correctional Needs in Massachusetts* (Boston: Massachusetts Department of Correction, 1972), mimeographed.

14 Irving A. Spergel, *Community Problem Solving: The Delinquency Example* (Chicago: University of Chicago Press, 1969), pp. 58–105.

Chapter 8

Chemical Dependency Programs: Alcohol and Drugs

Chemical dependence on drugs and other substances has been present in man since the dawn of history. In ancient Egypt, rich and poor alike drank a beer that they made by baking coarse barley leaves, crumbling them in a vat with water, stirring and straining the fermented liquid, and bottling it in jars closed with a lump of mud. Wine was a drink of the wealthy. Throughout history, the extent, intensity, and results of the use of alcohol and drugs can be broadly classified as (1) normal usage, (2) habituation or abuse, and (3) addiction. Excessive use of these substances has always been a problem. The Old Testament indicates that "the drunkard and the glutton will come to poverty" (Proverbs 23:21—written about 350 B.C.).

The basic elements that enter into the problem of chemical dependence are (1) physical tolerance, (2) physical dependence, and (3) psychological dependence. Sufficient physical tolerance to any foreign substance has to be developed before it can have a serious effect on the personality and body. For example, even half an aspirin might relieve headache pain if one has not had aspirins before. After a prolonged period of taking aspirins, it may be necessary to take two or three to produce the same effect. Similarly, the first taste of whiskey "burns all the way down," but after a prolonged period of usage, considerable quantities can be consumed before drunkenness results.

Physical dependence occurs when the body becomes used to changes in chemical composition, whether endocrinal changes because of stress, endocrinal imbalance, or the introduction of large amounts of foreign substances, such as alcohol or drugs. It is apparent that Selye's "adapta-

123

tion syndrome" may be operative; the body, including the endocrinal system, accommodates to change in order to retain homeostasis or chemical balance in the body as a reaction to change.[1] A cell in the body accommodates to other cells around it in terms of temperature, pressure, and chemical composition; the endocrinal system also accommodates to change, and the general adaptation syndrome is the accommodation of the entire body to change in temperature, pressure, and chemical composition. When the chemical composition of a body is saturated with alcohol or drugs or other foreign substances (or, for that matter, with an unusually heavy secretion of adrenalin as a consequence of stress over a long period of time), the cells and the body accommodate to changes and the cells accommodate to the use of available nourishment or to damage in an adaptation syndrome. Then, when the substance is missing, the resulting reaction is uncomfortable, called withdrawal.

Physicians have indicated that this dependence is in a wide spectrum of degrees. Only when there is physical dependence that results in extreme and agonizing withdrawal symptoms is the condition considered to be an *addiction*. Physical dependence appears, however, in association with many substances producing a condition less than the extreme withdrawal symptoms found in addiction. For example, many people who do not get their morning coffee develop headaches. Inveterate chain smokers trying to quit have what is commonly called "nicotine fits." Persons can, therefore, become *habituated* to a substance without being *addicted* to it. In summary, addiction involves extreme and agonizing withdrawal symptoms, while habituation is much less serious, involving minor discomforts or extreme nervousness. Fortunately, the majority of those who use these foreign substances can be still classified as "normal," as opposed to the habituated problem drinker or drug abuser or, at the extreme, the addict.

Psychological dependence is really an emotional dependence on a foreign substance, whether it is coffee, tobacco, alcohol, or drugs. The stress of life develops anxieties and tensions. Coffee, tobacco, alcohol, drugs, and other narcotics that have the effect of reducing anxiety and tension become part of the lifestyle of people who need them. This is why the success rate of the narcotics program in the United States Public Health Service Hospitals at Lexington and Fort Worth has been so disappointing. The *physical* tolerance and dependence can be treated by cutting off the foreign substance. The *psychological* dependence, however, cannot be so easily cut off. This is what makes addiction so

---

[1] Hans Selye, *Textbook of Endocrinology* (Montreal: Acta Endocrinologica, Inc., 1949), pp. 837–67. Also Hans Selye, *The Story of the Adaptation Syndrome* (Montreal: Acta, Inc., Medical Publishers, 1952).

difficult to treat. This is also why community-based programs in this field are so important, because they enable the habituated or addicted person to stay in his social setting, where emotional support from his therapist, caseworker, or his peers can be mobilized to handle the psychological dependence.

Alcoholism results from long-term use of alcohol, during which time physical tolerance and psychological dependence are developed. Drug abuse and narcotic addiction begin in a variety of ways. Much addiction has begun with direct injections of morphine or other narcotics in military hospitals, general civilian hospitals, and among members of the medical profession under stress. The classical heroin addiction begins with taking the drug orally, probably a three-grain "cap" (capsule) of 6 percent stuff until tolerance is developed, then injections into the muscle as a "flesh pop," and finally, intravenous injections.

CHEMICAL DEPENDENCE IN HISTORICAL PERSPECTIVE

Ancient man experienced chemical dependence on alcohol, as we have mentioned. Chemical dependence upon plants with narcotic qualities also began early. There were also dependency problems with substances such as coffee and tobacco. At one time or another, all these substances have been subject to penal sanctions. To understand modern problems in chemical dependency, particularly regarding alcohol and drugs, a quick review of chemical dependence from a historical perspective may help place the problem in proper context in terms of human behavior and emotional needs.

Coffee was originally discovered in Kaffa, a province in Southwest Ethiopia, where it grew wild. The name "coffee" derives either from a corruption of "Kaffa" or the Arabic word "gahwh." About 850 A.D., a goatherd noticed queer antics in his flock after they had eaten berries of this evergreen bush. The stimulating effect of coffee was thus discovered and was brought into the religious rites of the Muslims, although the strictly orthodox or conservative section of the priesthood claimed it was intoxicating and therefore prohibited by the Koran. Severe penalties were imposed among the Arabian Muslims, but coffee drinking spread widely because of its exhilarating effect. It was placed under cultivation in Southern Arabia in the fifteenth century and was brought to Ceylon and Java in the seventeenth century. In the eighteenth century, it was introduced into the Central and South American countries. By the twentieth century, coffee had become responsible for much of the income in tropical countries and the legal sanctions against it had disappeared. Coffee is now a normal and accepted beverage. Still, it involves an element of physical dependence.

Tobacco was used in ancient Mayan religious ceremonies. It was first cultivated by the Indians of North and South America. When Columbus and other early explorers arrived in America, they found the natives using tobacco in ceremonials, such as smoking the peace pipe, and in religious ceremonies. Cigarettes originated around 1856 during the Crimean War, when pipes were found to be too bulky and inconvenient to carry and the soldiers began to roll their own tobacco in paper. By 1556, tobacco was introduced into Europe for medical purposes. Nicotine and related alkaloids of tobacco provide the habit-forming and narcotic effects that account for general worldwide use. Legislation in several countries prohibited its use because of its effects. Several czars of Russia even deported people to Siberia for using it and had other sanctions, even to the extent of cutting off noses! No amount of legislation, however, has been able to prevent its use. In the United States, probably 100,000 doctors stopped smoking after research related it to cancer, but its use has increased in the general public despite the warnings that are now required by law to be stamped on packages. Tobacco is now legal and its use is considered to be normal.

Alcohol in the form of beer and wine has been a part of man's lifestyle since the dawn of history, although heavy drinking probably started around 3000 B.C. when man began to cultivate grapes. Ancient man evaporated the alcohol out of the various beers, wines, and other liquors to obtain stronger liquors. By 800 B.C., rice, molasses, palm sap, mare's milk, and wine formed the basic fermented liquor from which the distillants were produced. By 500 A.D., honey was fermented into mead in Britain and this, in turn, was distilled. By 1000 A.D., wine was distilled into brandy in Italy. Ireland developed beer from oats and barley malt. Vodka was introduced in Russia in the fourteenth century with potatoes as its base. Cognac was produced in France, also in the fourteenth century, with grapes and wine as its base. Whiskey was introduced in Scotland in 1500 A.D.; it was made from malted barley made into beer and then distilled. Rum was developed in the British West Indies in the seventeenth century as a by-product of sugar manufacturing. Gin was developed in the seventeenth century in Holland for medical purposes. Alcohol has been declared illegal and penal sanctions attached to its manufacture, possession, and use in many areas at different times. Nevertheless, it is obvious that its use has increased steadily and significantly in the civilized world throughout history. Today, alcohol is legal in most countries.

Narcotics from plants were discovered early in the history of man. Primitive societies had discovered caffein independently in many parts of the world from different sources, such as in the seeds of coffee, cocoa, and cola; in leaves, including tea, maté, and yaupon; and in bark, such as yoco. Tea was first used as medicine in China and is now drunk by more people than any other caffein beverage, although coffee is commercially more important. Cocoa was used by the Aztecs before the Spanish conquest and gained popularity in Europe after its introduction in 1502. Cola came from Africa and is consumed locally; it is exported mainly for carbonated drinks. Nonalcoholic narcotics include excitants like tobacco, hypnotics like kava, and hallucinogens, such as peyote, agaric, and marijuana. Euphorics include coca and opium and still remain of considerable medical importance; they are considered to be both a blessing and a bane to humanity. Native to Asia Minor, opium has many alkaloids, the principal ones being morphine and codeine. Coca leaves are rich in cocaine and are chewed by millions of South American Indians. The pistillate buds of the hemp plant yield marijuana, bhang, ganja, and hashish, which are different forms of the same narcotic and originally came from North Africa and India. The hallucinogens induce fanciful and brilliant-colored visions, and their psychological effects make them interesting as possible medicines for mental treatment, both in religions and in experimental psychiatry. Plants have been the source of nearly all medicines, although synthetics have been developed, generally modeled on the chemical structure of the natural drug. The United States has probably 400 toxic species, and the tropics are considerably richer in them. Primitive societies in the Western hemisphere —particularly Mexico and Colombia—have made extensive use of narcotic plants. The discovery of "wonder drugs" has renewed medical interest in plants. Among the later plant-derivative drugs are muscle relaxants, hypertensive agents, cortisone, penicillin, streptomycin, aureomycin, and many other antibiotics. Narcotics still appear in essentially four classifications: (1) excitants, (2) hypnotics, (3) hallucinogens, and (4) euphorics. Alcohol, not a narcotic drug, is a depressant. It was during the Civil War that morphine, an opium derivative and a euphoric, was given to wounded soldiers as a pain killer. The result was that many persons became addicted, which gave rise to the present problem of narcotic addiction in America. Simultaneously, patent medicines and traveling "medicine men" with their shows selling patent medicines distributed many drugs with morphine base for "female troubles." The result was that many people became addicted. By 1914, the Harrison Act was passed by Congress, having been initiated and promoted by Senator Harrison, whose daughter had become addicted.

In summary, the use of alcohol and narcotic plants has been present throughout the history of man. The modern alcohol and drug problem results from increased sophistication and refinement in the production of drugs and narcotics available to people who have a psychological dependence on them.

ALCOHOL PROGRAMS

The number of alcoholics in the United States was estimated in 1967 as ranging from 4,500,000 to 6,800,000.[2] Estimates in the early 1970s have ranged between 6 million and 10 million. In 1975, the National Institute of Mental Health estimated that mental illness drains the economy by about $21 billion annually through costs of care and treatment and through lost productivity. At the same time, alcoholism costs about $15 billion, and drug abuse and addiction cost about $10 billion every year. Consequently, chemical dependency on alcohol and drugs amounts to a major social and personality problem in America.

The National Council on Alcoholism estimates that 80 million people in the United States use alcohol as a beverage, but only about 9 percent of them have serious problems with it.[3] Even though it is a major problem medically, socially, and psychologically, Coleman points out that little substantively is known about it and it is not yet really understood.[4] Recent research by psychiatrists and others in the field has perceptibly increased the knowledge of it. Jellinek, for example, has identified the phases of alcoholism as (1) the pre-alcoholic symptomatic phase, typified by the beginning drinker who finds that alcohol relieves tension, so goes from occasional relief-drinking to continual relief-drinking; (2) the prodromal phase, in which the individual experiences occasional blackouts, but can carry on a conversation and show little or no outward signs of intoxication; (3) the crucial phase, characterized by loss of control over drinking, loss of self-esteem, and compensatory behavior; and (4) the chronic phase, in which alcohol plays a dominant role in a person's life.[5] Acute pathological or psychotic reactions after prolonged use of alcohol are pathological intoxication, delirium tremens, acute alcoholic hallucinosis, and Korsakoff's psychosis. Pathological intoxication occurs with people of low tolerance, such as epileptics and unstable people, who suddenly become disoriented with alcohol usage. Delirium tremens (the DTs) are characterized by disorientation, hallucinations (snakes, rats, etc.), fear, suggestibility, and coarse tremors of the hands, tongue, and lips. Acute alcoholic hallucinosis generally involves auditory hallucinations (hearing voices). Korsakoff's psychosis, first described by

2 Richard H. Blum, "Mind-Altering Drugs and Dangerous Behavior: Alcohol," Appendix B in *Task Force Report: Drunkenness* (Washington, D.C.: The President's Commission on Law Enforcement and Administration of Justice, 1967), pp. 29–49.

3 *Alcoholism* (New York: Metropolitan Life Insurance Company, 1972), p. 2.

4 James C. Coleman, *Abnormal Psychology and Modern Life*, 3rd ed. (Chicago: Scott, Foresman, 1964), p. 420.

5 E. M. Jellinek, "Phases of Alcohol Addiction," *Quarterly Journal in the Studies of Alcohol*, 13 (1952), 673–78.

When Pioneer Fellowship House first opened in Seattle, there was no other sanctuary for alcoholic men without resources except Skid Row.

Courtesy of Pioneer Cooperative Affiliation, Seattle, Washington.

the Russian psychiatrist in 1887, involves primarily memory defect, particularly for recent events, coupled with falsification to conceal the problem: it is probably due to vitamin B deficiency. Chronic alcoholic deterioration involves gradual intellectual, moral, and personality decline.

Alcoholism has been defined as a disease by many health organizations, including the World Health Organization and the American Medical Association. It is seen as having both physiological and emotional components. Neither can be de-emphasized when working with the alcoholic.

Studies have indicated that there is more drinking in societies caught in a struggle for subsistence, in societies generally more permissive, by members of deprived minority groups, by people from broken marriages, and by members of certain religious groups.[6] McCord and McCord have found evidence that sons who reject harsh fathers are more inclined to become alcoholics.[7]

---

[6] Bernard Berelson and Gary A. Steiner, *Human Behavior: An Inventory of Scientific Findings* (New York: Harcourt, Brace & World, 1964), p. 633.

[7] William McCord and Joan McCord, with Jon Gudeman, *Origins of Alcoholism* (Palo Alto: Stanford University Press, 1960).

A. E. Ross, one of the founding fathers of sociology in America, proposed the concept of alcoholic elimination among peoples. He noted that alcoholism is low in the Mediterranean countries and other areas where alcohol has been consumed over many centuries. On the other hand, when it is newly introduced to peoples who have not undergone "alcoholic elimination," the alcoholism rate is high (Ireland, the American Indian, and the Eskimo). This, together with other factors, suggests a biological base for some alcoholism and drug dependency.

Alcoholism has been viewed as characteristic of a "bankrupt idealist." The typical alcoholic is portrayed as trying to achieve goals, attempting to support his family, and with other high aspirations but frustrated by his inability to attain them or even, in some instances, his inability to make a good showing. Alcohol as an escape tends temporarily to ameliorate that problem. It may be that if he could give up on his aspirations and lower his goals to ones within his grasp, he might not need alcohol as an escape.

Although the alcoholic spree tends to ameliorate disturbing problems temporarily, the hangover is a period when the defenses are down, any attempt to escape has gone, and the individual is susceptible to diagnosis and therapy. The hangover is a period when the problems become accentuated. Consequently, this period is probably the best time in which to attempt to diagnose physical and emotional problems that cause an individual to become alcoholic.[8] Hangovers include suicide feelings, desires to masturbate or have sex, occasional leanings toward homosexual activities, and crying spells, according to Karpman. All these factors are important in the physical and emotional diagnosis of alcoholism or the heavy use of alcohol. The physical symptoms of headache or numbness are accompanied by emotional symptoms that include love and hate, fear and anger, depression and despair, sex stimulation and sorrow, and the ever-present remorse and guilt. The pattern of the emotional problem determines the theme of the hangover, although remorse and guilt are always there. The physical symptoms range from the "Anvil Chorus" type of headache to a mild and generalized feeling of numbness. The dominant themes in hangovers are anger, sex stimulation, boredom, anxiety, inferiority, inadequacy, and depression, depending upon the nature of the basic problem. Alcoholism is an escape mechanism. Many alcoholics or nonalcoholic acute drunks admit the escape mechanism, while some others deny it. Dominant themes in escape are boredom, compensation, defiance, ameliorating generalized anxiety (relaxation), lack of security, and guilt-generated specific anxiety.

---

8 Benjamin Karpman, *The Hangover* (Springfield, Ill.: Charles C Thomas, 1957). Also Benjamin Karpman, *The Alcoholic Woman* (Washington, D.C.: Linacre Press, 1948).

Escape is cyclical, however, and the individual runs into the same factors during the hangover that he was trying to escape. Alcohol is compulsive and progressive, in addition to its failure to provide a satisfactory escape for the drinker.

Although alcohol and crime have been associated for a long time, it is difficult to develop a causal relationship between them. The vast majority of alcoholics are not criminals. Nor are most criminals alcoholic. Nevertheless, a close association remains. A questionnaire study of 2,325 male felons in the California Department of Corrections indicated that 98 percent had used alcoholic beverages, as compared with the estimated 70 percent of the general population of males 21 years of age and over. Of the alcoholic beverage users in prison, 29 percent claimed they had been intoxicated at the time they committed the offense.[9] The types of crime committed during an alcoholic spree ranged from a high of 50 percent for automobile theft to a low of 10 percent for narcotics offenses. It is apparent that "impulse" crime is committed more frequently under the influence of alcohol than "planned" crime. This writer questioned 2,000 consecutive incoming prisoners at the State Prison of Southern Michigan for one year in 1942 to 1943 regarding the contribution of alcohol to their offenses. At that time, approximately 65 percent said that they had been drinking when they committed the offense, but only 20 percent blamed their offenses on alcohol.[10] It would appear that crime and alcoholism are both symptoms of a deeper personality maladjustment or social problem in terms of interaction with other people in society.

Two major problems confuse the attempts to develop a theory relating criminal behavior to alcohol: one relates to whether or not a person who is under the influence of alcohol will violate laws he would not violate if he were not under the influence. Another concerns the inability to determine whether alcoholism is the result of a clinical condition, such as psychopathy or neurosis.[11] Probably one of the best reviews and analyses of the studies attempting to link alcohol and crime appeared in the 1967 reports of The President's Commission on Law Enforcement and Administration of Justice.

On the basis of available information it is plausible to assume that alcohol does play an important and damaging role in the lives

---

[9] *Criminal Offenders and Drinking Involvement*, California Department of Public Health, Division of Alcoholic Rehabilitation, Publication Number 3, 1960, pp. 7–14.

[10] Vernon Fox, *Introduction to Corrections* (Englewood Cliffs, N.J.: Prentice-Hall, 1972), p. 239.

[11] In Edwin H. Sutherland and Donald R. Cressey, *Criminology*, 9th ed. (Philadelphia and New York: J. P. Lippincott, 1974), pp. 164–65.

of offenders, particularly chronic inebriates, and the production of crime. Yet one cannot be sure on the basis of the work done to date that alcohol use of offenders exceeds that of nonoffenders with similar social and personality characteristics (if any such match is possible). One cannot be sure that the alcohol use of offenders is any greater at the moments of their offense than during their ordinary noncriminal moments. One cannot be sure that the alcohol-using offenders would not have committed some offenses had they not been drinking. One is not sure that the alcohol use of offenders differs from that of persons possibly present in the same or like situations which inspired or provoked the criminality of one and not the other. Finally, and this is an important point in view of the fact that all studies have been done on apprehended offenders, one does not know the relationship now shown between alcohol use is not in fact a relationship between being caught and having a drinker rather than being a criminal and being a drinker.[12]

Intoxication in most cases results in such activities as singing, exchange of dirty stories, and other forms of interaction in which alcohol is known as a "social lubricant." The vast majority of alcoholics are not criminals and the vast majority of criminals are not alcoholics. The "average" alcoholic has been described as a middle-class citizen with a good job. "Skid Row"-type alcoholics, however, comprise the largest number of misdemeanants, with charges of public intoxication and disorderly conduct. They are a major problem for jails.

Diagnosis of alcoholism is basically physiological and clinical as evidenced by dependency and deterioration of some vital organs and behavior—the alcoholic continues to drink despite obvious medical and social contraindication.

Many church groups have developed programs to assist the Skid Row alcoholic and homeless men and women. A survey of 102 halfway houses for alcoholics in the United States and Canada was made by the Volunteers of America.[13] This group found that most residents like to have the house administered by recovered alcoholics because they have less trouble with communication. The Salvation Army has "Harbor Lights" in many Skid Row areas for alcoholics; it maintains 126 Men's Social Service Centers.[14]

The National Institute of Alcohol Abuse and Alcoholism provides as-

---

[12] Blum, "Mind-Altering Drugs," p. 43.

[13] Leo G. Ruffing, "Halfway Houses and the Alcoholic Offender," Proceedings of the One Hundred and Third Annual Congress of Correction, Seattle, Washington, August 12–17, 1973 (College Park, Md.: American Correctional Association, 1974), pp. 45–49.

[14] Warren C. Johnson, "Alcoholic Offender in the Community," in ibid., pp. 49–55.

sistance for and information regarding alcoholism treatment programs within the governmental framework. As part of the Public Health Service, the NIAAA functions within the Alcohol, Drug Abuse, and Mental Health Administration of the United States Department of Health, Education and Welfare. *Alcohol & Health Notes* is published monthly by the NIAAA's National Clearinghouse for Alcohol Information.

Childhood and teenage alcoholism has attracted the attention of some psychiatrists interested in the subject, such as Dr. William Rader of Los Angeles. Undoubtedly, childhood and teenage alcoholism may have always been present, but sheltered by the family; it took an affluent, sophisticated, and mobile society to bring it to professional attention. The youngest "alcoholic" brought to the attention of this writer was a 9-year-old girl who began drinking at age 4 or 5 when the father and mother encouraged her to taste their drinks, undoubtedly thinking it was "cute." Unfortunately, parents with a drink in their hands cannot tell their children not to use alcohol. The pattern of childhood and teenage alcoholism appears to begin at home with parents letting young children taste their drinks. By the early teens, probably 14 or 15, many of these young people can be termed to be "alcoholic." The peer pressure on them in a drinking society to continue their participation on a social basis makes successful treatment difficult.

The Manhattan Bowery Project began in November 1967, under the auspices of the Vera Institute of Justice, beginning as an alcohol detoxification unit with a medical ward, nursing care, and follow-up. An after-care center and clinic was opened in July 1969; it was designed to help in the after-care problem. A majority of out-patients live at the Salvation Army Memorial Hotel where staff members go twice a week. The New York Alcoholic Rehabilitation Unit, begun in 1971, has based its program on the Bowery Experience.

The Boston South End Center for Alcoholics and Unattached Persons offers assistance to Skid-Row inebriates approached on the streets who agree to accept the help. Medical and welfare services are available, as are job placement and housing. The St. Louis Detoxification and Diagnostic Evaluation Center provides similar services.

New Jersey has a statewide toll-free hotline aimed at helping people with alcoholism and related problems. The number is (800) 322-5525 and is sponsored by Volunteers for Ala-Call. More than 1,200 calls were handled during the first nine months of operation in 1974. About 50 percent of the calls were from people identifying themselves as non-alcoholics worried about problem drinkers in their own families. About 10 percent came from people who were concerned that they may be alcoholic.

The Church of St. Thomas More in Littleton, Colorado, had its application for a liquor license approved by Arapaho County officials in late 1974. Father Frederick D. McCallin has indicated that the days of large, dark churches is over if they want to be effective, further stating, "Let's face it. The first bartender in the church was Christ at the marriage feast of Cana." [15] At least 12 million Americans drink enough to qualify as alcoholics, according to the U.S. Surgeon General.[16]

A psychiatric treatment center for alcoholism at West Palm Beach, Florida, encourages patients to keep a private journal as a self-help tool during the six to eight weeks of residence.[17] Dr. Ronald J. Catanzaro, medical director at the Palm Beach Institute, indicates that the procedure opens new insights into the patient's feelings and maximizes his opportunity to express himself freely and openly. Over a period of weeks, he can see the bits and pieces fitting into a pattern. The therapist does not need to see the journal unless the patient offers to show it to him.

Indian alcohol programs in Kansas, Oklahoma, and Texas have jointly formed the United Indian Recovery Association, Inc.[18] Seven alcoholism treatment and rehabilitation programs now comprise the Association's membership. A primary goal is to upgrade the services offered to clients at Indian treatment and rehabilitation centers and the establishment of an Indian desk within the Alcoholism Division of the Oklahoma Department of Mental Health.

The Veterans Administration operates the largest single alcoholism rehabilitation system in the United States. When the program began in 1946, alcoholism was considered to be "a non-service-connected condition as well as a result of willful misconduct," but now the VA's Alcohol and Drug Dependence Service combines treatment of alcoholism and drug problems as a medical concern.[19]

Community-based alcoholism programs operating from neighborhood facilities easily accessible to the people they are designed to serve, located in the same social, economic, and behavioral environment in which the alcoholic lives and functions, have been observed as the most successful

15 "Colorado Church Granted License to Serve Alcoholic Beverages," *Juvenile Justice Digest*, 2, No. 15 (December 20, 1974), 1–2.

16 Ibid., p. 2.

17 "Patients' Private Journals Are Valuable Therapy Tools," *NIAAA Information & Feature Service*, IFS No. 12 (Rockville, Md.), National Institute on Alcohol Abuse and Alcoholism, May 1975, p. 4.

18 "Indians in 3 States Organize Coalition of Alcoholism Programs," *Alcohol & Health Notes*, published by National Clearinghouse for Alcohol Information, National Institute of Alcohol Abuse and Alcoholism (Rockville, Md.), January 1974, p. 5.

19 "Combined Alcohol, Drug Therapy Tested by VA," *NIAA Information & Feature Service*, published by the National Clearinghouse for Alcohol Information of the National Institute on Alcohol Abuse and Alcoholism, November 1974, p. 5.

programs in the treatment of alcoholics.[20] Fleetwood Roberts, director of the Poverty Program, Special Projects Branch of the National Institute of Alcohol Abuse and Alcoholism, indicates that the target population for these programs are people who exist under conditions of poverty and violence so prevalent that "outside counselors" cannot understand and communicate with the despair engendered by the environment in which their clients live. The National Institute on Alcohol Abuse and Alcoholism funds approximately 200 small, community-based projects for this purpose. Guidelines for estimating withdrawal symptoms for treatment are seen in Table 8-1.

Pretrial hospitalization for drunks picked up on other charges refers to therapeutic programs offered by community mental health centers, psychiatric in-patient programs in local hospitals, or other mental health programs designed for alcoholics who have been arrested. It may include day care, evening care, night care, or weekend care, but is generally limited to 24-hour or other short-term care.

Arizona State Health Department's Alcohol Abuse Division has established several LARC programs (Local Alcoholism Reception Center). South Tucson was the first municipality to establish a program and it serves approximately 2,400 patients a year. It is staffed by six paid professional counselors on a 24-hour basis and referrals are made to halfway houses or other treatment centers. The staff has learned to know quite well the local habitual inebriates. Although the recidivism rate of first admissions has been high, successive referrals have resulted in improvement of a portion of the drinking population. The LARC in Douglas, a town situated on the Mexican border, is located in a popular "Skid Row saloon" and when the walk-in clientele come into their old drinking haunt, they are offered coffee.

The length of time an alcoholic spends in the hospital has no significant effect on recovery. A study of 631 admissions to Napa State Hospital in Fairfield, California, made by Guy Grenny, psychiatric social worker with the Solano County (California) Mental Health Service over a 42-month period, indicated that a 7-day stay was sufficient to handle acute alcoholic complications.[21] Longer stays did not result in better long-term results. Alcoholic patients hospitalized for longer than 90 days have complicating medical or psychiatric problems. Consequently, local nonhospital services appear to be better for treating alcoholics because this type of care leaves them in their family or social setting, is cheaper,

20 "Community-Based Programs Held Best for Disadvantaged," *Alcohol & Health Notes,* published by National Clearinghouse for Alcohol Information, January 1974, pp. 1, 4.

21 "Longer Hospital Stay Said to Be No Aid to Recovery," *Alcohol & Health Notes,* published by National Clearinghouse for Alcohol Information, March 1974, p. 4.

TABLE 8-1   Detoxification

Guidelines for Estimating Withdrawal Reactions

Mild	Moderate	Severe
1. Drinking is done only after work	1. Drinking is done during the work day and evening	1. Drinking is done around the clock
2. Drinking is done only on weekends	2. Benders last for 3–6 days	2. Benders last for a week or more
3. Daily consumption less than 1 pint of whiskey in 24 hrs.	3. Daily consumption between pint and fifth in 24 hrs.	3. Consumption 1 fifth or more in 24 hrs.
4. Age under 35	4. Age 35–40	4. Age over 40 years.
5. Excessive drinking for less than 5 years	5. Excessive drinking has existed 5–10 years	5. Excessive drinking has existed for more than 10 years
6. Little previous withdrawal reaction	6. Shakes have been troublesome when sobering up	6. Hallucinations, DTs, or convulsions have occurred previously
7. Regular eating and living habits	7. Regular living habits with at least one balanced meal per day	7. Eating is irregular and poor
8. No evidence of malnutrition	8. No specific nutritional deficiencies but some weight loss is usual	8. Poor nourishment with specific deficiencies often present
9. No use of other sedative, tranquilizing or stimulant drugs	9. Occasional use of sedative drugs but no misuse of these	9. Frequent use of sedative or tranquilizing drugs to excess
10. No major medical illness	10. No major medical illness	10. Any major medical illness
11. No recent injury	11. No recent injury	11. Recent injury
12. No evidence of infection	12. No evidence of infection	12. Any infection

Harve E. Olsen, *Administration of Transitional Facilities* (Avon Park, Fla.: Florida Bureau of Alcoholic Rehabilitation, 1972), p. 58.

and provides therapy and other emotional support to handle the psychological dependence.

Alcoholism begins with occasional brief drinking, proceeds to constant relief drinking, memory blackouts, decrease of ability to stop drinking when others do, periods of lengthy intoxication, obsessive drinking, and

ALCOHOL ADDICTION AND RECOVERY

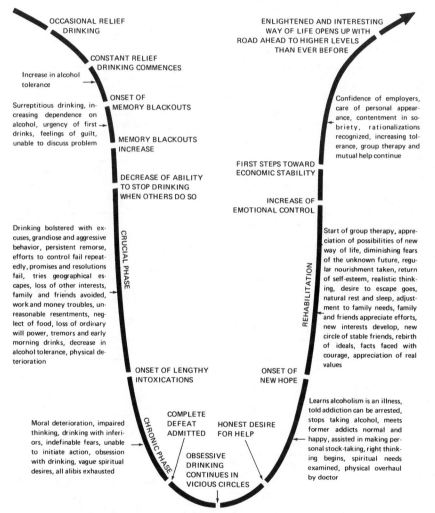

Figure 8-1.   Alcohol Addiction and Recovery.

James C. Coleman, *Abnormal Psychology and Modern Life*, 3rd ed. (Chicago: Scott, Foresman, 1964), p. 430. Redrawn from M. M. Glatt, "Group Therapy in Alcoholism," *British Journal of Addiction*, 54, No. 2 (1957). Permission has been granted from the editors of the *American Journal of Psychiatry* and the *Annals of Internal Medicine*.

DRUGS		SCHEDULE	OFTEN PRESCRIBED BRAND NAMES	MEDICAL USES	DEPENDENCE PHYSICAL
NARCOTICS	Opium	II	Dover's Powder, Paregoric	Analgesic, antidiarrheal	High
	Morphine	II	Morphine	Analgesic	High
	Codeine	II, III, V	Codeine	Analgesic, antitussive	Moderate
	Heroin	I	None	None	High
	Meperidine (Pethidine)	II	Demerol, Pethadol	Analgesic	High
	Methadone	II	Dolophine, Methadone, Methadose	Analgesic, heroin substitute	High
	Other Narcotics	I, II, III, V	Dilaudid, Leritine, Numorphan, Percodan	Analgesic, antidiarrheal, antitussive	High
DEPRESSANTS	Chloral Hydrate	IV	Noctec, Somnos	Hypnotic	Moderate
	Barbiturates	II, III, IV	Amytal, Butisol, Nembutal, Phenobarbital, Seconal, Tuinal	Anesthetic, anti-convulsant, sedation, sleep	High
	Glutethimide	III	Doriden	Sedation, sleep	High
	Methaqualone	II	Optimil, Parest, Quaalude, Somnafac, Sopor	Sedation, sleep	High
	Meprobamate	IV	Equanil, Meprospan, Miltown Kesso-Bamate, SK-Bamate	Anti-anxiety, muscle relaxant, sedation	Moderate
	Other Depressants	III, IV	Dormate, Noludar, Placidyl, Valmid	Anti-anxiety, sedation, sleep	Possible
STIMULANTS	Cocaine	II	Cocaine	Local anesthetic	Possible
	Amphetemines	II, III	Benzedrine, Biphetamine, Desoxyn, Dexedrine	Hyperkinesis, narcolepsy, weight control	Possible
	Phenmetrozine	II	Preludin	Weight control	Possible
	Methylphenidate	II	Ritalin	Hyperkenesis	Possible
	Other Stimulants	III, IV	Bacarate, Cylert, Didrex, Ionamin, Plegine, Pondimin, Pre-Sate, Sanorex, Voranil	Weight control	Possible
HALLUCINOGENS	LSD	I	None	None	None
	Mescaline	I	None	None	None
	Psilocybin-Psilocyn	I	None	None	None
	MDA	I	None	None	None
	PCP	III	Sernylan	Veterinary anesthetic	None
	Other Hallucinogens	I	None	None	None
CANNABIS	Marihuana Hashish Hashish Oil	I	None	None	Degree unknown

Figure 8-2. Controlled Substances: Uses and Effects

Schedule column indicates the seriousness of addiction with I being most addictive and V least.

POTENTIAL: PSYCHOLOGICAL	TOLERANCE	DURATION OF EFFECTS (in hours)	USUAL METHODS OF ADMINISTRATION	POSSIBLE EFFECTS	EFFECTS OF OVERDOSE	WITHDRAWAL SYNDROME
High	Yes	3 to 6	Oral, smoked	Euphoria drowsiness, respiratory depression, constricted pupils, nausea	Slow and shallow breathing, clammy skin, convulsions, coma, possible death	Watery eyes, runny nose, yawning, loss of appetite, irritability, tremors, panic, chills and sweating, cramps, nausea
High	Yes	3 to 6	Injected, smoked			
Moderate	Yes	3 to 6	Oral, injected			
High	Yes	3 to 6	Injected, sniffed			
High	Yes	3 to 6	Oral, injected			
High	Yes	12 to 24	Oral, injected			
High	Yes	3 to 6	Oral, injected			
Moderate	Probable	5 to 8	Oral	Slurred speech, disorientation, drunken behavior without odor of alcohol	Shallow respiration, cold and clammy skin, dilated pupils, weak and rapid pulse, coma, possible death	Anxiety, insomnia, tremors, delirium, convulsions, possible death
High	Yes	1 to 16	Oral, injected			
High	Yes	4 to 8	Oral			
High	Yes	4 to 8	Oral			
Moderate	Yes	4 to 8	Oral			
Possible	Yes	4 to 8	Oral			
High	Yes	2	Injected, sniffed	Increased alertness, excitation, euphoria, dilated pupils, increased pulse rate and blood pressure insomnia, loss of appetite.	Agitation, increase in body temperature, hallucinations, convulsions, possible death.	Apathy, long periods of sleep, irritability, depression, disorientation.
High	Yes	2 to 4	Oral, injected			
High	Yes	2 to 4	Oral			
High	Yes	2 to 4	Oral			
Possible	Yes	2 to 4	Oral			
Degree unknown	Yes	Variable	Oral	Illusions and hallucinations (with exception of MDA); poor perception of time and distance	Longer, more intense "trip" episodes, psychosis, possible death	Withdrawal syndrome not reported
Degree unknown	Yes	Variable	Oral, injected			
Degree unknown	Yes	Variable	Oral			
Degree unknown	Yes	Variable	Oral, injected, sniffed			
Degree unknown	Yes	Variable	Oral, injected, smoked			
Degree unknown	Yes	Variable	Oral, injected, sniffed			
Moderate	Yes	2 to 4	Oral, smoked	Euphoria, relaxed inhibitions, increased appetite, disoriented behavior	Fatigue, paranoia, possible psychosis	Insomnia, hyperactivity, and decreased appetite reported in a limited number of individuals

Figure 8-2. Continued

John H. Kabger, "Drugs of Abuse," *Drug Enforcement,* Drug Enforcement Administration, United States Department of Justice, 2, No. 2 (Spring 1975), 20-21.

complete defeat admitted. An honest desire for help precedes the onset of new hope. A beginning increase of emotional control precedes economic stability and sobriety. Figure 8-1 provides a diagram of the process of alcohol addiction and recovery.

DRUG PROGRAMS

Narcotic addiction and drug abuse has become a major social and personality problem in recent years, particularly through the 1960s and 1970s, with considerable acceleration during the Vietnam conflict. There are many different substances, but some are used more often than others. Another view of the uses and effects of controlled substances has been presented by the United States Drug Enforcement Administration. (See Figure 8-2.) There is common agreement about the effects of the drugs and risk of abuse or addiction. (Many other lesser drugs are not listed, such as jimson weed, maté, and other substances.)

Fashion, curiosity, group pressure, and search for new philosophies are not sufficient to motivate young people to habitual drug use. A French study by F. Davidson, M. Etienne, and J. Piesset has reported that the drug user's escape into a make-believe world results from longstanding and deep-rooted personal pathology.[22] There is little real difference between illegal drug abusers and many people legally misusing tranquilizers and sleeping pills. Consequently, the treatment cannot focus on a single physiological problem, but must focus on the personal and social pathology from which the drug abuser seeks relief. While there is evidence that anyone can become physically addicted to narcotics, there are personalities that are more vulnerable than others.[23] People who are most vulnerable are those with low frustration tolerance and high dependency needs. Impulsive, immature, inadequate persons are likely candidates. Many are "here-and-now" oriented, seeking an immediate "high" or relief from tension without considering future consequences.

There is a complex relationship between drug addiction and crime. A study of 269 narcotic addicts arrested by the New York City Police Department and treated at St. Luke's Hospital between March 1966 and January 1972 indicated that they were predominantly noncriminal before

---

[22] David Ehrlich, "Complex Pathology Behind Drug Abuse," *The Journal*, 3, No. 3 (March 1, 1974) (published in Toronto by the Addiction Research Foundation). From a study reported to the United Nations Division of Narcotic Drugs and to be published by the National Institute of Health and Medical Research.

[23] *A Federal Source Book: Answers to the Most Frequently Asked Questions about Drug Abuse* (Washington, D.C.: National Clearinghouse for Drug Abuse Information, 1971), p. 24.

addiction, but were arrested for crimes after addiction.[24] During heroin use, the increased arrests were primarily for violation of drug laws, prostitution, violence, property crime, and general misbehavior. During methadone maintenance, the arrests fell sharply for drug laws, prostitution, and property offenses, while violence and general misbehavior fell less sharply.

Narcotics programs in the United States include hospitalization, imprisonment, institutional group counseling, community surveillance and testing, casework programs in the community, and mutual aid organizations composed of ex-addicts.

Drug treatment on a self-help basis began in Santa Monica, California, where an ex-alcoholic opened Synanon House in 1958 as a therapeutic community in which addicts live and help each other. Yablonsky wrote of Synanon as an excellent approach that had good potential.[25] Subsequent reports have supported that view. The name "Synanon" was adapted from an uneducated resident addict's mispronunciation of "seminar." [26] It refers to a special type of intensive counseling session conducted by residents several times a week in small groups. Old and new residents are mixed and they emphasize breaking down rationalizations and deceptions with which they attempt to mislead themselves and others with regard to motivations and problems. Other Synanon Houses have opened elsewhere with similar programs. It has become an international program.

There is considerable uncertainty concerning the success of mutual aid organizations composed of ex-addicts and ex-alcoholics, despite their success with certain individuals. During training sessions in 1968, officers of the Bureau of Narcotics and Dangerous Drugs expressed such reservations to this writer. They felt that these groups may be successful with highly motivated addicts and drug abusers constituting perhaps less than 10 percent of all addicts, ". . . but let's see what they can do with the whole spectrum!" Three points have been advanced regarding the mutual aid programs in drug and narcotic treatment.[27] First, only those who remain in the organization for a number of years are counted and those who lapse or fail to cooperate are rejected from the program. Second, mutual aid programs seem to be attractive to the more literate addicts in which middle-class background and some education are dis-

[24] Paul Cushman, "Relationship between Narcotic Addiction and Crime," *Federal Probation*, 38, No. 3 (September 1974), 38–43.

[25] Lewis Yablonsky, "The Anti-Criminal Society: Synanon," *Federal Probation*, 26 (September 1962), 50.

[26] Daniel Glaser and Vincent O'Leary, *Parole Decision-Making: The Control and Treatment of Narcotic Use* (Washington, D.C.: Office of Juvenile Delinquency and Youth Development, 1968), p. 40.

[27] Ibid., pp. 40–41.

Since 1958, Synanon has been reeducating people who became addicted to drugs, alcohol, and criminal behavior. Now Synanon has created the Synanon Punk Squad so that the same process can be put to work to change the lives of kids under eighteen who are in trouble with drugs, alcohol, or the law. In January 1976, when this photo was taken, 130 kids were enrolled in the Synanon Punk Squad.

Courtesy of Synanon Foundation, Inc., Marshall, California.

proportionately represented. Third, these organizations do little to re-integrate addicts into society, but tend rather to become a substitute family; consequently the addicts living there tend to feel socially deprived and alienated when they are in the outside world among persons who are neither addicts or ex-addicts.

Daytop Lodge began in 1963 as an ambitious project with 25 residents. It started with the idea that probationers would serve as volunteers. Begun as Daytop Lodge in 1963, it has become Daytop Village, with the original facility on Staten Island, one at Swan Lake, another on 14th Street in Manhattan.[28] Under the leadership of David Deitch, Daytop's objectives became redefined to make the residents leaders in a social movement with utopian goals over and above a mere rehabilitation program. Now under the leadership of Msgr. William B. O'Brien, with headquarters in Manhattan, a special facility in the Catskill Mountains is used for the residents. Daytop Village now has 100 residents and is a

---

[28] Barry Sugarman, *Daytop Village: A Therapeutic Community* (New York: Holt, Rinehart and Winston, 1974), p. 121.

Daytop Midtown Headquarters houses 150 re-entry residents, 30 inductees, and administrative offices of Daytop Village, Inc., New York City.

Courtesy of Daytop Village, Inc., New York City.

culture and an institution existing to change people. An important feature is the balancing of discipline, conformity, and confrontation as a mutual concern among its members. Daytop Village adopted the concepts developed at Synanon in 1958. During an administrative conflict, several staff members left in 1967 and 1968 and established other programs elsewhere —Marathon House, Inc., in Rhode Island; an independent Daytop House in New Haven, Connecticut; a Concept House in Rhode Island; and a Gaudenzia House in Philadelphia. In spite of the conflict, Daytop Village has grown and still serves addicts well.

Daytop, Synanon, and the "Concept House" therapeutic communities have followed the same model. The movement deplores the materialism of modern America and the "Protestant Ethic," which encourages the overcoming of obstacles and the competitive spirit. In the hippie movement of the 1960s thosands of young people rejected the traditional value system. The difference between the self-help drug programs and the hippie movement, however, is that the drug programs do not reject it completely but seek to co-exist with it.

The Delancy Street Foundation has about 270 ex-addicts living in the old Russian and Egyptian consulates in San Francisco. It was started by John Maher, who began taking drugs at age 12 and spent the next ten years shoplifting, burglarizing, procuring, pushing drugs—in short, doing anything to support his habit. He started Delancy Street with a $1,000 gift from an underworld loan shark in 1970. A basic principle in this organization is that everybody works; the foundation runs five businesses which pay most of the expenses. Prospective members are interviewed by

A session at Delancy Street Foundation in San Francisco.

Courtesy of Delancy Street Foundation, Inc. Photo by Edward Turnbull.

veteran Delancy Streeters. The treatment is attack therapy, called "games," in which participants try to make one another angry. The theory is that by learning to withstand provocative behavior, they learn to control other problems and accept responsibility.[29]

Treatment Alternatives to Street Crime (TASC) is operated jointly by

---

[29] Michael S. Serrill, "From 'Bums' to Businessmen: The Delancy Street Foundation," *Corrections Magazine*, 1, No. 1 (September 1974), 13–28.

LEAA, the White House Special Action Office for Drug Abuse Prevention, and the National Institute on Drug Abuse. It identifies drug users entering the criminal justice system and refers eligible candidates for pre- and post-trial release into appropriate community-based treatment facilities. It has been in operation since August 1972, and more than 800 new clients are referred to the program each month.[30]

The Alternative Community Service Program in Multnomah County (Portland), Oregon is often used for drug-addiction-related offenses. It permits judges to sentence minor offenders to constructive public service work. A variety of jobs are available, such as teaching a blind person to cook, helping landscape a public building, instructing at a music center for young people, refereeing a sports contest in the recreational program, packaging food for the needy, individually tutoring elementary and high school students having academic difficulty, and any of a variety of other helpful tasks.

ADAPT is a methadone maintenance treatment clinic at Provident Hospital in Baltimore for hard-core heroin addicts. This type of methadone maintenance clinic has developed rapidly in large cities for the purpose of reducing crime related to heroin addiction. Methadone maintenance programs appear to be successful. The California Department of Corrections has had a methadone maintenance program designed to change illicit users of heroin into law-abiding and legally employed persons. There are approximately 41,000 addicts in Los Angeles County alone, and the program is not yet large enough to handle the problem adequately. Of those served, however, most are taking advantage of the supportive services offered to enhance the resocialization process.[31] Among opinions of 316 respondents in the California Methadone Maintenance Program, the best setting for such a program was divided as follows:[32]

Community program	36.1 percent
County medical center	19.3 percent
Private clinics	19.0 percent
University	7.9 percent
Veterans Administration hospital	7.0 percent
California Department of Corrections	5.1 percent
Don't know	2.8 percent
Ex-addict program	2.2 percent
None	0.6 percent

[30] "TASC participation hits 10,000," *LEAA Newsletter,* 4, No. 9 (April 1975).

[31] Welton A. Jones and John E. Berecochea, *California Department of Corrections Methadone Maintenance Program: An Evaluation* (Sacramento, Cal.: Department of Corrections, 1973), p. 4.

[32] Ibid., p. 57.

A nonprofit organization in Minneapolis, called 180 Degrees, Inc., helps ex-felons and felons in prison with chemical dependency problems. All staff are ex-felons. This organization provides personal contact, counseling, referrals, follow-up, and felon-to-felon counseling, with 24-hour phone service, a drop-in center, and residential care.

There are probably over 400 major drug treatment agencies in the United States, and the variety of approaches to treatment varies widely. There are many more smaller agencies, with New York State alone having more than 350 drug agencies.[33]

A review in 1973 of twelve private drug treatment agencies based in New York City and financed by the New York State Narcotic Addiction Control Commission found a wide variety of treatment approaches being used.[34] The modalities included therapeutic communities, methadone maintenance, detoxification, out-patient service, individual and group psychotherapy, vocational training, and so forth. The clients were just as diversified, including Blacks, whites, Puerto Ricans, men, women, adults, juveniles, offenders, and a wide variety of backgrounds. The programs reviewed were Addicts Rehabilitation Center, Daytop Village, Exodus House, Greenwich House, Inward House, Lower Eastside Service Center, Odyssey House, Quaker Committee on Social Rehabilitation, Reality House, Salvation Army, Samaritan Halfway Society, and Village Haven.

The Addiction Research and Treatment Corporation (ARTC) became operational in Brooklyn's Bedford-Stuyvesant section in October 1969 with funds from New York City, New York State, and federal agencies. The purpose was to expand the methadone treatment program for New York City addicts, particularly in districts with serious public health problems, generally referred to as "catchment" areas, because they seemed to "catch" these problems. The program included (1) complete medical assistance, (2) educational programs, (3) job counseling and placement, (4) psychological therapy through groups, (5) a residential therapeutic community in the catchment area, (6) a day-care unit for individuals who do not respond satisfactorily, (7) a crisis unit which offers individual help with personal problems of any nature 24 hours a day, (8) referrals, and (9) legal assistance.

There is apparently no way to know exactly how many drug treatment centers there are at any given time in the United States. Of course, New York and a dozen other states have the greatest drug problem, so there is a heavier concentration of treatment centers in those areas. More than

---

[33] "State Supports More than 350 Drug Agencies," *The Attack on Narcotic Addiction and Abuse* (generally called *The Attack*), 6, No. 1 (Fall–Winter 1973), 3–8. (Variance in No. 2 and No. 1 not a misprint.)

[34] "Commission Reviews 12 NYC Treatment Agencies," *The Attack,* 6, No. 2 (Spring 1973), 1, 10.

41,000 addicts were in New York State treatment programs in 1973, with 25,000 on methadone.[35] There were more than 66,000 addicts and users being treated. And more than 80,000 addicts have been admitted since the State Narcotic Addiction Control Commission began in 1967.[36]

It is very difficult to obtain accurate and objective information about narcotics and drug abuse. Unfortunately, much of the published material is likely to be slanted according to the views of the writer or producer, who either wants to promote stronger enforcement and stiffer penalties or wants to decriminalize drug abuse and narcotic addiction for any of several reasons. Nearly 100 drug abuse films were evaluated by the National Coordinating Council on Drug Abuse Education and Information, Inc., a private, nonprofit agency.[37] One primary conclusion was that many of the films were scientifically unacceptable.

TREATMENT STRATEGIES

The treatment strategies for alcoholism and narcotic abuse and addiction generally follow the standard patterns in therapy: (1) exploration, (2) confrontation, (3) explanation, and (4) termination. *Exploration* is a search for causes, generally involving a neurotic emotional situation. The cause of addiction could be rooted in such things as social deprivation in delinquent peer groups, isolation, economic deprivation, physical suffering and illness, loss of primary ties with family members, criminal linkage to support a habit, or searching for a feeling of well-being and adequacy. *Confrontation* involves breaking down old patterns of antisocial responses and negativism toward social mores, and creating a desire to want to learn to function independently. There must be a development of responsible behavior. *Explanation* involves gaining an understanding of behavior, translating old behavior into here-and-now patterns of adjustments, developing the capacity to sustain change, and achievement of personal autonomy. *Termination* comes about as a result of sufficient exploration of realistic goals in relationship with significant persons and a personal evaluation of the wide choices of problem solving as they relate to future behavior.

Self-help organizations rely considerably on the group counseling, reality therapy, and guided group interaction methods. There is a great

35 "More than 41,000 Addicts in State Treatment Programs; 25,000 Are Using Methadone," *The Attack*, 6, No. 1 (Fall–Winter 1973), 1.

36 "More than 80,000 Addicts Have Been Admitted to State Treatment," *The Attack*, 6, No. 3 (Summer 1973), 1.

37 "Chaplains Call Religion Aid to Successful Therapy," *The Attack*, 6, No. 3 (Summer 1973), 5.

emphasis on emotional support from other addicts who are trying to "kick the habit," in order to reduce the pressure of the psychological dependence.

Many chaplains in institutions and community-based programs consider religion to be an aid to successful treatment of chemical dependency, whether alcoholic or narcotic. One of the chaplain's most important functions is that of a caring therapist dealing with the whole person.[38] His training in theology and philosophy makes him more humanistic and less clinical than are many psychologists and psychiatrists.

Psychological dependency is the most difficult part of an addiction to handle. Conventional treatment programs generally just do not have the time for follow-up. This is why self-help organizations report a better success rate than do most hospitals, even though their caseloads are viewed as selective. The wide variety of approaches used is an advantage in many ways, because of the wide range of people and problems that must be served. All three frames of references—sociological, psychological, and biochemical—are useful and necessary for a balanced understanding of the causes of drug dependency and the potentially useful avenues of treatment available. It is not a single set of influences that produce drug or alcohol use and abuse but a multifaceted interaction of many forces. The society and time into which an individual is born have a great effect on the basic patterns of addiction behavior. The personal development history of a person will mold his or her emotional predisposition as well as the responses to various drugs and treatments. Finally, the chemical makeup of the drugs eventually taken will have an important, perhaps even determinative, influence on the long-term pattern of use that follows. The multiple causes of alcohol and drug dependency result in a wide variety of treatment needs among abusers which can only be met through availability of a broad range of treatment modalities.

CONCLUSIONS

Chemical dependence on foreign substances introduced into the body to relieve tension and anxiety has been present since the beginning of civilization. Legislation against these foreign substances, particularly alcohol and drugs, has not prevented the rapid expansion of their use, although how much such legislation has hindered faster expansion is difficult to estimate. It is obvious that the susceptibility of an individual to alcohol and drugs is related to his personality pattern, familial and developmental background, and other physiological, psychological, and

---

[38] "Chaplains Call Religion Aid to Successful Therapy," *The Attack*, 6, No. 3 (Summer 1973), 5.

sociological factors. Treatment programs have to account for the emotional dependence and psychological supports in order to be successful.

Legal problems over and above suppression and control have entered the field of alcohol and drug treatment programs. In 1966, the *Driver* v. *Hinnant* case (356 F.2d 761, 4th Circuit, 1966, 256 n3) held that conviction of alcoholics on charges of drunkenness was tantamount to conviction of sick persons for displaying symptoms of a disease and was therefore unconstitutional. Earlier, in 1962, the courts held that laws making addiction a crime are cruel and unusual punishment, with the statement that drug addiction is an illness comparable to leprosy, insanity, and the common cold (*Robinson* v. *California, 370* U.S. 660, 1962). Legal diversion of addicts from the criminal justice system includes the right to treatment, confidential privilege of communication, confidentiality and expungement of records, and liability of staff for neglect or misconduct.[39]

Regulations affecting the confidentiality of alcohol and drug abuse records have been developed jointly by the Department of Health, Education and Welfare and the Special Action Office for Drug Abuse Prevention. They follow guidelines set up in the Comprehensive Alcohol Abuse and Alcoholism Prevention, Treatment and Rehabilitation Act of 1970 and the Drug Abuse Office and Treatment Act of 1972. The safeguarding of individual privacy in case records and other personal information has become an issue between agencies with different objectives, such as police and other law enforcement agencies on the one hand, and social work and other treatment agencies on the other.

Chemical dependence on alcohol and drugs is a complex medico-legal problem. So much has been written about it and so little is known about it that there are not uniform standards for treatment programs. However, community-based programs seem to have better success than institutional programs, partially because of the selective factor in which the most serious cases must be institutonalized, and partially because the individual can be left in the community in a familiar social setting where treatment can include attempts to develop wholesome contacts and diminish the unwholesome ones. Most important of all is the ability of community-based agencies to make use of recovered alcoholics and addicts to provide psychological support for people involved in the treatment programs.

---

[39] H. S. Perlman, *Legal Issues in Addict Diversion—A Layman's Guide* (Washington, D.C.: American Bar Association, 1974), p. 60.

Chapter 9

Governmental Programs in the Community

Governmental programs in the community include those agencies that are routinely federally funded and result directly from congressional action. Eligibility for these programs varies according to the objectives of individual programs and the people they serve. The Social Security Administration, of course, serves almost everyone; over 90 percent of American workers are covered in one way or another. Vocational rehabilitation is available to those who are handicapped and have good prospects of recovery with assistance in preparing for and obtaining employment. Many of the programs are focused directly or indirectly toward offenders and ex-offenders, such as many programs funded by the Law Enforcement Assistance Administration (LEAA) of the Department of Justice. Other agencies serve people because they are poor, rather than because of their status as offenders—but of course ex-offenders often fall into this category. The community services agent, officer, or manager and the community-based correctional administrator and practitioner can use many of these programs for assisting offenders and ex-offenders.

VOCATIONAL REHABILITATION

The Vocational Rehabilitation Act of 1920 was designed to fund state vocational rehabilitation programs for persons with physical, emotional, and personality disorders. Although it did not specifically exclude offenders and ex-offenders, many practitioners questioned their prospects

150

for rehabilitation; consequently, up until 1965, many were not included in such programs. The programs are decentralized, in that each state has its own program to distribute federal funds under a plan approved by the national Vocational Rehabilitation Office in Washington. This arrangement is generally on a contractual basis.

The 1965 Amendments to the Vocational Rehabilitation Act specifically included rehabilitation of offenders and ex-offenders who qualify. Though vocational rehabilitation service to persons in prison having mental and behavioral disabilities has technically been permitted since 1943, the actual assistance had been limited in practice. The number of cases closed in state vocational rehabilitation agencies rose from 48,000 in 1963 to 218,000 in 1967. By 1967 there were 21,142 claims referred by correctional institutions (about 1 percent)—3,645 cases of alcoholism (less than 2 percent), 255 cases of drug addition (0.1 percent), and 9,968 character, personality, and behavior disorders (about 5 percent). This means that approximately 8 percent of all the cases closed by vocational rehabilitation agencies in 1967 were persons who could have been in the correctional caseloads, although only 1 percent of the total or one-eighth of the 8 percent with these problems were referred by correctional institutions.

The procedure taken by the vocational rehabilitation counselor and his office can be itemized in twelve steps: (1) initial evaluation, (2) determination of eligibility on the basis of need and prognosis, (3) case analogy to determine strength and weaknesses, (4) plan development, (5) treatment and counseling by a vocational rehabilitation officer, (6) training (academic, vocational, on-the-job, etc.), (7) provision of transportation where necessary, (8) provision of maintenance where necessary, (9) purchase of tools and equipment when needed, (10) provision of licenses and stock if vocational rehabilitation includes the establishment of a business, (11) placement in a job, (12) follow-up to determine whether or not the program has been successful. Eligibility includes the described handicap—whether of physical, emotional, personality, or cultural and social deprivation—and positive prognosis or prediction of successful rehabilitation. Even though the problem is present, the individual may not be eligible for vocational rehabilitation assistance if a positive prediction of response to treatment and assistance cannot be provided.

The Federal Vocational Rehabilitation Act of 1973 mandated that priority be given to individuals with the most severe disabilities. People with "behavioral disorders" are no longer considered to be eligible. "Severely disabled" people are now considered to be those with physical and mental impairment that seriously limits mobility and self-care. These people are unable to cope with the physical and mental demands of gainful employment. Some agencies have continued to serve offenders and ex-offenders from grant funds, including those from LEAA. With those funds declining in 1975, however, offenders and ex-offenders are receiving assistance from vocational rehabilitation only if they meet the other criteria, specifically, the "severely disabled" clause.

VETERANS ADMINISTRATION

Veterans in America have always received benefits of some sort. The first veterans' benefit on record was enacted by the Pilgrims of Plymouth Colony in 1636, providing that any soldier injured in defense of the colony should be maintained by the colony for life. Other colonies did the same, and by 1776, the concept of veterans' benefits was well established. The first Congress of the United States passed a federal pension law for veterans, but Congress kept the power of determining eligibility until 1819, when this power was given to the Secretary of War. The original Bureau of Pensions had been reorganized in 1813 into an Office of Pensions, which became part of the Department of the Interior in 1849, where it remained until the Veterans Administration was organized in 1930. Medical care for veterans was established on a national scale in 1861 to look after the health conditions of Union soldiers, and a Home for Disabled Volunteer Soldiers was established in 1865 and taken over by the Veterans Administration in 1930.

Veterans of the Spanish-American War, World War I, World War II, the Korean conflict, Vietnam, and peacetime service are eligible for benefits under different acts and regulations. Though the Veterans Administration was not organized as such until 1930, compensation for disability and other services were available to veterans. It was the American Legion, organized in 1919, that pressed for the organization of a Veterans Administration.[1] Besides disability pensions, treatment for alcohol or drug dependence and insurance, assistance to veterans is available for burial, clothing allowance, medical and dental treatment, hospitalization, job-finding assistance, loans for various reasons, and other services.

The Veterans Administration is available to the public through the various Veterans Administration regional offices and through the 166 Veterans Administration hospitals. The community services officer or community-based correctional coordinator must know about these services, because his clients are often veterans needing medical services, drug dependence treatment, and alcoholism treatment, as well as edu-

---

[1] *Federal Benefits for Veterans and Dependents* (Washington, D.C.: Veterans Administration IS-1 Fact Sheet, 1975).

cational benefits and other available services. Specialized alcoholism treatment units in forty-one VA hospitals and a variety of approaches are used. In the fiscal year, 1971–72 above, there were 91,000 veterans discharged with difficulties related to alcoholism. The peak age for alcoholism in veterans is forty-five to fifty-four. Because there were 25,000 veterans from World War II and the Korean conflict with alcohol problems, this program will last for a long time. Vietnam veterans are now beginning to come into the units for treatment for alcohol-related problems. It has become apparent, however, that many more Vietnam veterans will need treatment for drug-related problems.

The massive size of the American military forces since 1940 has increased the likelihood that many offenders and ex-offenders on present caseloads will be veterans. The requirement for all young men to register for the Selective Service Act when they reach their eighteenth birthdays and the possibility of inducting many of the physically and mentally capable young men into the military has broadened the proportion of veterans in the total population, including the offender and ex-offender population. A few received discharges under conditions other than honorable, but the vast majority were released with honorable discharges and are eligible for Veterans Administration services and benefits; some are receiving pensions for service-connected disabilities.

As indicated previously, drug dependence has appeared as a problem among veterans, especially among those from the Vietnam conflict. The first five drug treatment centers were established in 1971; thirty-one more were started in 1972, eight more in 1973, and because the problem is increasing, even more will be needed. There were 3,198 admissions to Veterans Administration hospitals for drug problems between January and June 1971, and 15,803 during the first several months of 1972. More than 65 percent of the admissions were for heroin addiction. Drug treatment consists of two to eight weeks of hospitalization followed by various periods of out-patient care. Drug treatment, of course, is not a simple medical problem. The average hard-drug addict has emotional, social, legal, financial, and other problems requiring a broad spectrum of services. The objective is not just to *get* him away from drugs, but to *keep* him away, which means that emotional and psychological dependency problems must be resolved.

The Veterans Administration has published guidelines that describe all the programs it offers to veterans. These are available from any Veterans Administration regional office. In addition, counseling assistance is provided for persons with service-connected disabilities to determine eligibility for pensions. Counseling is also available in legal and other areas.

DEPARTMENT OF JUSTICE PROGRAMS—LEAA

Programs supported by the Law Enforcement Assistance Administration are probably the most important to directors or coordinators of community-based corrections. The Law Enforcement Assistance Administration became part of the implementation of the Omnibus Crime Control and Safe Streets Act of 1968 (PL90–351). Part E of this act created the Law Enforcement Assistance Administration. Under this program, state planning agencies were developed by each state in order to distribute federal funds under a plan approved by the LEAA. The plans have involved "block" grants to the states to be distributed in accordance with their judgment, with a smaller number of discretionary grants to award direct funding to states, cities, counties, and other units of government to support projects. In addition, LEAA provides technical assistance to aid states in criminal justice efforts. The beginning of revenue sharing in 1974 represented an extension of the block grant concept.

These LEAA funds have been used to support a variety of community-based services, such as the construction of detention facilities and attendant juvenile services in the community. Model community correctional programs have been established. Police programs have been supported in the areas of working with juveniles and family crisis intervention. Many drug problems have been supported by LEAA funds in response to the rise in drug problems, particularly among youth.

The United States Bureau of Prisons has its own community services program, with five regional offices designed to coordinate and guide institutional and community activities throughout the United States. In addition, the United States Bureau of Prisons has contracted with over sixty correctional and other facilities in over forty cities to provide community-based programs for offenders. Other contracts with more than fifty private organizations are designed to provide community after-care treatment to releasees from rehabilitation facilities.

The Community Relations Service (CRS) relies on its professional staff to persuade and encourage local citizens and institutions to solve their problems. The CRS promotes the establishment of local criminal justice coordinating councils, which are composed of private business representatives, labor, education, and religious groups, as well as other interested citizens, to handle the broad spectrum of problems in the criminal justice system from control to corrections. Community-based correctional directors and coordinators can use these councils where they exist in their communities to develop resources and assist in the coordination of efforts in community-based corrections.

A state-by-state listing of the projects that have been funded by LEAA would be formidable. They have covered all the areas and phases in community-based corrections possible to establish. Halfway houses, alcohol and drug treatment programs, training programs for criminal justice personnel and offenders, counseling services, and research efforts to evaluate existing programs and to develop new ones are all included. Establishment of Youth Service Bureaus, a Community Reintegration Project that involves the AFL-CIO Placement Project, a Volunteers in Corrections (VIC) Program, a Narcotics Treatment Administration Program that includes methadone maintenance and detoxification, Project Straight Dope to prevent drug abuse among juveniles, a Family Crisis Project, and a Community Center Approach to Residential Juvenile Offenders involving YMCA and YWCA are only a few examples of the projects supported by LEAA in the community.

The IMPACT program, sometimes referred to as a therapeutic community rehabilitation project, is the largest program presently funded by the Law Enforcement Assistance Act. It is designed to reduce stranger-to-stranger crime in seven target metropolitan areas in the United States. It is based on the concept of the therapeutic community as an alternative to present incarceration and release procedures. The therapeutic community in this sense (as we have seen) enables selected offenders to be housed within transitional centers, and to participate in specific kinds of therapy. The program includes work release, educational release, and pre-release programs. Some programs divide the caseloads into (1) first offenders probated directly to the centers for 60 days before returning to probation supervision, (2) first offenders probated directly to the center for 120 days before being returned to probation supervision, (3) first offenders and recidivists presently incarcerated in the correctional system for 120 days before release, and (4) long-term group housing for both first offenders and recidivists with a minimum of one year before release.

DEPARTMENT OF LABOR

Since 1967, the Department of Labor has been actively involved in offender rehabilitation programs under the Manpower Development and Training Act. The Department of Labor was created by Congress in 1913 (37 Stat. 736; 5 U.S.C. 611) as a separate department in the executive branch, succeeding a Bureau of Labor established in 1884. Although much of the effort of MDTA has been in prison inmate training programs, offender rehabilitation programs have also been established in several communities. CETA (Comprehensive Employment Training Act of 1973) subsequently replaced MDTA to achieve the same objectives. A pretrial intervention program removes some persons accused of economically motivated crimes from the criminal justice system for several months, during which time they receive intensive counseling, education, and job training. For those who respond successfully, charges may be dropped. Further, an important program permits bonding for persons with criminal records who have been refused employment because they could not obtain commercial bonding (see Chapter 7). This program has led to the employment of about 2,500 persons with a default rate of less than 2 percent.

The Employment Service Model Program (ES) suggests ways to involve state employment agencies in efforts to serve inmates and ex-offenders more effectively. This model provides for a central unit to coordinate agency efforts in corrections within the state. A specialized staff to deal with offender employment problems is maintained.

A State Comprehensive Manpower Model attempts to bring together other state services and assistance from the private sector to assist in prisoner rehabilitation under a coordinated program. Planning assistants for these programs are available under contracts between the Department of Labor and the states. In addition, two offices of the Manpower Administration provide research and technical assistance in the area of offender training and employment. These are the Office of Research and Development and the Bureau of Apprenticeship and Training. These services may be coordinated by directors or coordinators of community-based corrections.

The Office of Employment Development Program (OEDP) is part of the Manpower Administration under the Assistant Secretary of Labor for Manpower. This office has a rather extensive program for manpower training in offender rehabilitation. Because training for prisoners and offenders has limited effect when it is offered without other supportive services, the program has been administered jointly by the Manpower Administration and the Office of Education of the Department of Health, Education and Welfare. Projects are developed at the local level with vocational education agencies. These projects are implemented after consultation with LEAA officials and state correctional officials. All but one or two states have taken advantage of this program. An interesting feature of this program in institutions is the incentive allowance for inmate trainees and the use of the "gate money" concept for release. Trainees can earn up to $20 per week while in training and may be augmented $5 per week for each dependent, up to $30.

The pretrial intervention program has been successful. Two experimental and demonstration diversion projects—the Manhattan Court Employment Project in New York City and Project Crossroads in Washington, D.C.—were funded as early as 1967 and 1968. Those who completed the course committed fewer further criminal acts by more than 50 percent, as compared with a control group without these project services. Because the approach was so promising, the Department of Labor initiated programs in Atlanta, Baltimore, Boston, San Francisco, Cleveland, Minneapolis, Newark, San Antonio, and other cities.

The pretrial intervention project works toward two goals: (a) improving employability of the offender and (b) avoiding a criminal record with the hope of avoiding subsequent commission of crime. The intervention program recommends to the court that the charges be dropped if the accused offender responds in a positive manner to the services.

A neglected area of endeavor regarding the female offender in employment was brought into focus by a joint program between the Department of Labor and the American Bar Association. Employment of females presents a special problem.

DEPARTMENT OF HEALTH, EDUCATION AND WELFARE

Health, Education and Welfare all have programs for the prevention and control of delinquency. Many delinquency programs are in the National Institute of Mental Health; there are programs in the Office of Education and in the welfare programs.

The Center for Studies of Crime and Delinquency focuses on basic research in the nature and causes of crime and delinquency, development and better coordination of community resources, and increasing utilization of community-based treatment programs. In addition, it develops innovative and more effective programs for offenders in institutions and other auxiliary services. The community services officer or the director of community-based corrections can use NIMH (National Institute of Mental Health) as a resource in providing technical assistance to agencies in the community and for direct services for narcotic addicts.

The Narcotic Addiction Rehabilitation Act of 1966 (PL. 89-793) (NARA) provides for narcotic addiction treatment by the United States Bureau of Prisons in case of addicts under criminal conviction and by NIMH for narcotics addicts who are civilly committed to the U.S. Surgeon General. Title I of NARA covers narcotic addicts who are charged with certain nonviolent federal offenses and who desire to be committed for treatment instead of prosecution, thereby providing pretrial diversion. Title III of that act covers narcotic addicts who are not charged with criminal offenses and who may apply for commitment to treatment. The community services officer may use this resource for addicts in his area.

The Comprehensive Drug Abuse Prevention and Control Act of 1970 (P.L. 91-513) broadened the scope of all existing community-based treatment programs. It authorized these programs to accept for treatment abusers of drugs other than opiates. This provides another excellent resource for the community services officer.

The Youth Development and Delinquency Prevention Administration was established under the Juvenile Delinquency Prevention and Control Act of 1968 (82/Stat. 462; 42/U.S.C. 3801), which was a successor of the Juvenile Delinquency Prevention and Control Act of 1961. Title I, Part A, of the act provides financial assistance to states and local cities to prepare comprehensive plans in the community. All but three states have used this act, with the others choosing to go with LEAA for the total criminal justice program. An interesting development under this act was a regional approach to planning by the Mississippi-Arkansas-Tennessee Council of Governments located in the Memphis Metropolitan Area. The effort of the project was to identify juvenile delinquency and its causes and mobilize public and private prevention and control resources in the three-state area. The provisions of this act can be used by the community services officer in advising and guiding local agencies in the area of technical assistance.

The Office of Education was established in 1867 (14/Stat. 434; 20/U.S.C. 1) and became an agency of HEW with the 1953 reorganization. The Bureau of Educational Personnel Development administers the Education Professions Development Act of 1967 and the Teacher Corps. Federal funding of educational programs for disadvantaged children was expanded in late 1966 (P.L. 89-750) to include services to improve the education of neglected and delinquent children in institutions. Working with local agencies, this agency promotes of community awareness and human development training in new treatment approaches, such as behavior modification, differential treatment, and team treatment. The Teacher Corps participates in the instruction of children with behavior problems. The Bureau of Elementary and Secondary Education (P.L. 89-750) operates several programs in institutions for delinquents. The Office of Child Development monitors and reports on selected youth development programs around the country, and conducts research on new methods of child care and identification of the needs of children. All these programs can be used in technical assistance.

The passage in 1975 of Title 20, a new amendment to the Social Security Act, affords states an opportunity to implement new services. New provisions of Title 20 could make available to the eligible residents of the states the following services:

1. Homemaker services when mothers must go to the hospital
2. Foster homes for mentally retarded adults ready to leave an institution but not yet ready to live alone

3. Emergency and follow-up services to protect children from abuse or neglect

4. After-school care for children so their mothers can have job training and a job

5. Chore services for elderly couples who may have to go to an institution unless they receive such services

6. Referral of unemployed teenagers to community agencies that specialize in job counseling for older youths

7. Emergency shelters to protect young runaways from exploitation while plans are being made for him or her to return home or live independently

8. Information and referral services for people who don't know where to turn for help in a crisis

9. Transportation to senior centers with varied activities for older persons otherwise confined to a rented room

10. Halfway houses for drug-addicted youth who need treatment and a supportive environment

11. Counseling to help families of newly blind individuals

12. Competent part-time care for handicapped children or senile older persons

13. Guardianship for older persons no longer able to manage financial affairs [3]

A community services officer can make use of all these services, which are distributed by the various state welfare departments.

DEPARTMENT OF HOUSING AND URBAN DEVELOPMENT

The Department of Housing and Urban Development (HUD) was established in 1965 (79 Stat.667; 42 U.S.C.3531-3537) to address all problems in urban areas, particularly crime and delinquency. The relationship of crime and delinquency to physical surroundings and communities and neighborhoods have become of central concern for HUD.

The Model Cities Program of HUD is aimed at eliminating slums and blighted neighborhoods, which are seen as breeding grounds for crime and delinquency. There are many different types of projects being funded under this program. Authority for the program derives from

---

[3] *A Citizen's Handbook—Social Services '75—Program Options and Public Participation under Title 20 of the Social Security Act* (Washington, D.C.: United States Department of Health, Education and Welfare, 1975), pp. 4–5.

Title I of the Demonstration Cities and Metropolitan Act of 1966. Funding involves planning grants, the payment of up to 80 percent of the cost of administering approved comprehensive demonstration programs in cities, supplemental funds in block grants to augment programs viewed by cities as beng important, and making use of and coordinating other existing federal grant programs for the purpose of improving cities and neighborhoods. The Office of Community Development encourages cities to undertake projects that improve all aspects of the criminal justice system. These projects include enforcement, pretrial release, and correctional programs of various types. About 150 cities are using the program.

Legal assistance is an important need for the poor in several areas, civil and criminal. Since 1968, however, legal assistance has been unavailable to the defense of adult offenders; it is still available for juvenile delinquency and civil matters. At this time there are at least thirty-five government-sponsored projects designed to rehabilitate alcoholics and narcotic addicts. More than seventy federal projects are designed to prevent and control juvenile delinquency. A few projects exist to educate and train state and local law enforcement officers and provide public education on law observance, enforcement, and crime prevention. Despite restrictions, many of these projects provide poor people with criminal law advice. Nearly fifty cities have implemented projects providing correctional services. HUD encourages all Model Cities projects to provide working relationships with all available criminal agencies. This means that community services officers and directors of community-based corrections can use these resources.

The Federal Insurance Administration, operating within the Department of Housing and Urban Development, administers several federal programs aimed at reducing losses caused by civil disorders, riots, or crime. The purpose is to increase the availability of coverage within the more volatile areas of the inner city; it assures that insurance proceeds will be available to restore or rebuild structures following a normal fire or riot. It is designed to provide federal reinsurance against riot and civil disorders to companies that participate in an insurance pool known as the Fair Access to Insurance Requirements plan. This plan exists in more than thirty states and has covered more than 75 percent of the property insurance market in the United States.

An amendment to the Housing and Urban Development Act of 1970 provides for crime insurance where it is critically needed but is not available at affordable rates. Requirements for the plan are that adequate precautions be taken in installation of alarm systems and other devices, and that crimes on which insurance claims are based must have been reported to local law enforcement agencies. The plan is available for states that can show that insurance rates against crime are sufficiently high that hardship would be caused by reliance on private companies. A problem of public policy arises as to how much private insurance should be taken over by government. (This same problem arises on the part of bail being required, and problems of compensation to victims of crime when private insurance is available.) The moves in recent years have been toward governmental responsibility when private insurance premiums become too high for most individuals who would purchase them. For example, Social Security is, in fact, an income maintenance protection program, as is Unemployment Compensation and Workmen's Compensation. Consequently, the introduction of federal insurance plans is in line with recent trends.

DEPARTMENT OF AGRICULTURE: FOOD STAMPS

The Food Stamp Act of 1964 is a program funded by the United States Department of Agriculture and administered by state departments of public welfare, primarily divisions of family services, although the names of the agencies vary among the states. Food stamps are purchased at reduced cost and used as money in grocery stores at their face value. Eligibility for food stamps is based on the "adjusted net income" formula. Beginning with the family's annual income, 10 to 30 percent is deducted for essentials. Mandatory expenses, such as Social Security tax, necessary child care, alimony, medical expenses, and other essential expenses are deducted. Eligibility to purchase food stamps is determined by matching the size of the family to the adjusted net income. One person would be eligible if the adjusted net income were $194 per month or less; a couple would be eligible with $280 or less; a family of four would be eligible with $513 or less per month. Thus, an eligible family of four could purchase $154 worth of food stamps, with the cost based on a sliding scale from zero to $130. The food stamp plan replaced the old "commodities" program in which surplus agricultural goods were distributed to people on welfare. The commodities program continues in some areas, but is generally restricted to institutions, such as state hospitals.

OFFICE OF ECONOMIC OPPORTUNITY

The Office of Economic Opportunity was established by the Economic Opportunity Act of 1964 (78 Stat.508; 42 U.S.C.2701) to "eliminate the paradox of poverty in the midst of plenty" through providing opportunity for education, training, opportunities to work, and the opportunity to live in decency and dignity. On the theory that young people living in high-delinquency areas may be drawn into a cycle of criminal activity, OEO programs attempted to attack basic conditions in the neighborhoods by providing assistance to relevant agencies to plan and implement community action programs and to improve educational and employment opportunities. The development of new jobs and the seeking of new job openings to provide employment for poor people has been a primary objective. Training projects in vocations and skills, followed by job placement services, comprise a central effort of OEO.

The Opportunities Industrialization Centers are manpower training programs to provide a complete range of activities for underemployed and unemployed men and women. School-age education includes guidance, testing, counseling, tutorial and remedial education, cultural activities and special education programs. Adult education projects teach English as a second language and offer basic literacy training. Emergency financial assistance programs are available to provide loans or grants to meet immediate and urgent family needs, including housing, clothing, and employment-related needs.

Youth development programs were initiated in May 1970 to stress the active participation of poor youth 14 to 25 years of age in planning, operation, and evaluation of programs designed to serve them. Recreation programs have been a central concern.

Economic development programs include assistance in small businesses and services operated by local individuals and groups, location of outside industry in the community, tourism projects, and development of natural resources.

Project NewGate, mentioned in an earlier chapter, has been funded by OEO since 1967. This project incorporates three basic principles: (1) counseling and intensive technical or educational preparation before release; (2) a post-release program of counseling, guidance, and therapeutic support; and (3) a continuation of the education and skill training program. The program includes release time or furlough for student-inmates, social and cultural activities not usually available in a prison, and job placement. Community people and resources are involved in the community-based systems into which the student-inmates can move upon final release. Support from the prison is continued in the post-release community phase, in which the inmate can live in a university dormitory or other facility as any other student would live.

OEO funds aid experimental programs for disadvantaged inner-city youth. The Neighborhood House in North Richmond, California, attemps to bridge the communications gap with 100 participating young people who print their own community newspapers, present plays, and produce videotapes on various problems and programs. The United Planning Organization in the District of Columbia sponsors the Teen Corps, which is an employment service for inner-city youth. The Community Action Agency of Hillsborough County, Florida, delegates its funds to the Commission on Human Relations, which created a Youth Council to serve as an advisory role in community decisions. The National Urban League Street Academies in New York City encourage inner-city youth to enroll in college preparatory educational programs operated by the Urban League. The School District of Philadelphia, Pennsylvania, administers the Hartranft Community Corporation Youth Project to establish multipurpose youth centers in the area to provide community service projects and work to improve housing conditions. The School District of Philadelphia also received a grant to operate the North Philadelphia Economic Development Program to operate job training and tutoring services projects. The Las Colonias del Valle group in San Juan, Texas, gathered information on the background of Chicano youth to develop a Mexican-American studies curriculum at the University of Utah. The project has also helped to get water to the low-income Mexican-American neighborhood, established a clinic, help to get streets paved, operate a mobile food store, and survey the needs of residents in public housing.

The Pilot District Project (PDP) is an experimental program aimed at discovering ways to improve police-community relations in ghetto areas. Beginning in 1968, the project includes attempts at improvement of police protection, crime prevention and detection, noncriminal dispute settlements, and emergency social services.

Community liaison programs sponsored by the Department of Human Resources of the District of Columbia government are geared to provide information to members of the community about significant events, available services, and other important facts. A *Problem Solver's Guidebook,* a newsletter, bulletin boards, and other methods of disseminating information have been developed. Community services in the form of nighttime and weekend emergency service centers to receive referrals and provide assistance by referrals or advice were also established. These and similar programs elsewhere can be used by the community services officer.

OEO also supports the Volunteers in Service to America (VISTA) under authority of Title VIII of the Economic Opportunity Act. It was formerly known as ACTION, an independent agency of the executive branch, by the reorganization plan 1 of 1971. There are about twenty projects in this program in which volunteers interview persons in jail to determine bail-bond problems and whether release is feasible. In many other such projects, volunteers work with street youngsters in neighborhoods with a history of crime to provide counseling. Volunteers at the California Department of Corrections Project in Oakland attempt to reduce recidivism among released offenders by assisting in job placement. Volunteers in Redwood City, California, provide tutoring and job counseling to inmates in the jail. In San Francisco, the Real Alternatives Program, Inc. is designed to provide alternatives to detention and arrest of juveniles. The Denver Juvenile Court Program provides social services to probationers and their families. Volunteers in the Golden Gate Youth Camp in Golden, Colorado, work intensively with boys in the camp and when they return to Denver. The Youth Opportunities Unlimited in Chicago operates throughout the city in ghetto communities to counsel youth groups. The Turner House in Kansas City provides conseling, tutoring, and recreation for juveniles referred by the courts. The VISTA program in Baltimore, associated with the University of Maryland's School of Social Work, provides social welfare services to juvenile ex-offenders. VISTA volunteers in New York City work with offenders as they are released and become employed and work with the families of ex-offenders. The Vespra Project in Puerto Rico works extensively with ex-addicts. Volunteers assigned to the Shelby County Penal Farm in Memphis, Tennessee, work in the prison providing adult basic education to the inmates and work with the families to facilitate the offender's return to the community. Although many other programs could be described, this provides an example of the VISTA approach funded by OEO. Community services officers can make use of these resources.

The debilitating isolation of the group known as the poor will continue as long as access to other crucial institutions in society remains closed to them. Consequently, legal aid is a basic requirement in a democratic society.[4] The objectives of OEO and the traditional legal services are to provide quality service to economically disadvantaged people. Referral to a legal resource can be made with (1) recognition of the client's problem as potentially legal, (2) knowledge of an appropriate legal resource, and (3) an effort to bring the client and resource together.[5]

NATIONAL SCIENCE FOUNDATION

The National Science Foundation was established by the National Science Foundation Act of 1950 (64 Stat.149; 42 U.S.C.1861-1875) and was given additional authority by the National Defense Education Act of 1958 (72 Stat.1601; 42 U.S.C.1876-1879) to carry out research in a variety of areas. Research in crime and delinquency are concentrated in two programs: (1) Research Applied to National Needs (RANN), oper-

---

[4] F. Raymond Marks, Jr.,*The Legal Needs of the Poor: A Critical Analysis* (Chicago: American Bar Foundation Series—Legal Services for the Poor, 1971), p. 17.

[5] Dorothy Linder Maddi, *Public Welfare Case Workers and Client Referrals to Legal Services* (Chicago: American Bar Foundation Series—Legal Services for the Poor, 1971), p. 8.

ated by the Research Applications Directorate, and (2) Social Science Research, operated by the Division of Social Science Research. RANN concentrates on specific environmental societal and technical problems. Social Science Research concentrates on social problems, including crime, from the perspective of sociology, economics, and other social sciences. Typical grants by RANN are provided for assessing efficiency of science and technology in law enforcement, and studying the nature of crime as a social phenomenon, with evaluations of recent innovations and changes in the criminal justice system. Typical research projects under Social Science Research include economic analysis of illegal activities and cost benefit analysis of policies to control them; effectiveness of various methods of police activity in reducing crime; assessment of educational and occupational levels on juvenile delinquency; and other similar social and economic problems. The community services officer can use the National Science Foundation as a resource for technical assistance, but it does not provide direct service.

CONCLUSIONS

As the major funding agency in the United States, the federal government funds state and local projects aimed at analysis and control of crime and delinquency. Through various departments and agencies, federal funds can be provided to states and localities to provide direct services to offenders and ex-offenders. The community services officer needs to know what the community has obtained from federal funding; moreover, he must assist in planning new funding by identifying areas of need.

Many agencies do not provide direct services, but can be used for technical assistance, which is also a function of the community services officer. Technical assistance is available from all governmental agencies in some form. How it is used is sometimes dependent upon the ingenuity of the community services officer and his associates in the community. Agencies of the federal government are excellent resources in community-based corrections.

Poverty programs use an indirect approach to end violence and crime. Education, job training, and efforts at community involvement have been traditional, but the opportunity structure for participation of all does not exist. Many wonder how the richest and most powerful society in the world can produce so many poor and powerless people.[6] Identification of these people and their needs is nceessary before constructive community action can occur.

---

6 Richard E. Rubenstein, *Rebels in Eden* (Boston: Little Brown, 1970), p. 192.

Chapter 10

New Careers
and Ex-Offender Groups

The use of offenders and ex-offenders in assisting and counseling other offenders emerged in the late 1960s and early 1970s.[1] It was directly influenced by the concept of "New Careers," which began with having poor or indigent people receiving welfare payments counseled and assisted in income management by other persons who had previously received welfare payments but who had become self-sufficient.[2] About the same time, ex-offenders were beginning to be used by the Los Angeles County Probation Department on an experimental basis on the theory that there would be some common understanding between offenders and those who had "reformed."

The traditional stance in the criminal justice system toward the use of ex-offenders in law enforcement or corrections had been one of unconditional rejection. The idea has appeared to many administrators and policymakers in the criminal justice field as a policy of "the blind leading the blind." Applicants for positions in police departments, prisons, and other phases of the criminal justice system have traditionally been subjected to fingerprinting and extensive background checks, in addition to being required to fill out a detailed application form followed by written and oral examination. The question, "Have you ever been convicted of a felony?" always appeared on the application. It was customary to elimi-

---

[1] Robert Pruger and Harry Specht, "Establishing New Careers Programs: Organizational Barriers and Strategies," *Social Work*, 13, No. 4 (October 1968), 21–32.

[2] Arthur Pearl and Frank Riessman, *New Careers for the Poor* (New York: Free Press, 1965).

nate all persons with felony records, as well as those with arrests for drunkenness, vagrancy, and other offenses. The theory was that if a person cannot handle his own affairs adequately and stay out of all trouble, then he or she is not really capable of helping others stay out of trouble. This position has also been traditional in many licensed professions and occupations, and in many private business and industrial corporations.

But recently, this policy has been changing. Louis Randall, himself an ex-prisoner, presented a strong case for using ex-offenders in correctional services in 1970.[3] He made an eloquent plea, saying that people can change and the functional relationship between the helper and the helped should not be permanently categorized. Even though there was (and is) resistance to this concept, it is now a fact that more and more ex-inmates are being included in the correctional field, particularly in community-based programs.

NEW CAREERS

New Careers was first introduced in the area of welfare and income maintenance, as previously mentioned. It was a consequence of the governmental opportunity programs and the general thinking related to them. By 1967, the concept of New Careers had been expanded to the area of corrections. Dr. J. Douglas Grant of Oakland, California, president of New Careers Development Organization, achieved success by having prospective New Careerists, in Oakland in 1969 applying for admission to the program, selected by the offenders in an anonymous vote to assure acceptance. In his program, offenders still under supervision were identified as inmate leaders and were used to counsel inmates at the California State Prison at San Quentin and in the community. The advantage of this technique is obviously the personal identification—these individuals "have been there" and have knowledge that provides common ground for communication. This type of knowledge is not available to middle-class social workers or people of different cultural or racial backgrounds from prisoners. Milton Luger, director of the New York State Division of Youth, supported this idea when he said that he wants offenders as part of the rehabilitative effort because he *needs* them, and not because he is sorry for them.[4]

---

[3] See his "The Role of the Ex-Offenders in Corrections," Proceedings of the 100th Annual Congress of Correction (Cincinnati), October 11–15, 1970 (College Park, Md.: American Correctional Association, 1971), pp. 147–48.

[4] *Correctional Briefings*, Number 4 (Washington, D.C.: Joint Commission on Correctional Manpower and Training, 1969).

LINKERS

The term "linkers" has been used informally by many community services agents to refer to persons living in a neighborhood who have sufficient leadership ability and positive attitude that they can counsel and lead others in their peer group. The people who serve as linkers in community-based programs frequently have criminal records and have already demonstrated the antagonism toward the Establishment that is shared by other people in the neighborhood. Informal discussions with police, probation and parole agents, and community service coordinators have confirmed that the most effective linker is a person who has been in a correctional institution, juvenile or adult, and who therefore understands his neighborhood's antipathy toward society's power structure.

Most criminal justice personnel have a difficult time communicating or being effective in urban ghetto and slum neighborhoods. It has become obvious that most representatives of the "white power structure," which establishes the laws and the social order in the United States, have difficulty in being effective in different ethnic, racial, and cultural neighborhoods. Even a black policeman originally from a neighborhood might meet resistance because it appears that he has "traded sides" and joined the enforcement arm of the white power structure in return for a good paycheck.

Convincing a person to serve as a linker is a delicate and difficult task. After a person has been identified as a leader, the approach to him must be cautious and diplomatic. He must not be asked to "inform," "cooperate," or otherwise appear to be subservient to the police, probation and parole agents, or community services coordinator. Negotiation for his services must respect the values of the neighborhood he represents. The linker will be called upon to represent the best interests of his neighborhood and his people. The criminal justice people, including the community-based corrections agent, represent constituted authority and the power structure *in negotiation* with the linker and his neighborhood. Both sides must perceive their common interests and objectives—essentially, keeping people out of jail and improving conditions in the neighborhood.

Experience with linkers in large cities has demonstrated that good interpersonal relationships between representatives of the power structure and leaders in the community can reduce friction, conflict, and problems. Specific procedures are frequently concerns of interpersonal relationships. Specific problems are frequently the function of local conditions. The exchanges of ideas and proposals between community and criminal justice people can contribute significantly to improved conditions and a lowering of the crime rates.

EX-OFFENDER GROUPS PROVIDING DIRECT SERVICE

Direct service refers to face-to-face counseling and assistance, as compared with services that relate to more impersonal and political concerns, such as prison reform. There are many ex-offender groups that have been organized throughout the country to assist offenders in reintegrating into society after institutionalization and to provide counseling service and other assistance during emergency and stress. Although a complete listing is impossible, we will briefly describe a few significant organizations.

Volunteer Sister Mary Jane Wilcox and tutors Teddy Jones and Tina Smith (Ex-offenders).

Courtesy of The Fortune Society.

The Fortune Society was begun in 1967 by David Rothenberg, who was at that time producing a play about prison experiences, entitled *Fortune and Men's Eyes*. After some performances, audiences were invited to stay and discuss the play. The interest impelled Rothenberg to begin this group,[5] and by 1975, it had helped between 4,000 and 5,000 people.

---

[5] "The Fortune Society—Championing the Ex-Offender," *Corrections Magazine*, 1, No. 5 (May/June 1975), 13–20.

Rothenberg now works full time with the Fortune Society, which presently has a staff of fifteen. Members of the Fortune Society assist offenders and ex-offenders in coming back into society. They counsel people, obtain jobs, and provide emotional support as needed. A basic purpose is to create a greater public awareness of the prison system in America to help people realize the problems and complexity confronted by inmates during their incarceration and when they rejoin society. The Fortune Society sends out teams of speakers comprised of what they call "ex-convicts" to talk to school groups, church and civic groups, and on radio and television to relate first-hand experiences of prison life and to help create a greater understanding of the causes of crime in America.[6]

In several places on the West Coast and in some communities as far east as Kansas City, Kansas, the late Bill Sands [7] established centers manned by ex-prisoners to help ex-offenders to adjust to society. Referred to as the Seven Step Program, it has many similarities to the Twelve Steps of Alcoholics Anonymous. The seven steps are *included* in Figure 10-1, identified by number, together with four others accepted by The Fortune Society. (Note that the first letters in the steps spell FREEDOM.) Sands also assisted in organizing the chapter inside the Kansas State Penitentiary. It is from this nucleus that the present program known as These Seventh Steps developed.

In the mid-1960s, many similar organizations were developed in the United States and Canada with many different names. Some were independent ventures and did not relate to other chapters. For example, Seven Keys to Freedom existed in Columbia, South Carolina, in the late 1960s with a similar program. The need to organize into a national chapter was recognized, and so one was established in Cincinnati,[8] with a permanent full-time staff. An outside board of directors is composed of ex-convicts and free citizens. Each chapter now is chartered by the national organization, and the program is becoming more cohesive and uniform. The members in the various prisons and the community programs and halfway houses are bringing their objectives and the method closer together. By 1975, there were sixty-eight chapters, both inside and outside prisons. This organization emphasizes (1) pre-release programs, (2) post-release programs, (3) employment, (4) a juvenile program, and (5) a public information program.

Efforts from Ex Convicts (EFEC) in Washington, D.C., operates a halfway house through a yearly contract with the District of Columbia

---

6 The Fortune Society also publishes *Fortune News,* which is concerned with prison affairs and the reintegration of ex-prisoners into society.

7 Bill Sands, *My Shadow Ran Fast* (Englewood Cliffs, N.J.: Prentice-Hall, 1964).

8 The 7th Step Foundation, 28 East 8th Street, Cincinnati, Ohio 45202.

I THINK, THEREFORE, I AM ...

As a thinking person, I believe that I am worthy of being loved and accepted. I believe that my ability to accept myself is a part of my real freedom. It is vital that I develop a foundation of belief about myself—for freedom and love and respect are not an "end result" but, rather, a process which changes, refines and grows. My ability to offer love and respect and my acceptance of freedom is a reflection of my view of myself.

SUGGESTED STEPS

---

1. Facing the truth about ourselves, we decided to change.

2. Realizing that there is a power from which we can gain strength, we decided to use that power.

3. Evaluating ourselves by taking an honest self-appraisal, we examined both our strengths and weaknesses.

   Admitted to God (as we understand him), to ourselves, and to another human being the exact nature of our weaknesses.

4. Endeavoring to help ourselves overcome our weaknesses, we enlisted the aid of that power to help us concentrate on our strengths.

5. Deciding that our freedom is worth more than our resentments, we are using that power to help free us from those resentments.

   Made a list of all persons we had harmed and become willing to make amends to them all.

   Made direct amends to such people wherever possible, except when to do so would injure them or others.

6. Observing that daily progress is necessary, we set an attainable goal toward which we can work each day.

   Continued to take personal inventory, and when we were wrong promptly admitted it.

7. Maintaining our own freedom, we pledge ourselves to help others as we have been helped.

Figure 10-1. I Think, Therefore, I am . . .

"The Fortune Society—Championing the Ex-Officer," *Corrections Magazine,* 1, No. 5 (May/June 1975), 19.

"The Last Offenders," who are members of the institutional chapter of The
Seventh Steppers leaving the Blackburn Correctional Complex, Lexington, Ken-
tucky, on parole. Originally published in the *Kentucky Inter-Prison Press*.
Courtesy of the Kentucky Bureau of Corrections.

Department of Corrections and an emergency shelter house for men and
women being released from prison but who have no place to stay. It also
runs Project TAP (Training Assistance Provisions), which attempts to
secure meaningful employment or institutional training for females, and
EFECtivity, Inc., a profit-making project of EFEC that represents an
economic development concept to engage in business, therefore making
jobs for ex-offenders. In 1975, EFEC received a license from the metropolitan police department to operate a detective agency, thereby providing employment to ex-offenders as security guards.

One organization begun by EFEC is BONABOND, which was designed
to provide bail and bond money for persons awaiting trial. Originally
operated by ex-offenders, the venture is still operative, but is staffed by
persons who have never been convicted.

Ex-Cons for a Better Society, Inc., was established in Ohio in 1974.
The purpose of this group is to assist ex-offenders in adjusting to society
and helping society to better understand the ex-offender and the correctional system. This organization published a newspaper entitled *Ex-Cons
for a Better Society*.[9] Its funding ran out in mid-1975, however, and the
future became uncertain.

---

9 Ex-Cons for a Better Society, Inc., 2426 Salem Avenue, Dayton, Ohio 45406.

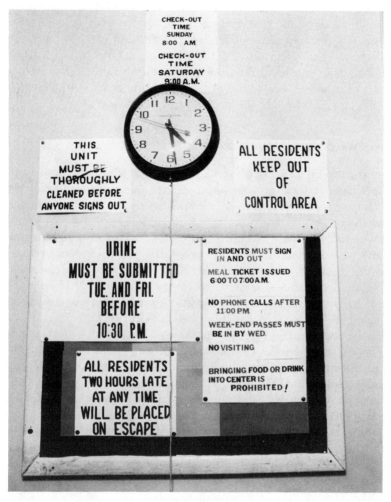

Figure 10-2.   Bulletin Board at Community Treatment Center for Youth.

Michael S. Serrill, "Profile/District of Columbia," *Corrections Magazine*, 1, No. 4 (March/April 1975), 49.

The Bridge is an organization in East Orange, New Jersey,[10] that is designed to assist ex-offenders to find employment and to stabilize their lives. A similar group, Bridge, Inc., in Rochester and Buffalo, New York, was formed by the Rochester and Buffalo Ecumenical Council of Churches after the Attica uprising of September 9, 1971.[11] Ex-offenders

---

10 The Bridge, 90 Washington Street, East Orange, N.J. 07019.

11 Bridge, Inc., 750 Main Street West, Rochester, N.Y. 14611.

and non-offender citizen volunteers are used for counseling. The purposes are to establish, maintain, and operate a help and support program for prison and jail inmates and ex-offenders in the state of New York; to provide services and programs for the physical, intellectual, spiritual, occupational, and emotional development of members; and to conduct or participate in projects or action programs in connection with research projects undertaken to study the problems of ex-prisoners.

EX-OFFENDER GROUPS PROVIDING INDIRECT SERVICES

There are several organizations of ex-offenders whose purpose is to accomplish penal reform and to improve the conditions of former inmates who have returned to society. We will briefly describe a few of the significant ones.

The National Prisoners' Alliance was established in 1971 to promote public understanding and to generate political support for penal reform and the improvement of the conditions of offenders and ex-offenders in society.[12] The first national conference of this group was held in 1972. Unfortunately its organizers have violated parole or returned to prison or absconded, so it was no longer in existence by 1975.

The Penal Reform Institute was established in Virginia in the early 1970s. This organization was designed to improve prisons directly. It has since merged with the Prisons Project of the American Civil Liberties Union in Washington, D.C.

The American Justice Guild, Inc., was established in Jacksonville, Florida, in 1972. Established by an inmate of the Florida State Prison in cooperation with an attorney in Jacksonville, this group only lasted about a year. But its existence, like that of other similar groups, was important because it represented a need and an attempt to meet that need.

The largest and most effective of these organizations has been prisoners' unions. The United Prisoners' Union, established in California at the California State Prison at Folsom, was the first of such groups. It established headquarters in Sacramento and offices in San Francisco, Los Angeles, San Diego, and other places and became a militant political body with definite political concerns. By 1975, however, it did not appear to be functional. The Prisoners' Union publishes *The Outlaw* and is a separate group.[13]

The National Penal Reform Institute was established by inmates behind the walls of the maximum security unit of the Rhode Island Maxi-

---

12 National Prisoners Alliance, 215 South East 9th, Portland, Ore. 97214.

13 Prisoners' Union, 1315 18th Street, San Francisco, Cal. 94107.

mum Security Facility at Cranston.[14] Its primary purpose is to reform prisons and to make them humane places in which to live.

EX-OFFENDERS WORKING IN CORRECTIONS

Ex-offenders have been working in corrections in perceptible numbers from the late 1960s to the present time. A few had worked in prisons and other correctional programs for some time, but their numbers were limited. A successful warden in a small correctional institution in the Georgia prison system previously served as a prisoner in that system; there is a superintendent of a juvenile institution in Florida who also served time. And in recent years, an ex-offender became supervisor of the data processing center for the South Carolina Department of Corrections—he presented two papers at the annual meeting of the American Correctional Association in 1968.[15]

Since that time, the Los Angeles Probation Department, the New York State Division of Youth Services, Florida Division of Corrections, Florida Division of Youth Services, and other jurisdictions have joined the United States Bureau of Prisons in employing ex-offenders. As indicated previously, there are also jobs in Federal Prison Industries, Inc., in which inmates can earn Social Security credit.

Many public correctional agencies employ ex-offenders. (Table 10-1 lists state hiring practices of American correctional agencies; offenses that prohibit the hiring of ex-offenders by American correctional agencies are listed in Table 10-2. In Table 10-3 is a list of positions held in correctional agencies by ex-offenders.)

Many private correctional agencies have recently been using ex-offenders in functions usually performed by professionals. This is generally accepted as a positive contribution that improves communication. St. Leonard's House in Chicago is staffed almost entirely by ex-offenders.[16] Located in a large, economically deprived Black community, the New Careers Program at St. Leonard's House has had a significant impact on the community and the entire field of corrections. Using ex-offenders to help offenders actually provides peer pressure on the individual so that

---

[14] National Penal Reform Institute, Maximum Security Facility, P.O. Box 8273, Cranston, R.I. 02920.

[15] See William L. Perrin, "Data Processing as a New Prison Industry," Proceedings of the Ninety-Eighth Annual Congress of Correction (San Francisco), August 25–29, 1968 (Washington, D.C.: American Correctional Association, 1969), pp. 96–100; and William L. Perrin, "Administrative Uses of Data Processing in a Correctional System," Proceedings of the Ninety-Eighth Annual Congress of Correction, pp. 189–200.

[16] Earl L. Durham, "St. Leonard's House: Model in the Use of Ex-Offenders in the Administration of Corrections," Crime and Delinquency, 20, No. 3 (July 1974), 269–80.

176   CHAPTER 10

TABLE 10-1   Ex-Offender Hiring Practices of American Correctional Agencies

Correctional Agencies Authorized To Hire Ex-Offenders	Ex-Offenders Working in Agencies		Year Policy of Hiring Ex-Offenders Began
	Yes	No	
Alabama	X		No Date Reported
Alaska	X		1971
Arizona	X		1968
California	X		1960
Colorado	X		No Date Reported
Connecticut	X		1968
Delaware		X	No Date Reported
District of Columbia Department of Corrections	X		1969
Federal Bureau of Prisons	X		1969
Florida	X		1971
Georgia	X		1968
Hawaii	X		1961
Idaho	X		1969
Illinois	X		No Date Reported ("Always")
Indiana	X		No Date Reported ("Old Policy")
Iowa	X		1969
Kentucky	X		1962
Louisiana	X		No Date Reported ("Several Years")
Maine	"Unknown"		1972
Maryland	X		No Date Reported ("About 15 or 20 Years")
Massachusetts	X		1972
Michigan	X		1969
Minnesota	X		1971
Mississippi	X		1971
Montana	X		No Date Reported
Nebraska	X		1962
New Mexico		X	No Date Reported
New Jersey	X		1967
New York	X		No Date Reported
North Carolina	X		1962
North Dakota		X	No Date Reported
Ohio		X	No Date Reported
Oregon	X		No Date Reported ("Never Prohibited")
Pennsylvania	X		1971
Rhode Island	X		1960
South Carolina	X		No Date Reported ("Long Standing")
Tennessee	X		1968

TABLE 10-1   (Continued)

Correctional Agencies Authorized To Hire Ex-Offenders	Ex-Offenders Working in Agencies		Year Policy of Hiring Ex-Offenders Began
	Yes	No	
Utah	X		1970
Virginia	X		1967
Vermont	X		1969
Washington	X		1968
West Virginia		X	No Date Reported ("Has Always Been in Effect")
Wisconsin	X		No Date Reported ("Several Years")
Wyoming	X		1965

Robert R. Smith, Larry F. Wood, and Michael A. Milan, *A Survey of Ex-Offender Employment Policies in American Correctional Agencies* (Montgomery, Ala.: Experimental Manpower Laboratory for Corrections, Rehabilitation Research Foundation, 1974), p. 3.

he or she cannot easily claim exploitation by the white, middle-class power structure.

EMPLOYMENT FOR OFFENDERS

There are many organizations that focus directly on obtaining employment for offenders and ex-offenders. A position paper adopted by the American Correctional Association in Houston, Texas, in 1974 strongly encouraged that public and private agencies concerned with the rehabilitation of law violators hire ex-prisoners.[17] The American Bar Association maintains a National Clearinghouse on Offender Employment Restrictions designed to try to eliminate any restrictions to the employment of offenders and ex-offenders.[18]

Job Therapy, Inc., headquartered in Seattle, Washington, is an organization that attempts to serve offenders and ex-offenders in employment and job training. Headed by Richard Simmons, it is active in sixteen states, Canada, and Mexico, and has a budget of about $2 million. It reports that since its inception in 1966, it has cut recidivism rates among its participants by about 75 percent.

The Citizens Committee for Employment provides the same service

17 "Editor's Notes—Employ Ex-Offenders, Position Paper Urges," *American Journal of Correction*, 36, No. 5 (September–October 1974), 39–40.

18 National Clearinghouse on Offender Employment Restrictions, American Bar Association, 1705 DeSales Street, N.W., Washington, D.C. 20036.

TABLE 10-2   Offenses Prohibiting the Employment of Ex-Offenders
Reported by Correctional Agencies Authorized to Hire Ex-Offenders

Types of Offenses That Prohibit Employment

Correctional Agencies	Narcotics or Drugs	Alcohol	Sex Offense	Notorious or Heinous	Against Person	Against Property	Other
Alabama			X	X	X		
Arizona	X		X				
California			X	X			
Connecticut			X	X			
Federal Bureau of Prisons							Xa
Florida				X			
Georgia							Xb
Hawaii							Xb
Idaho							Xb
Illinois							Xb
Indiana	X	X	X	X	X	X	X
Louisiana	X		X	X			
Minnesota							Xb
Montana	X		X				
Nebraska							Xb
New Jersey	X						
Pennsylvania	X	X		X			
Tennessee	X		X				
Washington							Xb
Wisconsin							Xb

a The Federal Bureau of Prisons indicated that they could not hire persons convicted of treason, bribery of governmental officials, professional thieves, persons associated with organized crime, or persons who give no evidence of stability or participation in the rehabilitation process.

b These agencies responded to the "Other" category and commented that employment depends on the "need" or the "man" with no further explanation.

Robert R. Smith, Larry F. Wood, and Michael A. Milan, A Survey of Ex-Offender Employment Policies in American Correctional Agencies (Montgomery, Ala.: Experimental Manpower Laboratory Laboratory for Corrections, Rehabilitation Research Foundation, 1974), p. 5.

for ex-offenders in Chicago. An inmate self-help committee was organized in the Essex County, New Jersey, Corrections Center in 1975 to assist persons in finding jobs through work release in the community.[19]

The Wildcat Service Corporation was developed by the Vera Institute of Justice and funded by LEAA to help ex-offenders and ex-addicts learn good work habits, reduce their participation in criminal activity, and

---

[19] Inmates Self-Help Committee, Essex County Corrections Center, Box 349, Caldwell, N.J. 07006.,

TABLE 10-3 Positions Held by Ex-Offender Employees in American Correctional Agencies

Positions Held by Ex-Offender Employees	Number of Ex-Offenders Employed	Percent of Ex-Offenders Employed
Maintenance and Service	68	28.3
Counselors	51	21.3
Line Staff Correctional Officers	40	16.7
Teachers and Teachers' Aides	34	14.2
Clerical Staff	33	13.8
Administrators	11	4.6
Minister	1	.4
Physician	1	.4
Other (Not Identified)	1	.4

Robert R. Smith, Larry F. Wood, and Michael A. Milan, *A Survey of Ex-Offender Employment Policies in American Correctional Agencies* (Montgomery, Ala.: Experimental Manpower Laboratory for Corrections, Rehabilitation Research Foundation, 1974), p. 6.

stabilize their life patterns.[20] A big hurdle for ex-offenders is finding work in the first place, and good work habits and performance are necessary to keep it. Evaluation of a study of this group indicated that ex-offenders provided employment were productively employed for most of the year, while a sample of ex-offenders not in the program averaged only eleven weeks' work during the year. The supportive program appeared to discourage illegal activity—fewer Wildcat participants were arrested the year after entering the program. Excessive alcohol use was a problem for each group, but the control group reported twice as much daily alcohol use as the Wildcat group. Supported work appeared to have stabilized the lives of the participants; more Wildcat participants married or entered into common-law arrangements and fewer were divorced or separated, as compared with the control group.

Wildcat is being supported by approximately $6 million to support 1,500 jobs in the demonstration project funded by LEAA and five other federal agencies. It has been expanded into the Manpower Demonstration of Labor, Department of Health, Education and Welfare, Department of Housing and Urban Development, the White House Special Action Office for Drug Abuse Prevention (SAODAP), and the Ford Foundation. The areas participating are Jersey City and Newark, New Jersey; Philadelphia; St. Louis; San Francisco; the Puget Sound Area of Washington; five northwestern counties of West Virginia; Fond du

20 "Ex-Offenders' Work Program Cracks Employment Barriers," *LEAA Newsletter,* 4, No. 9 (April 1975), 5–7.

180 CHAPTER 10

Lac and Winnebago Counties in Wisconsin; Atlanta; Chicago; Hartford, Connecticut; Boston and Springfield, Massachusetts; and Oakland,

Several publications recently have encouraged people to hire offenders and ex-offenders, outlining procedures and techniques by which this can be accomplished.[21]

The use of ex-offenders in the military services has also been encouraged. An army regulation of 1878 rendered persons convicted of a felony ineligible to serve. Early in World War II, however, President Franklin D. Roosevelt suspended the regulation. As a result, between 50,000 and 60,000 men were released from state and federal prisons for military service. After the war was over, a survey indicated that the records of these men were equivalent to those of persons who had not been convicted; [22] the incidence of court martials, bad conduct and dishonorable discharges, and similar disciplinary problems did not differ markedly. In fact, the aggressive behavior that made them a "danger" to the community may have been the very quality that made them good soldiers.

CONCLUSIONS

During the decade 1965 to 1975, attitudes and practices concerning the employment of offenders and ex-offenders in correctional institutions and agencies has changed dramatically. Although in the past many prisons used offenders as teachers and in other supervisory functions, in most instances, this was a case of economics. In prisons in which there was enough money to hire civilian staff, this type of use of prisoners rarely occurred. Even so, some prison systems, such as in Michigan, used selected older recidivists to counsel young "wayward minors" and other functions. By the 1970s the use of offenders and ex-offenders in counseling and in other jobs, including technical and administrative jobs, was increasing.

In the 1960s universities were very reluctant to accept ex-offenders in studies in criminal justice, even though they may have been accepted in other fields. Today, however, most major universities with criminal justice programs have ex-offenders in their student bodies. Many work part-time with the division of corrections as counselors, and many have

---

[21] For example, Roberta Rover-Pieczenik, *A Review of Manpower R&D Projects in the Correctional Field (1963–1973)* (Washington, D.C.: Criminal Justice Research, Government Printing Office, 1973). Also P. G. McCreary and J. M. McCreary, *Job Placement and Training for Offenders and Ex-Offenders* (Washington, D.C.: Law Enforcement Assistance Administration, 1974).

[22] Hans Mattick, "Ex-Cons Prove to be Good Soldiers; Prison Returns Fall to New Low," *The Menard Times* (Illinois State Penitentiary), 17, No. 2 (March 1, 1966), 8.

been offered similar positions upon graduation. The traditional distance between the keeper and kept in the field of criminal justice, especially in corrections, has been significantly reduced. As Milton Luger, former director of the New York State Division of Youth Services, has pointed out, they are not being hired for rehabilitative purposes or because of sentimentality—they are being hired because they are needed for what they can do.

On the other hand, nobody would hire a person *because* he is an ex-offender. He still goes through a selection process. But if he has all the other credentials and capabilities, his experience as an offender gives him a realistic "edge" in terms of understanding and common ground for communication over those who have not "been there." It becomes apparent that personnel policies in the future in corrections will still emphasize ability and competence, but will not deny ex-offenders jobs for which they are qualified.

In summary, offender and ex-offender groups have been gaining political and social power, generally through the shift in the courts' policy of "hands off" the prisons in the 1950s to almost a "hands off" the offender to protect his rights as a citizen. Prisoners' unions have formed under the right of assembly of the First Amendment. Ex-offender groups are in almost all urban centers, with thirty-five to forty identifiable groups in the Chicago area alone.[23] The 7th Step Foundation and The Fortune Society are probably the strongest. The formation of the American Association for Ex-Offenders was announced in St. Louis at the February 1976, midwinter meeting of the American Correctional Association.

---

[23] Patrick D. McAnany, Dennis Sullivan, William Kaplan, and Edward Tromanhouser, *Final Report: The Identification and Description of Ex-Offender Groups in the Chicago Area* (mimeographed, Chicago: University of Illinois at Chicago Circle, Center for Research in Criminal Justice, August 1974), 68.

Chapter 11

Private
Community-Based Corrections

Private groups have historically taken the lead in advances in the criminal justice system. In local policing, the Bow Street Runners in 1750 preceded by more than three-quarters of a century the first municipal police department housed at Scotland Yard in London in 1829. It was the Quakers in Pennsylvania, organized as the Philadelphia Society for Alleviating the Miseries of the Public Prisons, that established the first "penitentiary" at the old Walnut Street Jail. Probation was initiated by a shoemaker from Boston who became interested in the offenders who went to the court. John Augustus bailed many people out and accepted supervision for many from 1841 until his death in 1859, whereupon a private group assumed his work. Massachusetts approved hiring a probation officer to be paid with tax funds for the first time in 1879. The first juvenile court resulted from the pressure of the Cook County Women's Clubs on the legislature and the Chicago Bar Association to prepare an act that would meet constitutional challenge. The National Congress of Parents and Teachers (PTA), which had been organized in Washington, D.C., in 1897, was also active in this juvenile court venture in 1899 in Chicago. Community-based corrections was also a product of the leadership of private organizations and individuals.

Religious and philanthropic organizations have always assisted people in trouble and in need, from the Bible's Good Samaritan to the modern John Howard Societies and religious groups. From the fourth century through the Middle Ages, church groups provided assistance to strangers, vagabonds, and people in trouble.[1] St. Vincent de Paul built the first asylum for wandering children in Paris in 1648.

In England, the Discharged Prisoner's Aid Society movement began before the 1770s.[2] By 1772, there were several such societies to relieve the distress of discharged poor persons who had been imprisoned for offenses or small debts. These pioneering societies were officially recognized in 1862 when a Discharged Prisoner's Aid Act was passed by Parliament.

RELIGIOUS GROUPS

Religious organizations have considered the obligation to be charitable to one's fellow man as a fundamental tenet. During the Middle Ages, for example, the monasteries were open for vagabonds and other travelers, although English law limited their stay to two nights. Charitable efforts have traditionally been part of most religious groups. Joseph Tuckerman, a Unitarian clergyman, pioneered in social work with the poor in Boston during the middle nineteenth century,[3] and another minister, Stephen Humphreys Gurteen, originated the Charity Organization Society which, in turn, gave rise to community welfare councils and the family agencies. The YMCA movement was an expression of nineteenth-century evangelical Protestantism. An orphange was founded by the Ursuline Sisters in New Orleans in 1727. Counseling and service to homeless people and disturbed children were also provided. After the 1840s, the mass immigrations of Catholics from Ireland and Italy and Jews from Germany and Russia brought widespread services by Catholic and Jewish welfare organizations at local and national levels. Most visible, of course, are the residential institutions which in 1966, held 57,000 dependent and neglected children in Catholic and Protestant facilities, as compared with 106,000 children in secular institutions, the majority of which (76,000) were in facilities operated with tax funds. More than a third of the dependent and neglected children institutionalized in the United States, then, are in church-sponsored facilities. Churches are known to be active in community affairs [4] and are available for appropriate service at the

---

[1] C. J. Ribton-Turner, *A History of Vagrants and Vagrancy and Beggars and Begging* (London: Chapman & Hall, 1887. Reprinted Montclair, N.J.: Patterson Smith, 1972), particularly Chapters I and II, pp. 1–33.

[2] Martin W. Pinker, "Toward New Horizons," Proceedings of the Eighty-Second Annual Congress of Correction (Atlantic City), 1952 (New York: American Correctional Association, 1953), p. 207.

[3] Robert H. Brenner, *From the Depths* (New York: New York University Press, 1956).

[4] Thomas Sherrard and Richard Murray, "The Church and Neighborhood Community Organization," *Social Work*, 10, No. 3 (July 1965), 4.

Personal counseling on a one-to-one basis is an important tool in helping a man
regain his rightful place in society. There is also group, marital, and job development counseling by the Family Service Department of The Salvation Army. The
residents also receive spiritual guidance. Weekend passes enable the men to stay
in close touch with their families.

request of the community services coordinator or director of community-
based correctional programs.

The Salvation Army began as a simple mission to reach the outcasts
of London's East End in 1865; it has continued that tradition to the
present time. This organization maintains lodging places for homeless
people, generally limiting them to one or two nights, but remaining flexible on this point to accommodate hardship cases. In fact, many community services coordinators have found that when all other solutions to
emergencies in terms of lodging or meals fail, the Salvation Army responds positively. Their Florence Crittendon Homes are available to
serve unwed mothers. The Prisoners' Hope Brigade is another group designed to provide services, counseling, and religious worship in jails and
prisons.[5]

5 Sallie Chesham, *Born to Battle: The Salvation Army in America* (Chicago: Rand
McNally, 1965), p. 93.

The Volunteers of America began in January 1896, and have provided similar community service to that offered by the Salvation Army. In fact, the Volunteers of America have been more active in the establishment of halfway houses.

Other religious groups have provided counseling and other services for persons in trouble. The Juvenile Rehabilitation Ministry of the Home Mission Board of the Southern Baptist Convention, Youth for Christ, and many other religious groups have programs for prevention and control of delinquency. In addition, there have been many individual clergymen who have embarked on careers in the delinquency control area.

PRIVATE GROUPS IN COMMUNITY CORRECTIONS

There are many other agencies in the community sponsored by private groups and individuals to help offenders and ex-offenders. Many of these reflect specific interests of the individuals and groups supporting them. W. Clement Stone, the Chicago millionaire, for example, has developed several projects. He also supports the Lewis University Special Services Center, which makes university courses available for inmates in the Illinois State penitentiaries. (Their publication, *The Candle: Correctional Program News,* includes articles on correctional concerns and suggestions to families and ex-offenders for better adjustment.[6]) The World Correctional Service, headed by Harry Woodward, provided grants in a multiplicity of correctional efforts until 1975, when their interests shifted to child abuse. Guides for Better Living is a motivational course or program under the same auspices.

Legal aid and counseling on legal problems is always a problem for the offender and ex-offender. Since governmental agencies (OEO and Model Cities) withdrew from counseling in criminal cases, private organizations have increased their activity. Project TACT (Temporary Assistance Counseling and Training), for example, is a division of the Legal Aid Bureau of Buffalo, Inc.[7]

The Personal Aid Bureau of the Jewish Family Service in Philadelphia has been in existence since 1941 to provide assistance in personal matters to Jewish offenders. Counseling and other services are provided in prison, and assistance is provided individuals being released from prison. When parole is forthcoming, the agency assists in formulating a plan and a private sponsor from the agency. This group also works with the families

---

[6] See "Families Do the Hardest Time," *The Candle: Correctional Programs News,* 4, No. 1 (February 1975), 1–2; and Boots Scobie, "And So I Wait" (Chicago, 1974), pp. 3, 7.

[7] Project TACT, Fifty-One Court Street, Buffalo, N.Y. 14202.

of prisoners during the incarceration to prevent their "closing the gap" left by the missing family member. A lay sponsorship program in which youthful offenders are provided with a volunteer to help them is a most recent development.[8]

The Gateway Hospital and Community Health Center in Los Angeles conducts several programs of service to offenders and ex-offenders. There is a center for mentally disordered offenders that provides treatment and other services for sociopathic offenders.[9]

The Ex-Offender Contact Center began in Grand Rapids, Michigan, in 1973, having been initiated by a group of citizens originally interested in jail ministry. The Center provides counseling, legal advice, job referrals, transportation services, educational and training counseling and guidance, and related activities to assist the ex-offender trying to rejoin society. The "jobology" program assists in the preparation of résumés, generates letters of reference, and provides counseling to help ex-offenders seek employment successfully. The "Link" organization is for Kent County residents (Grand Rapids) with relatives in Michigan's prisons. Group counseling is provided in the various prisons in which persons from Kent county are incarcerated.[10]

Special Social Services in New York City was incorporated in 1943 to work with the children of offenders, without working directly with the offender. Casework services, seasonal programs, camp placement, Christmas giving, and limited scholarship funds are provided. This group serves only the poor; and no fees are charged.[11]

The SEK, Inc., program was begun in the mid-1960s in the Sarasota-Bradenton-St. Petersburg area by three young men identified with Youth for Christ. It is a nonprofit organization aimed at delinquency control. It has a walk-in camping program, halfway house, and a ranch. It aims at working with delinquents from a physical, mental, social, and spiritual approach.[12]

The National Congress of Parents and Teachers, popularly known as the National PTA, is also interested in working with youth in delinquency prevention. Its local Child Protective Committees work with various degrees of effectiveness in various localities. During 1971 to 1973,

[8] Personal letter from Robert H. Stern, supervisor of the Personal Aid Bureau of the Jewish Family Service, Philadelphia, dated October 23, 1974.

[9] Personal letter from Jeanette Lazeroff, Gateway Hospital and Community Mental Health Center, Los Angeles, dated October 17, 1974. Also "Treatment of the Mentally Disordered Criminal Offender," *The Gateways Newsletter*, 2, No. 1 (April 1974), 1, 4.

[10] Ex-Offender Contact Center, 334 Rumsey Street, Grand Rapids, Mich. 49503.

[11] Personal letter from Sylvia Ranchlin, Special Social Services, New York, dated July 7, 1974.

[12] SEK, Inc., 4051 12th Street, North, St. Petersburg, Fla. 33703.

.

the PTA combined with the National Council of Juvenile Court Judges in a project to encourage volunteers to work with the juvenile courts throughout the country. *A Handbook for Volunteers in Juvenile Court* resulted from that project.[13] In fact, the national PTA was central in establishing the first juvenile court in Chicago in 1899. Mrs. Alice Mc-Lellan Birney initiated the concept of a National Congress of Mothers and combined with Mrs. Phoebe Apperson Hearst to form the national PTA in Washington, D.C., in 1897. Two years later, they joined efforts with the Cook County Women's Clubs to initiate the juvenile court.

The Minneapolis Rehabilitation Center was established in October 1964, as a Research and Demonstration Project supported by the Department of Health, Education and Welfare and in which participating agencies were the Minnesota Division of Vocational Rehabilitation and the Minnesota Department of Corrections. The purpose was to provide group counseling and other assistance to parolees from the Minnesota State Reformatory for Men. After three years, the persons receiving this treatment had a considerably better record than those who had not participated, both in terms of recidivism and in the seriousness of offenses when they did occur. In recidivism, the experimentals had a 63.4 percent success as opposed to 54.9 percent success for the control group.[14]

Reachout Today is another agency in Minneapolis that works with ex-offenders to assist them in successful return to society from prison.[15] The City Youth Center in Minneapolis also serves youth in delinquency control programs.

There are many Bridge organizations. Bridge in Buffalo and Rochester, New York, is an organization of volunteers that we mentioned in the last chapter.[16] Each sponsor within Bridge is supported by a group of four to twenty people known as a "support group"; these people provide the volunteers with material goods in the aid of food, clothing, housing, education, employment, and other assistance.

Project Bridge refers to an organization in San Francisco that maintains several private halfway houses. The concept is to make a "bridge" from the prison to the free community. Bridge at Walla Walla, Washington, was a self-help organization centered around therapy and group

---

13 Vernon Fox, *A Handbook for Volunteers in Juvenile Court,* Special Issue of *Juvenile Justice,* 23, No. 4 (February 1973).

14 Richard C. Ericson and David O. Moberg, *The Rehabilitation of Parolees—Minnesota Rehabilitation Center—Summary* (Minneapolis: Minneapolis Rehabilitation Center, 1968), p. 6.

15 Reachout Today, 1828 Park Avenue, Minneapolis, Minn. 55404.

16 Bridge Volunteers/Associates, Inc., 1766 Main Street, Buffalo, N.Y. 14208 and 750 Main Street West, Rochester, N.Y. 14611.

work in preparation for release and job finding.[17] Financed by an up-
holstery business and LEAA, Bridge was phased out at the end of May
1975, because of ending of LEAA funding. It had been in existence for
three years. The Bridge in Grand Rapids, Michigan, is a home for runaways. It is operated locally with community support as a crisis counseling intervention center for youth.

Job Therapy, Inc., a nonprofit organization, was begun in March
1965 by Richard Simmons to assist offenders in getting out of prison and
staying out. In five years, this group recruited, screened, and matched
over 500 reputable business, labor, and professional men as volunteer
citizen-sponsors with almost 600 confined men.[18]

The Citizens Committee for Employment in Chicago is concerned
with the employment of ex-offenders and assists in counseling in a manner
that promotes their keeping those jobs.

Family visits began in May 1974 on an organized basis at the Washington State Penitentiary through ATICA, Inc. (Alternative Treatment
to Implement Concept Advocates), a private group that provides inmates'
families in the Seattle–Puget Sound area with transportation to visit incarcerated relatives.[19] Most of the families are on public assistance, so
this project has been most helpful in maintaining family contacts.

The National Council on Crime and Delinquency (NCCD) (formerly
the National Probation and Parole Association) began its first citizen's
council in the State of Washington in 1955. By 1974, twenty-two states
had citizen action councils sponsored by NCCD. The purpose was to
work on criminal justice problems ranging from the creation of probation and parole systems to the upgrading of courts and education of
business community. In the late 1960s, NCCD shifted its emphasis from
fostering new citizens councils to working with service organizations,
labor unions, and church groups, while providing technical assistance
to states and communities from their five regional service centers.

PRISONERS' AID SOCIETIES

Private prisoner help societies began in America in 1797 when the
Quakers organized the Philadelphia Association for Alleviating the
Miseries of the Public Prisons. This organization still exists today as
the Pennsylvania Prison Society. The purpose of this type of group has

---

17 Personal letter from Superintendent B. J. Rhay, Washington State Penitentiary,
Washington, dated May 19, 1975.

18 Arthur Gordon, "They Go to Prison on Purpose," *Reader's Digest*, August 1970,
also published in *The Rotarian*, August 1970.

19 "Special Bus for Walla Walla Visitors," *Target*, 4, No. 4 (April 1975), 3–4.

been to provide direct and indirect assistance to both offenders and ex-offenders. Direct services take the form of counseling, assistance in employment, and sometimes a little financial aid. Indirect services take the form of political activity in attempting to support and promote penal reform, humanitarian treatment, and legislative activity. For example, the Correctional Association of New York, formerly known as the New York Prison Society, has a legislative mandate to bring recommendations in the area of prison reform and correctional progress to the New York Legislature every session. The focus in community-based corrections, however, is on direct services, with a peripheral interest in indirect services.

The Pennsylvania Prison Society has been offering casework services to offenders and ex-offenders since 1925.[20] This group has been concerned with assisting individual prisoners and parolees find and use their inner strengths for more socially responsible and individually satisfying behavior. Seeking help from the society has to be voluntary on the part of the offender and must stem from a genuine need and desire for help. The lay sponsor has traditionally been a citizen who takes responsibility for a paroled offender when caseloads are too high for the parole officer or parole agent to handle adequately. Consequently, part of the casework service involves finding lay sponsors who can perform adequate counseling and serve responsibly as a stabilizing factor for the offender.

The Massachusetts correctional association was established in 1889 as the John Howard Industrial Home and remains one of the most active correctional associations in the country. This group, which became the Massachusetts Correctional Association in 1967, issues excellent publications in the field of corrections, has a legal service program, is active in promoting legislation, and provides direct service to offenders and ex-offenders in the form of casework services.[21] The objectives have been to educate the public in the treatment of crime, to advance constructive penal legislation, to secure progressive prison management, and to aid in the rehabilitation of discharged prisoners. In 1940, the resources of three social agencies—the John Howard Society, the Massachusetts Prison Association, and the Friends of Prisoners—were pooled to form the current organization.

The Women's Prison Association and associated Hopper Home were,

---

20 Alan Bookman, "Eligibility Requirements and Intake Practices as an Integral Part of the Helping Process in a Prison Society," Proceedings of the Seventy-Eighth Annual Congress of Correction (Boston), August 29–September 2, 1948 (New York: American Prison Association, 1948), pp. 299–306.

21 Harold Kramer, "The Philosophy of Intake and Eligibility Practices," Proceedings of the Seventy-Eighth Annual Congress of Correction, pp. 292–306.

founded in 1944 as a private nonprofit agency providing rehabilitation services to female ex-offenders. The Hopper Home is a twenty-bed halfway house with 24-hour supervision, three meals a day, personal laundry, sewing facility, and other services including personnel and group counseling.[22]

The Connecticut Prison Association was established in 1875 by a group of concerned private citizens. The Phoenix Mutual Life Insurance Company of Hartford has joined with this group to establish the volunteer sponsor program. Volunteeer parole aides, lawyer volunteers, and volunteer assistants to parole officers are among those who participate in this program.

The John Howard Association of Illinois was begun in 1901. Headquartered in Chicago,[23] it became a state group in 1969 with a professional staff. Its objectives include assisting ex-offenders to reintegrate into society and furnishing technical assistance and consultation in the field of corrections. Its original purpose was to provide indirect services of community welfare planning to ex-offenders. Primary functions today include training volunteers, and providing family and individual counseling. The prison family project is primarily a direct service program, but it is also designed to stimulate interest, education of the community in the correctional process, and otherwise bring the community into the correction process. Today the John Howard Association is active in surveying county jails, developing standards, assisting in approving living conditions and medical services, preventing brutality, and otherwise assisting in the total correctional process. It has also recently developed master plans for the state of Virginia, Maryland, Florida; and it has developed a survey on penal institutions in Illinois.

The John Howard Association of Hawaii, supported by the Aloha United Fund, has a broad program to assist offenders and ex-offenders coming back into society. Its Waianae Rap Center has 24-hour coverage for any offender or ex-offender who needs assistance, particularly with drugs. John Howard Associations are particularly active in Canada, England, Australia, and other English-speaking countries.

The Northern California Service League provides a full spectrum of direct service to offenders and ex-offenders. Counseling in jail, family contact, material assistance, and follow-up programs are available. Recently a pretrial diversion project has been established. Professional social work programs are also available.

The New Jersey Association on Corrections has 450 members dedi-

---

[22] Women's Prison Association and Hopper House, 100 2nd Avenue, New York, N.Y. 10003.

[23] John Howard Association, 537 South Dearborn Street, Chicago, Ill. 60605.

cated to the reform of penal and criminal justice systems in that state. Its Morrow Projects Division provides re-entry services to hundreds of former offenders and operates two comprehensive halfway houses, one in Trenton and one in New Brunswick. It also maintains "man-to-man" and "woman-to-woman" volunteer programs for ex-prisoners and prisoners from Newark.

The Bureau of Rehabilitation of Washington, D.C., was established in 1929 to provide counseling and help for persons in conflict with the law. This group provided probation and parole officers until the District of Columbia established its own program in 1936. Between 1968 and 1970, three residential facilities were opened and a full program has become self-sustaining under contract with governmental correctional agencies. In 1969, the Bureau contracted under Titles I, II, III of the Federal Narcotic Addict Rehabilitation Act of 1966. A neighborhood treatment was opened 1971 for out-patient drug treatment.

The Correctional Service of Minnesota sponsors the Citizens Counsel on Delinquency and Crime, which is a statewide agency sponsored by the United Fund. Its objectives are to improve law enforcement, courts, corrections, and programs of crime prevention; to test the effectiveness of promising new rehabilitative approaches in the areas of unmet needs; to promote scientific research in publications in the various fields of criminology; and to educate the public in respect to the problem of crime and delinquency and relative to the criminal justice program.

P-A-C-E in Indiana was organized in 1960 in Indianapolis as Prisoners Aid by Citizen Efforts, but the name was changed in 1972 to Public Action in Correctional Effort, thereby keeping the same initials. Its primary goals have been to call for the improvement of correctional institutions and programs in the State of Indiana. In 1974, P-A-C-E was particularly concerned with women's prisons, and suggested that a women's unit be housed in all-male institutions. The men and women were to live in separate areas, but would share the educational and vocational facilities and other programs in the institutions.[24] The rationale behind this idea was that the larger male institutions can afford better programs than can a single, small women's prison.

The Alston Wilkes Society in South Carolina is one of the largest prisoners' aid societies in existence. With 34 on its staff, it has a membership of 6,000, thereby generating a large number of volunteers, since nearly all the members perform some activities. Services include halfway houses, one-to-one volunteer work with offenders and ex-offenders, assistance to families, in-prison visitation, rebuilding broken homes and families, finding employment, and many other related services. The

---

24 "Disputes over Women's Prison," *The Pacesetter*, 5 (October 1974), 1.

Society's newsletter appropriately calls for reform and points out several areas of need in each issue.[25]

The problem of financial and material assistance has been a difficult one for prisoners' aid associations. It is obvious that it is needed in many cases, but the conditions under which it is given need careful examination.[26] Whether financial assistance should be in the form of grants or loans is a basic question. Money is considered to be a tool in casework planning and treatment for readjustment back into the community. In a survey of fifteen agencies, all agreed that marginal and emergency grants or loans were an integral part of the casework process and that the money is an integral part of casework planning.

The John Howard Society has suggested that the balance between dependency and independency in a former prisoner involves a number of questions that have to be considered when money is involved: [27]

1. What are the particular stresses inherent in this specific problem?
2. What degree of dependence and independence has this person achieved in life?
3. To what degree has he utilized regression as a means of coping with stress in the past?
4. To what degree is the individual vulnerable to this type of stress?

The caseworker must be able to distinguish between need and request while evaluating whether or not to provide funds. Lack of funds, of course, may preclude much discretion. Assessment of the client's ability to make constructive use of financial assistance is a primary consideration. In any case, the role of the private after-care agency is to fill the gap between an offender's release from prison and his rehabilitation into the community, as well as to provide crisis intervention assistance.

Prisoners' aid societies have generally reduced the offering of financial assistance to discharged offenders to a bare minimum, and then it is well controlled. Social workers have found that giving money to people increases dependency and unrealistic expectations to the point that it

---

25 *Alston Wilkes Society Newsletter*, 10, No. 1 (Spring 1975), 1.

26 Allan C. Hubanks and Jane Wells, "Workshop XII—Financial and Material Assistance—Sponsored by International Prisoners' Aid Association," Proceedings of the Eighty-Ninth Annual Congress of Correction (Detroit), September 7–12, 1958 (New York: American Correctional Association, 1959), pp. 261–63.

27 See Louie Zeitoun, "Philosophy and Practices of Material Assistance in Aftercare Agencies in Canada," Proceedings of the Eighty-Ninth Annual Congress of Correction, p. 269.

almost becomes addictive.[28] Funds may be provided on contingency or contract basis, always with positive conditions and controls. Social workers believe that funds should be provided only on a short-term basis to maintain life on a survival basis. Too much giving can be negative, because it establishes debt. This is why prisoners' aid societies have learned to counsel people about the budget and its management, rather than providing a dole.

Prisoners' aid societies have a function in job placement of offenders and ex-offenders and in interagency cooperation in the process.[29] Working with parole agents or parole officers and the state employment service, as well as using private contacts with employers, they can perform a constructive function and relieve parole agents of this responsibility so they can use their time in other services. The continuous process of rehabilitation can best be attained by integration of services of governmental and voluntary agencies working to serve the inmate and the community.

Private agencies have traditionally been concerned with prison conditions. In fact, there is record of inquiry into conditions of jails in England as early as 1334, instigated because "some reformer" cared enough to elucidate facts and compile statistics.[30] It was in 1775 that John Howard, with the assistance of Sir William Eden, succeeded in getting Parliament to pass the Penitentiary Act, which was the first significant concept of the prison as it came to be known. Forty years later, Elizabeth Fry found that conditions had changed little, and twenty years after that, Charles Dickens described what he saw on a visit to NewGate Prison and reported greed, cruelty, revenge, habit, and stupidity blocking the way to reform. The first private agency was established in America by the Quakers in 1787, as was mentioned earlier.

Direct aid to ex-offenders takes the form of provision of temporary food and shelter, clothing, tools, transportation to jobs, and other necessities common to living in society. Parole and probation services that are frequently offered before the government is ready to institute such services. Private organizations generally substitute. Parole planning and planning for post-release living is a frequent duty of prisoners' aid so-

28 Jeanne M. Giovanni and Margaret F. Purvine, "The Myth of the Social Work Matriarchy," in The Social Welfare Forum, 1973 (New York: National Conference on Social Welfare by Columbia University Press, 1974), p. 195.

29 Stanley M. Remez, "Inter-Agency Cooperation in the Job Placement of Inmates and Parolees," Proceedings of Eighty-Fourth Annual Congress of Correction (Philadelphia), October 24–29, 1954, pp. 196–202.

30 Walter Lemmon, "Functional Objectives of the Private Agency," Proceedings of the Eighty-Fourth Annual Congress of Correction, 206.

cieties. In all cases, cooperation is important between the institution, the agency, and the offender.

INTERNATIONAL PRISONERS' AID ASSOCIATIONS

All over the world, most community correctional work and even probation and parole supervision has traditionally been done by private organizations, sometimes on a voluntary basis and sometimes subsidized by the government. The International Prisoners' Aid Association is a

Furniture restoration at Onward Workshop in Manchester.

Courtesy of NACRO (National Association for the Care and Resettlement of Offenders), London, England.

federation of these agencies.[31] Headquartered in Milwaukee since its origin in 1950, it was moved to Philadelphia in 1973. Its functions are summarized in the *1970 International Directory of Prisoners' Aid Agencies*, the latest available directory. It is apparent that community-based corrections and voluntary private agencies serve the field of criminal justice around the world.

CONCLUSIONS

The private agency has the function of filling gaps in governmental services and taking the leadership in penal reform and correctional innovation. With greater flexibility, private individuals and groups can promote new ideas and provide services that governmental agencies cannot. Governmental agencies tend to stay with the "tried and true" traditional approaches, and an administrator who innovates in the field of corrections can be labeled as radical, violating the public safety and interest, and "soft on crime." Most of the significant progress in the history of corrections (in probation, the penitentiary movement, and the juvenile court, for example) has come from private individuals and groups.

Private correctional organizations still provide much of the community correctional service around the world. Portugal, for example, not listed in the *International Directory of Prisoners Aid Societies*, has such a society; it provides all the supervision of probationers and parolees with the help of governmental subsidy.[32] In summary, private community-based corrections programs can fill gaps in governmental services and provide innovative leadership that is needed by the community and by offenders and ex-offenders.

---

[31] International Prisoners Aid Association, 203 McNeil Building, University of Pennsylvania, Philadelphia, Penn. 19174.

[32] Pierre Cannat, "Le Système Pénitentiare du Portugal," in Louis Hugueney, H. Donnedieu de Vabres, and Marc Ancel, *Les Grands Systèmes Pénitentiares Actuels* (Paris: Reçueil Sirey, 1950), pp. 287–96.

Chapter 12

Group Homes, Foster Homes, and Juvenile Services

Assisting youth and children who are not yet eighteen to make successful social adjustments and to stay out of trouble is a vital service in the criminal justice system. All states have placed the top jurisdiction of the juvenile court at the seventeenth or eighteenth birthdays, and when persons must go to court, these dates provide lines of demarcation. For serious crimes, however, the juvenile court with original jurisdiction may certify a case to the adult criminal court at the minimum age of 14, 15, or 16, depending upon state law. Where the minimum age is not specified for these serious crimes, such as in Florida, the law reverts to English common law, and a child *could* be tried for a capital offense in adult court at age seven. In most informal and administrative services, however, the age demarcation is not so important.

The traditional services for juveniles in the community have been the juvenile court and the detention facility. Like probation, parole, and the jail at the adult level, these services are established and traditional in the community; therefore, we will not include them in a discussion of the newer concept of community-based corrections for juveniles. The newer approaches generally provide services to children and youth long before the juvenile court and detention facility has to bring "authority" into the case or situation.

Protection of the child from the criminal justice system is just as important as protecting society from the child, because they are circular or mutually reinforcing. The earlier a child gets into the criminal justice system, the longer he stays in it. Nevertheless, deviant behavior is not analogous to a disease when the criminal justice system is involved—that is, the earlier caught, the easier cured. If the traditional criminal justice system were effective, early detection, diagnosis, and treatment (the DDT of delinquency) could be effective. Unfortunately, it is not, and alternative methods need to be found to work with juveniles in the community.

Some of these alternatives lie with traditional agencies, such as the family, the school, welfare departments, and police. Newer alternatives are residential group treatment homes in the community, correctional day-care centers, agency-operated group homes, boarding homes and foster homes, specialized community services in probation and parole, and short-term residential programs. These newer programs offer some reason for optimism.

GROUP HOMES

Group homes for juveniles include a variety of types of facilities, such as halfway houses, group centers, small-group homes. large-group homes, day-care programs, and group foster homes. Halfway houses include community-based treatment programs for sixteen to thirty youths and are generally situated in large urban areas. Group centers are residential treatment programs for sixteen to twenty-five young people, but with educational and vocational programs within the center, the residents are not as actively involved in community activities as in halfway house. Small-group homes usually provide for four to eight young people under the supervision of a resident husband-and-wife team. Large-group homes are similar except that they handle nine to fifteen young people. Day-care programs are nonresidential programs providing group work; in some cases, these have an educational program in addition to a more intensive treatment program than would be provided on probation or parole. Group foster homes provide residential care for small numbers of youths in private homes; they are generally under contract with the juvenile court.

An excellent survey made by the Florida Division of Youth Services in 1974 indicated the distribution of these programs at that time throughout the United States and Canada.[1] Most states had one or more of these programs for children and youth. (Those that did not were Hawaii, Kansas, Louisiana, Montana, Nebraska, Nevada, New Hampshire, New Mexico, South Dakota, Tennessee, Utah, and Wyoming.) The programs in Arkansas are operated under private auspices and North Carolina has some locally operated programs funded by LEAA. Nebraska had some of these programs, but closed them because of financial reasons. All the

---

[1] *Directory of Halfway Houses and Group Homes for Troubled Children* (Tallahassee: Florida Division of Youth Services, 1974).

provinces of Canada, except for New Brunswick, had at least one of
these programs underway. Even the Yukon Territory had a home with
twelve boys and three girls in Whitehorse. (Distribution of day-care centers is shown in Table 12-1. That of group centers is shown in Table
12-2. Small-group homes distribution is shown in Table 12-3; and
Table 12-4 gives the distribution of large-group centers. Finally, halfway
houses for children are shown in Table 12-5.)

Group homes have been replacing detention homes in many communities. In fact, many counties simply do not have the money to con-
struct new detention homes. In addition, the National Council on Crime
and Delinquency has indicated that the detention home is a beginning
of institutionalization and depersonalization that is not as conducive to
rehabilitation as are the smaller, more intimate residences.[2] A past president of the National Council of Juvenile Court Judges has said that the
two most significant developments in recent years regarding juveniles
have been the use of volunteers and the development of group homes.[3]

Group homes are generally operated in the community by the juvenile court or under contract with the juvenile court. The patterns vary.
Some group homes have only boys, others have only girls, some have
both, and a few have mixed sexes and ages to approximate a family
situation.

Services of the community are used for the group homes. The residents go to public schools, attend church, and go to other functions in
the community just as though they were living at home.

Standards have been worked out for agency-operated group homes
in several places. In the majority of standards, three requirements
emerge in common:

1. A professionally trained social worker with experience in child welfare who is in the employ of the agency shall supervise the agency
   group home.
2. A professionally trained social worker in the employ of the agency
   shall make the determination as to the children to be placed in each
   agency group home, or such determination may be made by an inter-
   disciplinary team when it is the general practice of the agency to use
   such services.
3. Casework service is essential for each child in a group home. . . . The

---

2 Sherwood Norman, *Think Twice Before You Build a Detention Home* (New York:
National Council on Crime and Delinquency, 1968).

3 Personal conversation with Honorable G. Bowdon Hunt, Judge of the Polk County
Juvenile Court, Bartow, Florida, May 15, 1972.

caseworker should be responsible for helping the child in his or her parent-child relationship. . . . Whenever practical this shall be provided by a professionally trained social worker.[4]

As in all community-based correctional programs—as well as other programs—the staff's understanding of personality development and the ability to work with people determines the success or failure of the program.

At the local level, group homes are frequently established by the juvenile court. In some places, they have been established by other agencies, such as women's clubs, PTA, and other groups. In any case, they work closely with the juvenile court. Youth Home, Inc., was established in Little Rock, Arkansas, in March 1968, for six teenage girls between 13 and 17 years of age. Within a year, a second girls' Youth Home began operation. Local citizens and volunteers operate the homes, which were funded by private contributions, much of which came from the Rotary Clubs in Arkansas. Any community in Arkansas can establish a home under Youth Home, Inc., and minimum standards necessitate raising approximately $13,000 to provide matching funds under a contract agreement under Title IV-A of the Social Security Act to meet an estimated operating budget of $50,000.[5]

The staff of group homes must be prepared to work with parents. Parents of children in custody are generally in the same community and many become very defensive and hostile about having an agency maintain control of their children. Moreover, parents of delinquents are generally more disturbed than are parents of nondelinquents. A five-year study in the Delinquency Research Unit of the Judge Baker Foundation Center of Boston (Boston's Juvenile Court) has identified disorders in parents of delinquents that appear to a greater extent than those in parents of nondelinquents,[6] particularly cold and dominating mothers and inadequate or alcoholic fathers.

Other types of group homes are those developed in Massachusetts, where all juvenile schools were closed in 1972, and those like the Criswell

---

4 Martin Gula, *Agency-Operated Group Houses: A Specialized Resource for Serving Children and Youth* (Washington, D.C.: United States Children's Bureau, Department of Health, Education and Welfare, 1964), p. 26.

5 Carol Smelley, "'Venture of Faith': Youth Home, Inc.," *Alternative*, 1, No. 1 (November 1974), 6–7.

6 Beatrice Simcox Reiner and Irving Kaufman, *Character Disorders in Parents of Delinquents* (New York: Family Service Association of America, 1959). See also, Reiner and Kaufman, *Case Work with Parents of Juvenile Delinquents* (New York: Family Service Association of America, 1956).

TABLE 12-1   Day Care Centers

State	Cost of Construction	Cost of Purchase	Cost of Leasing	Annual Cost per Child	Annual Operating Cost	Funding Source	Staff to Child Ratio
Alabama	•	•	$ 1,200	$1,700	$ 70,000	HEW	1 to 12
Florida	•	•	12,111	2,834	85,035	State, LEAA, HEW	1 to 6
Georgia	•	•	36,000	2,500	70,000	State, IV-A	1 to 1.5
Idaho	•	•	•	•	•	State	1 to 14
Indiana	•	•	•	2,000	•	LEAA	1 to 6
Massachusetts	•	•	•	2,496	•	State, LEAA, IV-A	1 to 3
Pennsylvania	•	1.00	•	6,319	537,079	State	1 to 6

TABLE 12-1 (Continued)

State	Number of Programs Boys	Girls	Co-Ed	Average Number of Residents	Age Range of Youngsters	Average Length of Stay	How Admitted	From	Treatment Services
Alabama	1	0	1	50	12-15	6 months	Voluntary	Public School	Individual and group by staff and non-staff.
Florida	0	0	5	30	15-17	4 months	Committed	Court, Parole, Training School	Individual and group by staff.
Georgia	4	0	0	25	12-16	12 months	Committed	Court	Individual and group by staff and non-staff.
Idaho	2	2	0	•	11-17	6 months	Committed Probation	Court/Parole	Contracted for.
Indiana	•	•	•	•	16-18	6 months	Committed	Training School	Group by non-staff.
Massachusetts	•	•	120	•	•	•	•	•	•
Pennsylvania	0	0	1	85	15-18	6 months	Committed	Court	Individual and group by staff.

Directory of Halfway Houses and Group Homes for Troubled Children (Tallahassee: Florida Division of Youth Services, 1974), pp. 10–11.

201

TABLE 12-2 Group Centers

State	Cost of Construction	Cost of Purchase	Cost of Leasing	Annual Cost per Child	Annual Operating Cost	Funding Source	Staff to Child Ratio
California	•	•	$53,640	$3,000	$269,896	State	1 to 3
Colorado	•	•	•	5,110	•	State, LEAA	•
Florida	•	•	16,390	5,869	146,725	State, LEAA, Title I	1 to 2.5
Idaho	•	•	•	2,000	•	LEAA	1 to 2.3
Manitoba, Canada	•	•	•	7,300	•	Province	1 to 2
New York	$300,000	•	•	6,500	135,000	State, HEW, IV-A	1 to 2.5
Vermont	•	•	•	2,100	5,900	State	1 to 2.5

TABLE 12-2 (Continued)

State	Number of Programs			Average Number of Residents	Age Range of Youngsters	Average Length of Stay	How Admitted	From	Treatment Services
	Boys	Girls	Co-Ed						
California	5	•	•	12	14-25	4 months	Parole	Parole	Individual and group by staff and non-staff.
Colorado	•	•	•	•	10-18	5 months	Committed	Training School, Other	Individual and group by staff and non-staff.
Florida	3	2	0	25	13-15 15-17	5 months	Committed	Court, Parole, Training School	Individual and group by staff.
Idaho	1	0	0	30	11-16	8 months	Probation Committed	Court, Parole	Individual and group by staff.
Manitoba, Canada	1	1	0	25	12-18	12-18 months	Probation Committed	Court, Private Agency	Individual and group by staff.
New York	2	3	0	20	15-17	8 months	Voluntary Probation	Court, Training School	Individual and group by staff.
Vermont	2	2	0	20	9-17	8 months	Probation Committed	Court, Private Agency	Individual and group by staff.

Directory of Halfway Houses and Group Homes for Troubled Children (Tallahassee: Florida Division of Youth Services, 1974), pp. 10-11.

TABLE 12-3 Small-Group Homes

State	Cost of Construction	Cost of Purchase	Cost of Leasing	Annual Cost per Child	Annual Operating Cost	Funding Source	Staff to Child Ratio
Alabama	$30,000	•	$ 1,200	$3,400	$ 21,000	LEAA, private	1 to 3
California	•	•	420,000	2,100	420,000	State, LEAA	1 to 4
Colorado	•	•	•	2,100	•	State, LEAA	•
Connecticut	•	•	•	6,500	85,000	State, LEAA, HEW, private	1 to 2
Florida	•	•	3,940	5,730	40,108	State, LEAA, Title I	1 to 2.3
Georgia	•	•	3,600	8,000	20,000	LEAA, IV-A	1 to 1.5
Idaho	•	•	•	2,000	•	LEAA	1 to 1.5
Illinois	•	•	•	3,800	35,000	State	1 to 4
Indiana	•	•	•	1,800	•	State	•

TABLE 12-3 (Continued)

State	Number of Programs Boys	Girls	Co-Ed	Average Number of Residents	Age Range of Youngsters	Average Length of Stay	How Admitted	From	Treatment Services
Alabama	2	0	0	6	12-17	7 months	Committed Probation/Parole	Court, Training School	Individual and group by staff and non-staff.
California	25	•	•	8	14-25	5 months	Parole	Parole	Individual and group by staff and non-staff.
Colorado	•	•	•	•	10-18	5 months	Committed	Other Training Schools	Group and individual by staff and non-staff.
Connecticut	•	•	•	7	12-18	5 months	Probation Committed	Court, Training School, Parole	Individual and group by staff and non-staff.
Florida	5	1	0	7	10-12 12-14	8 months 6 months	Committed	Court, Parole, Training School	Individual and group by staff.
Georgia	3	2	0	8	13-19	12 months	Committed	Court, Parole	Individual and group by staff.
Idaho	4	3	0	4	12-18	9 months	Committed Probation	Court, Parole	Individual and group by staff.
Illinois	15	0	0	8	13-20	6 months	Voluntary	Parole	Individual and group by staff.
Indiana	•	•	•	•	12-18	8 months	Committed	Parole	Individual by staff.

205

TABLE 12-3 (Continued)

State	Cost of Construction	Cost of Purchase	Cost of Leasing	Annual Cost per Child	Annual Operating Cost	Funding Source	Staff to Child Ratio
Iowa	•	$30,000 to 150,000	$200 to 300/mo.	4,800	•	State	1 to 5
Massachusetts	•	•	•	6,760	80,000	LEAA	1 to 2
Kentucky	•	•	1,500	3,777	30,000	State	•
Minnesota	•	•	•	2,463	12,400	State, LEAA	1 to 2.5
Missouri	•	•	4,800	6,700	58,000	State, LEAA	1 to 2
Michigan	•	•	•	5,000	25,000	State, LEAA	1 to 2
New York	•	$50,000	6,500	6,500	45,000	State, HEW, IV-A	1 to 2.1
North Dakota	•	•	3,300	6,000	32,000	State, LEAA	1 to 2

TABLE 12-3 (Continued)

State	Number of Programs Boys	Number of Programs Girls	Number of Programs Co-Ed	Average Number of Residents	Age Range of Youngsters	Average Length of Stay	How Admitted	From	Treatment Services
Iowa	4	2	0	8	13-17	18 months	Committed	Court, Private Training School	Individual and group by staff and non-staff.
Massachusetts	5	3	0	8	10-21	•	Voluntary Committed	Court, Training School, Other	Individual and group by staff and non-staff.
Kentucky	•	•	•	10-12	10-17	4 months	Committed Probation	Parole, Court, Private Agency	Individual and group by staff.
Minnesota	42	28	0	5	12-18	9 months	Probation Committed	Court, Parole	Individual and group by staff and non-staff.
Missouri	7	3	0	8	12-17	4 months	Committed	Court, Training School	Group by staff.
Michigan	1	17	4	6	12-19	6 months	Committed	Court	Individual and group by staff.
New York	15	12	0	7	13-17	8 months	Voluntary Probation	Court, Training School	Individual and group by staff.
North Dakota	1	0	0	5	12-20	3 months	Committed	Training School	Individual by staff. Individual and group non-staff.

TABLE 12-3   (Continued)

State	Cost of Construction	Cost of Purchase	Cost of Leasing	Annual Cost per Child	Annual Operating Cost	Funding Source	Staff to Child Ratio
Ohio	•	27,000	1,800	3,300	20,000	State	1 to 2
Oklahoma	•	•	4,000	3,000	25,000	State, IV-A	1 to 2
Pennsylvania	•	•	•	3,615	14,680	State, LEAA	2 to 1
Rhode Island	•	•	1,800	5,600	44,000	State, LEAA	1 to 2
South Carolina	•	•	2,400	4,380	40,000	State, LEAA	1 to 2
Alberta, Canada	•	35,000	•	3,000	13,000	Province	1 to 3
Manitoba, Canada	•	•	2,000	•	•	Province	1 to 2.5
Ontario, Canada	•	•	•	4,800	350,000	Province	1 to 2

TABLE 12-3 (Continued)

State	Number of Programs			Average Number of Residents	Age Range of Youngsters	Average Length of Stay	How Admitted	From	Treatment Services
	Boys	Girls	Co-Ed						
Ohio	9	4	0	6	12-18	8 months	Probation	Court, Parole	Individual and group by staff and non-staff.
Oklahoma	1	2	0	7	14-18	•	Committed	Court	Individual and group by staff and non-staff.
Pennsylvania	6	2	1	4	18-21	•	Committed	Court	Individual and group by staff and non-staff.
Rhode Island	3	0	0	6	15-18	1 year	Voluntary Committed	Court	Individual and group by staff and non-staff.
South Carolina	0	2	0	8	11-17	3 months	Voluntary Probation Committed	Court, Training School, Private Agency	Individual and group by staff.
Alberta, Canada	11	3	0	6	12-17	6 months	Voluntary Committed	Training School	Individual and group by staff and non-staff.
Manitoba, Canada	4	1	0	16	14-18	12-18 months	Committed Probation	Court, Private Agency	Individual and group by probation staff.
Ontario, Canada	6	2	1	6	12-16	•	Committed	Training School	Individual and group by staff.

Directory of Halfway Houses and Group Homes for Troubled Children (Tallahassee: Florida Division of Youth Services, 1974), pp. 12–13.

TABLE 12-4 Large-Group Homes

State	Cost of Construction	Cost of Purchase	Cost of Leasing	Annual Cost per Child	Annual Operating Cost	Funding Source	Staff to Child Ratio
California	•	•	$327,000	$2,520	$327,000	State, LEAA	1 to 3
Connecticut	•	•		6,500	100,000	State, LEAA, HEW, Private	1 to 2
Delaware	•	$ 33,000	•	5,094	51,000	State, LEAA, Private	1 to 2
District of Columbia	•		4,800	8,855	125,000	D. C. Budget	1 to 2
Maryland	•	•	5,200	8,303	191,000	State	1 to 10
Montana	•	•	4,800	3,250	32,500	Local, LEAA	1 to 5
New York	•	300,000	•	6,500	135,000	State, HEW, IV-A	1 to 2.94

TABLE 12-4 (Continued)

State	Number of Programs Boys	Number of Programs Girls	Number of Programs Co-Ed	Average Number of Residents	Age Range of Youngsters	Average Length of Stay	How Admitted	From	Treatment Services
California	20	•	•	7	14-25	5 months	Parole	Parole	Individual and group by staff and non-staff.
Connecticut	•	•	•	11	12-18	5 months	Probation/ Committed	Court, Parole, Training School	Individual and group by staff and non-staff.
Delaware	1	2	0	9	12-20	7 months	Probation/ Voluntary	Parole, Training School	Individual and group by staff.
District of Columbia	5	2	0	12	7-17	2-12 months	Committed/ Voluntary	Court, Parole, Training School	Individual and group by staff.
Maryland	2	1	0	10	13-17	4 months	Committed	Court, Parole	Individual and group by staff and non-staff.
Montana	2	1	2	10	14-18	3½ months	Committed Voluntary Probation	Court, Private Agency, Parole	Individual and group by staff and non-staff.
New York	3	0	0	25	15-17	8 months	Voluntary Probation	Court, Training School	Individual and group by staff.

TABLE 12-4 (Continued)

State	Cost of Construction	Cost of Purchase	Cost of Leasing	Annual Cost per Child	Annual Operating Cost	Funding Source	Staff to Child Ratio
Ohio	•	•	2,500	5,200	50,000	State, LEAA	1 to 2
Pennsylvania	•	•	7,500	7,450	95,500	State, LEAA	1 to 1
South Carolina	•	•	3,600	5,834	60,000	State, LEAA, HEW	1 to 3
Virginia	•	20,000	3,600	5,455	60,000	State, LEAA	1 to 2
Washington	$105,000	•	200	5,500	70,000	State	1 to 2
Manitoba, Canada	•	•	•	2,900	•	Province	1 to 4
Ontario, Canada	•	•	•	4,800	150,000	Province	1 to 2

TABLE 12-4 (Continued)

State	Number of Programs			Average Number of Residents	Age Range of Youngsters	Average Length of Stay	How Admitted	From	Treatment Services
	Boys	Girls	Co-Ed						
Ohio	7	4	2	9	14-19	5 months	Probation	Court, Parole	Individual and group by staff and non-staff.
Pennsylvania	2	0	0	12	18-21	•	Committed	Court	Individual and group by staff.
South Carolina	2	0	0	9	11-17	4 months	Voluntary Probation Committed	Court, Training School, Private Agency	Individual and group by staff.
Virginia	4	1	0	11	16-19	8 months	Voluntary Committed	Training School, Parole	Individual and group by staff and non-staff.
Washington	3	2	0	11	8-18	7 months	Voluntary	Training School, Parole	Individual and group by staff.
Manitoba, Canada	2	0	0	16	14-18	12-18 months	Committed Probation	Court, Private Agency	Individual and group by probation staff.
Ontario, Canada	2	1	0	8	12-16	•	Committed	Training School	Individual and group by staff.

Directory of Halfway Houses and Group Homes for Troubled Children (Tallahassee: Florida Division of Youth Services, 1974), pp. 14-15.

TABLE 12-5   Halfway Houses

State	Cost of Construction	Cost of Purchase	Cost of Leasing	Annual Cost per Child	Annual Operating Cost	Funding Source	Staff to Child Ratio
Arizona	•	•	$ 4,800	$1,800	$ 83,000	State, LEAA	1 to 3
Florida	$250,000	$106,481	10,793	4,544	113,600	State, LEAA, HUD, Title I	1 to 3.78
Idaho	•	•	•	2,000	•	LEAA	1 to 2.5
Illinois	•	•	•	7,000	300,000	State	1 to 1
Maine	•	65,000	•	6,000	55,000	State, LEAA, HEW, HUD	1 to 2
Manitoba, Canada	•	•	•	9,200	•	Province	1 to 2
Maryland	•	•	32,500	7,434	282,517	LEAA	1 to 8

TABLE 12-5 (Continued)

State	Number of Programs			Average Number of Residents	Age Range of Youngsters	Average Length of Stay	How Admitted	From	Treatment Services
	Boys	Girls	Co-Ed						
Arizona	1	2	0	12	15-18	5 months	Committed	Training School	Individual by staff/group and individual by non-staff.
Florida	7	2	0	25	15-17	5 months	Committed	Court, Training School, Parole	Individual and group by staff.
Idaho	2	2	0	35	10-17	10 months	Probation Committed	Court Parole	Individual and group by staff.
Illinois	1	0	0	20	16-20	3 months	Voluntary	Parole	Individual and group by staff.
Maine	1	1	0	10	12-17	•	Committed	Court, Training School	Individual and group by staff.
Manitoba, Canada	2	2	0	10	14-18	12-24 months	Probation Committed	Court, Private Agency	Individual and group by staff.
Maryland	1	0	0	35	8-12	•	Committed	Court, Training School	Individual and group by staff and non-staff.

TABLE 12-5 (Continued)

	Cost of Construction	Cost of Purchase	Cost of Leasing	Annual Cost per Child	Annual Operating Cost	Funding Source	Staff to Child Ratio
Michigan	•	•	4,000	6,600	80,000	State, LEAA	1 to 2
Minnesota	•	•	9,000	8,482	162,000	State, LEAA, Private	1 to 1.3
New York	•	50,000	•	6,500	45,000	State, HEW, IV-A	1 to 2
Oregon	•	•	4,800	7,200	70,060	State, LEAA, IV-A	1 to .60
Texas	•	•	14,148	6,600	66,912	State	1 to 2
Vermont	•	•	3,750	7,177	150,458	State, LEAA	1 to 2.6

TABLE 12-5 (Continued)

State	Number of Programs Boys	Number of Programs Girls	Number of Programs Co-Ed	Average Number of Residents	Age Range of Youngsters	Average Length of Stay	How Admitted	From	Treatment Services
Michigan	11	2	0	12	12-19	5 months	Committed	Court	Individual and group by staff.
Minnesota	4	1	0	14	13-25	5 months	Committed Probation	Court Parole	Individual and group by staff.
New York	1	0	0	7	15-17	•	Voluntary Probation	Court, Training School	Individual and group by staff and non-staff.
Oregon	21	4	5	10	12-18	9 months	Committed	Court	Individual and group by staff and non-staff.
Texas	1	2	1	10	16-21	2 months	Voluntary	Parole	Individual and group by staff.
Vermont	1	0	0	15	16-23	4 months	Committed Probation	Court, Training School	Individual and group by staff.

Directory of Halfway Houses and Group Homes for Troubled Children (Tallahassee: Florida Division of Youth Services, 1974), pp. 8–9.

House in Florida—both are examples of alternatives to juvenile institutionalization, and both have been viewed favorably by outside observers.[7] Such programs are characterized by a residential facility in the community, and local schools and other services are used in much the same way they are used by local residents.

In September 1971, the students at the Amherst campus of the University of Massachusetts, in reaction to the Attica tragedy, examined what could be done in the area of corrections, particularly juvenile corrections. They established a program called Juvenile Opportunities Extension (JOE) as a means for college students to volunteer their skills and time working with young people at the Westfield Detention Center.[8] The students were able to be particularly helpful in 1972, at which time the juvenile institutions were closed, leaving the staff with high anxiety, bitterness, and feelings approaching vengeance. Soon afterward, two university dormitories were opened to youthful offenders under a program called Massachusetts Association for the Reintegration of Youth (MARY). Ten youths are housed on campus and the students work with them. More youths will participate as the program is expanded. This is one .example of group homes started by interested community (in this case, college) citizens.

FOSTER HOMES

Foster homes are used in two different ways. The traditional foster home involves a long-term placement in a family home without adoption. The newer concept of foster home as part of the community-based correctional program involves a short-term placement with a family as needed. Couples and families are evaluated according to suitability of their home for placement of children with behavioral problems. The general approach is for the juvenile court to contract with such families, who are on a stand-by basis. The family may receive a standard fee of $10 to $20 per week, more or less in different jurisdictions, and when a child is placed in the home, they may receive $5 or $10 per day as long as the child is there. Of course, the cost varies between jurisdictions and according to the national economy.

The child in this situation goes to school, attends church, and participates in community activities with other family members. The agency licensing, using, and supervising the foster home program must be sure

---

[7] John M. Flackett, "Juvenile Offenders in the Community: Some Recent Events in the United States," *The Howard Journal of Penology and Crime Prevention* (London), 14, No. 1 (1974), 22–36.

[8] Lynn Nichols, *Massachusetts Association for the Reintegration of Youth* (Amherst, Mass.: University of Massachusetts, mimeographed, undated, received March 19, 1975).

that the child is accepted in the home as a member of the family; the foster-home program must not be regarded merely as a source of supplemental income.

This type of foster home replaces the detention home. Even though the costs may sound high, closer examination indicates that they are only a fraction of the costs of operating a detention home, including salaries and maintenance. Further, the foster home is available on the basis of need, while the detention home is a permanent structure with a permanent staff and must be maintained whether there are children there or not.

Most of the foster homes used by juvenile courts are group foster homes, as compared with many used by private child-placing agencies as single foster homes. A summary of the number of group foster homes in 1974 is shown in Table 12-6.

As was mentioned in the section on group homes, Massachusetts' major training schools were unilaterally closed in 1972. By 1975, of the approximately 2,600 youngsters under care of the Department of Youth Services, there were about 300 in local detention, about 800 under conventional parole supervision, and approximately 1,500 scattered among a variety of community programs, including private boarding schools and YMCAs, foster homes, residential facilities in neighboring states; also, there were about 700 in nonresidential day programs.[9] Dare, Inc., a nonprofit corporation that operates eighteen different programs, most of them group homes, has been of considerable assistance with juvenile foster-home placement. Their Hastings House is a group home in Cambridge located in a middle-class residential neighborhood; it holds twelve to fourteen boys, age fourteen to seventeen. Many of the boys are chronic delinquents with as many as twenty arrests. Massachusetts officials are optimistic about this type of program. It appears clear that foster-home care is better for children with problems than is institutional care, except in cases where specialized care really requires an institution.[10]

SCHOOL PROGRAMS

School programs, in dealing with delinquent behavior, began with classroom discipline and enforcement of compulsory education laws. In-school discipline is a task inherent in public education under compulsory education laws that keep children and youth in school—and there are some who do not want to be there and may disturb others in the

---

9 "Massachusetts—Officials Say Juvenile System Works," *Corrections Magazine*, 1, No. 5 (May/June 1975), 33–36.

10 Howard W. Hopkirk, *Institutions Serving Children* (New York: Russell Sage Foundation, 1944), p. 24.

TABLE 12-6 Group Foster Homes

State	Number of Youngsters per Home	Bed Subsidy per Month	Boarding per Day	Number of Homes	Age Range	Average Length of Stay	Funding Sources
Alaska	•	210.00	•	30	13-16	•	•
Arizona	3	100.00	3.33	85	8-18	•	State
Florida	5	40.00	3.50	11	10-18	6-18 months	State, LEAA
Idaho	1	•	5.00	8	12-17	2 months	LEAA
Illinois	2	•	•	27	13-20	•	State
Indiana	3	150.00	•	10	12-18	8 months	State
Minnesota	5	50.00	3.00	74	12-18	•	State, County
Missouri	4	30.00	2.00	8	12-17	10 months	State, LEAA
Ohio	3	•	4.50	40	12-18	10 months	State
Pennsylvania	2	287.00	8.25	18	to 21	•	State, LEAA
South Carolina	3	•	2.50	•	9-17	12 months	State
Wisconsin	3	50.00	6.00	36	12-18	9 months	State, LEAA, HEW
Manitoba	6	•	6.30	5	14-18	6-24 months	Province
Ontario	6	13.00	•	12	12-16	•	Province

Directory of Halfway Houses and Group Homes for Troubled Children (Tallahassee: Florida Division of Youth Services, 1974), p. 16.

classroom situation. The principal in recent years has been replaced in many schools by a dean of students or vice-principal who serves as disciplinarian. Early compulsory education laws resulted in the establishment of the "truant officer"; his responsibility was to find children who were legally required to be in school and get them back. As a result of this function, these officers came into frequent contact with parents, police, juvenile courts, and other community agencies. After World War II, however, the "truant officer" became a "visiting teacher." With the change in title came a change in philosophy and function. While the old function of enforcing compulsory education laws still obtained, new functions in terms of counseling, social services, and casework appeared.

A more recent development in this field has been the social service division or counseling division within the public school system. Some excellent services have been created, providing trained social workers to counsel and give casework services to children and youth showing behavior problems, as well as to their families. The basic principle of their work stems from the observation that most young people who become involved in serious delinquency have first exhibited problems of school truancy. Some schools have entered into contractual agreements with the juvenile court by establishing the position of Teacher Probation Officer (TPO). The TPO is a teacher whose teaching load is reduced so that he or she can provide probation-type supervision of a case-load of students in the school. Many programs, such as those at Alexandria, Virginia, and a broader program in the state of Ohio, particularly Lucas County (Toledo), have shown great effectiveness. Administratively, some difficulty has arisen because of the resentment of other teachers who view the TPO as receiving a higher salary for less work! In fact, TPOs are selected for their ability to work with children and youth and really spend *more* time on their jobs because of the many problems they have to handle during evenings and weekends.

Many larger cities have established special schools for problem students. New York City, for example, has the "600 Schools," which are designed to take disciplinary problems from the other schools. (The number "600" has no significance, but is just used as a label to identify schools for problem students.)

The National Congress of Parents and Teachers (National PTA) has a child protective committee in each local chapter. Though these vary widely in activity and effectiveness, they are prominent in some areas in assisting schools in establishing and operating counseling and casework services for children in need.[11] The organization has combined with the

---

11 *The PTA Works for Children—In Your Community, In Your State, Throughout the Nation* (Chicago: National Congress of Parents and Teachers, undated).

National Council of Juvenile Court Judges in a study of absenteeism or truancy from school in the period 1973 to 1975 and hopes to increase the effectiveness of the local committees.

The program of the Providence Educational Center (PEC) in St. Louis, Missouri, provides an alternative to training school incarceration for youths aged 12 to 16 who are charged with stranger-to-stranger crimes and who have histories of poor academic achievement and social failure.[12] The basic premise underlying PEC's program is that the long-term rehabilitation of delinquents exhibiting these characteristcs is contingent on the development of the skill they need to experience success in school, in their family and social relationships, and on the job. PEC programs are comprised of three closely coordinated and functionally interrelated components. The *educational* component consists of an individualized approach to providing instruction and remedial assistance in reading, mathematics, and other academic subjects. The *social services* component performs diagnostic assessments, provides counseling to clients and families, and acts as a liaison with juvenile court officials. The *after-care* component is responsible for easing the transition back into the community after graduation. The program's effectiveness in reducing costs and lowering juvenile recidivism rates has earned it the designation of an LEAA Exemplary Project.

The school setting is an ideal place to identify beginning antisocial behavior. Elementary school teachers without special training can identify many potential behavior problems. By the time children are in junior high school (generally considered to be sixth through eighth grades), the patterns of social adaptation have been fairly well established. Counseling and casework services in the school for children with behavioral difficulties *and* their families are important at the elementary, junior high, and high school levels.

POLICE SERVICES

Police departments have historically provided services for juveniles, particularly juveniles with problems. Some professional organizations in the field of law enforcement, such as the International Associations of Chiefs of Police (IACP), do not view recreation departments and schools as appropriate police functions.

On the other hand, many police departments throughout the country carry on recreational and other programs to serve juveniles because "nobody else is doing it." The New York City Police Department, for

---

[12] *Providence Educational Center: An Exemplary Project* (Washington, D.C.: National Institute of Law Enforcement and Criminal Justice, 1974).

example, has for a long time sponsored the Police Athletic League (PAL), in which youth from the ghettos can participate in wholesome athletic competition and other programs.

The Montgomery, Alabama, Police Department has maintained an excellent program for children and youth since the early 1960s and the beginning of civil rights disturbances. At that time, the department maintained Boy Scout Troop 5, which required individual boys to be under police supervision before they could be admitted. The morale was high, and the boys won more than their share of ribbons and badges in competition with other troops. More important, of course, was that they identified with the law-abiding element of society and with the Montgomery Police Department. This Boy Scout program was typical of the Montgomery Police Department's voluntary involvement with the youth of the city. And that involvement has continued. In 1975, there were 467 sworn officers in the Montgomery Police Department, of whom 106 were in the Youth Aid Division. The School Relations Bureau within that division maintained offices in the various schools and were considered to be members of the school faculty. In full uniform, these officers counseled disturbed youth, amelioriated problems, and gave the youth of Montgomery a "helping" image. A professional psychologist with a Ph.D. was hired; selected officers were sent to Delinquency Control Institutes at Florida State University, University of Southern California, University of Louisville, and elsewhere; and training programs were established that brought "name" people in the field of juvenile delinquency to Montgomery for frequent training sessions. In addition, a summer camp and other programs are maintained to serve children and youth. Today police cars can ride into the ghetto area and attract groups of friendly youth. This is an example of how aggressive and antisocial tendencies and urges can be channeled into socially acceptable efforts.

Voluntary police supervision for juveniles is available in most cities. A juvenile taken into custody is generally turned over to the juvenile division; it is this group which decides whether supervision within the police department is adequate or whether the child must be turned over to the juvenile court. Because more than one million children are taken into custody each year and between 250,000 and 300,000 are referred to juvenile court, it is obvious that the majority are handled in police departments. Many are under ongoing and quasi-permanent supervision. Cases have been known of juveniles stealing several automobiles over a period of months and still remaining under police supervision because of circumstances and hope for improvement. In the majority of cases, police judgment has been vindicated by successful diversion of youngsters from the criminal justice system.

In addition, many police departments, sheriff's departments, sheriff's associations, and other law enforcement organizations provide scholarships, camps, and residential facilities for dependent children.

The community services officer or community-based correctional program coordinator will find that police know the community, both formally and informally, better than almost any other agency. Good relationships with the police are thus important in the exchange of information and in coordination of efforts to improve the perceptions of young people.

There is a significant difference in the number and types of offenses for which juveniles come into contact with police. Those from the central zone of the city tend to have much more frequent contact with the police than those in other zones, particularly for such offenses as theft and vagrancy.[13] Poverty areas in the city are characterized by juvenile crime and parent-child conflict. In the Bronx, New York, the Vera Institute and Fordham University devised in 1970 a Neighborhood Youth Diversion Program (NYDP), which was originally funded by LEAA but was subsequently taken over by the Human Resources Administration.[14] Boys and girls 7 to 15 years of age facing adjudication as delinquents or in need of supervision were provided advocates in the form of brother/sister figures to assist in mediation and counseling. By 1975, 1,200 clients had been assigned advocates and the community problems have significantly diminished.

Operation Peace of Mind was instituted in Texas after the bodies of twenty-seven young mass-murder victims were found in Houston in 1973. In September 1973, its hotline for runaways was instituted to serve the entire nation. Funded by LEAA, the project accepts calls from runaways who want to get word to their families and responds to the calls from anxious parents who want to contact their children. Before the formation of this agency, runaways had been handled only by police, welfare departments, and juvenile courts.

CHILD GUIDANCE CLINICS

The first child guidance clinic opened in Philadelphia in 1897. By World War I, there were approximately 600 such clinics in the United States. Today there are approximately 2,000 clinics serving children with emotional disturbances. Most of them are administered centrally by individual state departments of mental health.

The majority of problems handled by child guidance clinics have been

---

[13] See Lyle Shannon, "Types and Patterns of Delinquency in Middle-Sized Cities," *Journal of Research in Crime and Delinquency*, 1, No. 1 (January 1964), 53–66.

[14] "Diversion Program for NYC Kids," *Target*, 4, No. 4 (April 1975), 3–4.

a result of referrals from concerned parents and schools. Traditionally, full use of such facilities has not been made by agencies of the criminal justice system. But the community services officer and the coordinator of community-based correctional programs working in the juvenile area could find them a useful resource in many areas.

Emotional disturbances, like truancy, may precede delinquency by some time. Truancy is more likely to be antecedent to delinquency. Emotional problems may be antecedent to certain kinds of delinquency, particularly obsessive-compulsive types of behavior and some sex deviation, but it is more closely connected to mental illness than is truancy. In either case, the child guidance clinic can be helpful.

Adolescent girls with potential problems can be identified early in high school, as was shown in a study involving 260 problem girls and 531 "residual" or nonproblem girls in a New York City vocational high school. Here, 128 problem girls were treated by the Youth Counseling Service and 132 were not; the study indicated that social work counseling was of benefit in preventing further progress of problems.[15] Moreover, it was found that the initial contact and continued access to these adolescent problem girls was better and more effective when it was done in groups.

WALK-INS

Walk-ins can be storefronts or residences, similar to the old settlement houses. They are generally established in vacant stores in deteriorated neighborhoods to provide a place where children and youth with problems can go for recreation, counseling, or just to "rap." They are used in drug programs, by religious organizations, by government-sponsored programs (Office of Economic Opportunity and Model Cities), as well as in some groups without identification except a simple concern for people with problems. For example, in the late 1960s the Baltimore City Police Department began a successful program of neighborhood counseling in vacant stores in the area in which racial riots had occurred and in other problem areas in the city.

Some organizations have opened walk-ins in private residences, generally abandoned, or in old commercial buildings in deteriorated neighborhoods. Some of the popular names ascribed to these facilities have been "Divine Light," "Our Father's House," and other names with helping connotations. Many religious groups have used the ancient Christian

---

15 See Henry J. Meyer, Edgar F. Borgatta, and Wyatt C. Jones, *Girls at Vocational High: An Experiment in Social Work Intervention* (New York: Russell Sage Foundation, 1965).

symbol of two broad arcs connected at one end and crossed at the other to depict a fish, the symbol used by early Christians when they were meeting resistance from the Roman Empire.

The community services officer must learn for himself of such services in his community—there is no central organization, no directory, and no way to list these walk-ins on a national basis.

A drop-in center was established in Portsmouth, New Hampshire, in 1973 through the Junction 13 Youth Services System,[16] which receives extensive support from court and police personnel. The court refers over 60 percent of its juvenile cases to this group, and the police department refers over 30 percent. An average of 800 young people per month visit the drop-in center for recreational and counseling services. Participants also include young people who participate of their own volition. Counseling is provided not only for clients, but for parents as well. Major emphasis is placed on prevention of delinquency, and area schools serve as a focal point for this goal. Junction 13 staff members working at the junior high school can change a student's class schedule to allow for part-time work when necessary, or aid students having difficulties in class work. Tutoring is an ongoing function.

YOUTH ADVOCACY

"Youth advocacy" refers to a role that has been informally performed by some school, church, social welfare, and other groups to "front" for a child in trouble, primarily to keep him from going into the juvenile justice system. In some areas there are offices of youth advocacy, such as in Alaska and in Youth Service Bureaus. O. J. Keller has identified six roles as being particularly appropriate for the youth advocate: he or she must be (1) a friend of youth, (2) a locator of resources, (3) a coordinator of existing service systems, (4) an evaluator of existing services, (5) a check or control of bureaucracy when its needs are met at the expense of the children's needs, and (6) an omsbudsman who is partial to his or her youthful client.[17] Many children who come to court have been an annoyance rather than a serious threat to society. In many cases they have been victims of an unsatisfactory family situation. Because of the absence of proper resources to help such children, however, the court

---

16 Junction 13 Youth Resource Center, Portsmouth, N.H. 03801.

17 Quoted by Paul H. Hahn, *Community Based Corrections and the Criminal Justice System* (Santa Cruz, Cal.: Davis Publishing Co., 1975), p. 46, from a general session on Youth Advocacy at the American Correctional Association annual Congress on Correction, Seattle, Washington, August 1973.

frequently adjudicates them as delinquent—and "the helping hand strikes again." [18]

Jill McNulty names five areas in which the child advocate should be active: (1) he or she can help families obtain needed services, whether in medical, educational, or other areas; (2) he or she can represent the child in dealings with the school, frequently to seek reinstatement after behavior problems and sometimes to negotiate change if the school is being too restrictive; (3) the youth advocate can also work with police, attempting to secure confidence and cooperation in referral of troubled families and children to advocates rather than to the courts, and to encourage the use of juvenile officers; (4) he or she can provide adequate legal representation in court if it is not provided by parents; and finally, (5) the advocate can help to devise a system whereby a child-serving agency is primarily accountable to the client, rather than to external funding sources.[19]

Young Citizens for Action (YCFA) has a contract with the City of Santa Fe, New Mexico, as youth advocate. This group is well received by the city police, city council, business community, residents, and "the kids." [20] The YCFA was organized in about 1964 and has gained strength. It is active in organizing sports activities, and is well supported by volunteers from the community.

In 1972, students at the University of Florida established the Clinical Regional Support Teams program (CREST). They serve as volunteer student counselors and undergraduate tutors under the supervision of a paid doctoral student.[21] Referrals of youngsters exhibiting severe authority problems are made by the Florida Division of Youth Services. Between 1972 and 1975, 200 juveniles have been served at a cost of approximately $1 per day as compared with an annual cost of $10,000 per child in the state's training schools. Advocacy is included in the program.

Child Protective Service exists for children who are neglected, abused, or exploited. Physical, emotional, and intellectual growth and welfare are presumed to be jeopardized when the child is (1) malnourished, ill-clad, dirty, without proper shelter or sleeping arrangements; (2) without supervision and unattended; (3) ill and lacking essential medical care; (4) denied normal experiences that produce feelings of being loved,

---

[18] Jill K. McNulty, "The Right to Be Left Alone," *Journal of Family Law*, 12, No. 2 (1972–73), 243–46.

[19] Ibid., pp. 252–54.

[20] "Santa Fe Youth Advocacy Center Earns Community Respect," *Impact*, 1, No. 5 (May 1973), 7.

[21] "Florida Students Work with Delinquents," *Target*, 4, No. 4 (April 1975), 2.

wanted, secure, and worthy (emotional neglect); (5) failing to attend school regularly; (6) exploited, overworked; (7) physically abused; (8) emotionally disturbed due to continuous friction in home, marital discord, mentally ill parents; and/or (9) exposed to unwholesome and demoralizing circumstances.[22] Protective services become advocacy programs in many areas.

Juvenile advocacy is a basic practice in juvenile court.[23] Juvenile courts rely on social agencies more than any other court and try to provide services in the best interests of the child. But there are civil-criminal ambiguities in the juvenile court that need to be understood and are essential to the child's welfare. Further, the increasing adversarial nature of juvenile court hearings necessitates a knowledge of where and when to interject juvenile advocacy.

SHORT-TERM INSTITUTIONALIZATION

Several community-based programs have been designed to begin with short-term institutionalization, followed by probation-type supervision in the community. These programs are designed to use the short-term institutionalization for diagnosis, tests, interviews, and short-term treatment, either through individual counseling or group therapy, after which the individual is returned to his community. New Jersey began an early program of this type in the 1950s at the Diagnostic Center at Menlo Park under the leadership of Dr. Ralph Brancale.

In 1961, the California Youth Authority began an experiment known as the Community Treatment Project (CTP).[24] This was a study to determine the most effeffctive way of changing delinquents to nondelinquents. The procedure in this project was to have each youth spend four to six weeks at the CYA's Northern Reception Center and Clinic in Sacramento; then he or she was either sent to a CYA institution for several months or returned directly to the home community on parole status. It was the latter group that was considered to be involved in the community treatment program. The first phase of the experiment was from 1961 to 1969, and the second phase began in 1969. It was found that power-oriented youths performed worse in the community treatment program than in traditional settings. Passive conformists performed

---

22 Child Welfare League of America, *Standards for Child Protective Service* (New York: Child Welfare League of America, 1960).

23 See Douglas J. Besharov, *Juvenile Justice Advocacy—Practice in a Unique Court* (New York: Practicing Law Institute, 1974).

24 Ted Palmer, "The Youth Authority's Community Treatment Project," *Federal Probation*, 38, No. 1 (March 1974), 3–14.

somewhat better in the CTP than in traditional programs. Other, smaller groups, such as asocialized passive, situational emotional reactors, and cultural identifiers, were not represented sufficiently to draw full conclusions, but the cultural identifiers tended to perform better in traditional programs. It has been concluded that the original ideal of CTP of changing delinquents into lifelong nondelinquents is not being achieved in the majority of cases, though the reduction of deviant behavior on a short-term basis has been observed. Implementation and maintenance of such a program requires permanent commitments to sustain the quality of personnel and their enthusiasm to make a community-based program work over the long term.

The Marshal Program operated at the California Youth Authority's Southern reception center-clinic at Norwalk, California. Here a ninety-day program in a therapeutic community model was used to induce delinquent wards to examine their own deviant attitudes, problems, and conduct, and to find new outlooks in behavior styles.[25] The therapeutic community model was based on interpersonal and self-confrontation to work through behavior problems. The young participants were expected to account to themselves and their peers, as well as staff, working in the framework of a community. One significant conclusion was that delinquents with a minimum level of ego strength and social assertiveness tend to become differentially alienated and defensively reactive.

Great Britain began probation hostels for juveniles in 1914 to receive boys who had no proper home or surroundings, but did not need to be sent to the "reform school." [26] By 1967, there were about thirty-five such hostels, approximately one-third being for girls. These hostels are staffed by a "warden" and matron, who are usually a husband-and-wife team. There are one to three other staff members. There has been no systematic evaluation of the program, but the observation has been made that success or failure depends upon the personal qualities or personality of the persons involved, particularly the warden.

Outward Bound programs are designed to build up self-esteem and a feeling of self-worth in young offenders through achievement. Alper traces the beginnings of the concept involved in these programs to a World War II incident in Great Britain: a large number of seamen died without struggle when they had been forced to abandon ship in the cold waters of the North Atlantic, while some older seamen in poorer physical condition survived. A study of the reason for the older sailors'

---

[25] Doug Knight, *The Marshal Program: Assessment of a Short-Term Institutional Treatment Program, Part II: Amenability to Confrontive Peer-Group Treatment* (Sacramento: California Department of the Youth Authority, 1970), p. 92.

[26] Mark Monger, "Probation Hostels in Great Britain," *Federal Probation* (September 1967).

survival resulted in the establishment of the first Outward Bound School in Aberdobey, Wales, to develop more muscle in young merchant seamen. The experience resulted in the recognition of the value of structuring stressful situations to unify groups toward a common goal.[27] Following the British model, the Colorado Outward Bound Program School was opened in 1962 in the Rocky Mountains to emphasize mountaineering, back-packing, high-altitude camping, solo survival, and other related activities. In 1964, five Massachusetts adjudicated delinquents joined the program and twenty-five entered it a year later in programs in Minnesota and Maine. Massachusetts referred to its program as Homeward Bound and evolved this idea into a two-phase program lasting six weeks.

The Philadelphia Youth Development Center (YDC) is a century-old, battered, red brick building which provides the nucleus of a community-based effort to provide help for tough inner-city boys and girls between 15 and 18 years of age.[28] This facility became a juvenile center in 1958 and the state took it over in 1962. By 1972, there was both a day program and a conventional residential program with sixty beds for boys aged 16 to 18. The YDC has several other activities, including contracts with other agencies. One contract provides for three group homes run by Opportunities Industrialization Centers (OIC), a vocational training agency. One of these homes, the House of Umoja, is controversial because it is a grass-roots operation whose leaders lack formal training in social work. Residential living there is unorthodox because it serves youth who have been involved in gang wars. This facility opened in 1968 and has published six issues of a magazine called *Umoja* which (a Swahili word for "unity"). Its principles recognize "the strength of the family, tribal concepts, and African value systems," and it seems to be working.[29]

START (Short-Term Adolescent Residential Training) began in New York State in 1960 for 15- to 17-year-old delinquents. While it has several types of programs, the START project emphasizes group sessions in the evenings to allow for work or school during the day. It is a residential program in which the youths stay in the institution, going to school or working there as well, rather than going to community schools, as would be the case in most halfway houses. The STAY (Short-Term Aid Youth) program combines many of the START features, but the youth go back to their homes at night. Parent-youth group sessions under leadership of

[27] Benedict S. Alper, *Prisons Inside-Out: Alternatives in Correctional Reform* (Cambridge, Mass.: Ballinger, 1974), p. 136.

[28] Anthony Astrachan, "A Refuge from Gang Wars—Philadelphia Youth Utilizes Unusual Programs," *Corrections Magazine*, 1, No. 5 (May/June 1975), 41–48.

[29] Ibid., p. 45.

the director are also conducted. This is a relatively small program; each facility houses about twenty youths. There are boys' programs and girls' programs, but co-educational programs are rare.

The California Community Treatment Project in Sacramento pioneered in the differential approach to treatment of youthful offenders within the community setting. Since the beginning of Phases I (1961–1964) and II (1964–1969), the youthful offenders involved in the CTP have been classified according to their interpersonal maturity and assigned a parole agent selected for his ability to implement a treatment-controlled program developed at his level. The findings after the first two phases indicate that although more than 90 percent of the eligible youths appear to have been handled *at least as* effectively within the community as in traditional programs, no more than 50 percent have been handled *more* effectively. Phase III (1969–1974) corroborated this experience.

KEEPING NORMALS NORMAL

There are several agencies that serve *non*-delinquent children and youth. There is an old cliché that "a good, self-respecting delinquent wouldn't be found dead in a Boy Scout troop." In general, this attitude seems to be true. When young people have antisocial and resentful attitudes, their defensiveness usually prevents them from functioning in what they consider to be "Establishment" programs. Nevertheless, many of these programs are especially valuable for children who may be predelinquents—possibly the sons and daughters of offenders and ex-offenders—in an effort to keep them normal.

Big Brother, Inc., is designed to provide father figures—not substitutes for fathers—for children who need them.[30] The services of this group have been used effectively with nondelinquent children around the country.

The National Congress of Parents and Teachers, commonly called the Parent Teachers Association (PTA), maintains child protective committees, as mentioned previously. These committees are concerned with child abuses, dependency, and deviant behavior, including delinquency.

Boy Scouts, Girl Scouts, YMCA, YWCA, and similar organizations are resources that can be used for predelinquent and, sometimes, for delinquent children and youth.

Recreational programs have been considered to be helpful in communities, although their contribution to delinquency prevention has not been satisfactorily proved. Nevertheless, it is obvious that it is easier to

---

[30] Big Brother of America, Inc., 220 Suburban Station Building, Philadelphia, Penn. 19103.

get into trouble during leisure time than it is at work, at home, or during other activities. Theoretically, recreation could contribute much to keeping normals normal.

How the agencies that work generally with nondelinquents can be used in the criminal justice system by the community services officer is dependent upon the community resources and needs. A community services officer does well to know about all such community resources.

CONCLUSIONS

Community services for juveniles commonly focus on group homes, foster homes, and generalized services for juveniles in the community. These services are usually associated with the school, police, mental health clinics, and many private services, particularly walk-ins and programs for nondelinquents.

Delinquency prevention programs that center on the individual may miss their objectives. It is necessary to take a closer look at institutions. For example, schools under the present system can have a deleterious effect on adolescents in the lower socioeconomic groups who are bound to a working-class future at an early age. Suspension for truancy or misbehavior does not even approach resolving the problem, but is a way of eliminating it for the schools—not for society. Similar rejection techniques simply aggravate the problem for total society, whatever it does for the school administration. Failure in a system that has 95 percent or more of the people growing up under compulsory education is simply a perpetuation of the problem, regardless of how righteous a teacher or school administrator may feel. Failure in school tends to kill motivation; it fosters poor schoolwork and adjustment, and many students drop out as a result of this pattern. Negative labeling at an early age as "tough" or delinquent may encourage a child to "play the game." Continuous revision of school curriculum to meet realistically the needs of the students is needed. Community-based programs can do much to help in this area of delinquency prevention.

The family, particularly the father, is most important in delinquency prevention. A comparison of delinquents and nondelinquents on the basis of the presence or absence of the mother show a difference, but it is less statistically significant than is a comparison involving presence or absence of the father. In cultural terms, the father represents authority and the delinquent is in conflict with authority.[31]

The disastrous history of institutions for juvenile delinquents can be

---

[31] Keith J. Leenhouts, *A Father . . . A Son . . . And a Three Mile Run* (Grand Rapids, Mich.: Zondervan Publishing House, 1975).

linked to an unwillingness to discard old, ineffective concepts and to build on knowledge of the past. This chapter presents a case for institutional treatment of juvenile offenders that is community-based, involves the delinquent in his own fate, increases his self-respect, and allows him or her to experience positive human relations.[32]

---

[32] See Gisella Konopka, "Our Outcast Youth," *Social Work*, 15, No. 4 (1970), 76–86.

Chapter 13

The Youth Service Bureau

The Youth Service Bureau is an independent agency, either public or private, established to divert children from the criminal justice system. Because the criminal justice system can be damaging to children and youth, particularly if it places them in institutions and other settings in which all their peers have behavior problems, diversion from the system becomes important, particularly for those who are in the early stages of the development of deviant behavior patterns. The Youth Service Bureau serves to divert children and youth from the criminal justice system by (1) mobilizing community resources to resolve youth problems, (2) strengthening youth resources and developing new ones, and (3) promoting positive programs to remedy delinquency-breeding conditions.[1]

Recent changes in the juvenile court as a result of Supreme Court decisions have tended to move the informal court hearings "in the interests of the child" toward a more adversarial approach, and introduction of counsel and other changes have served to lengthen the formal procedures in the juvenile court. Consequently, some method must be found to retain the original intent of the juvenile court—which focused on the "interests of the child"—and, when possible, to divert as many children as possible from the formal criminal justice system. The Youth Service Bureau appears to perform that function; it is supported by the National Council on Crime and Delinquency along with other organizations and practitioners in the field of delinquency control.

---

[1] Sherwood Norman, *The Youth Service Bureau: A Key to Delinquency Prevention* (Paramus, N.J.: National Council on Crime and Delinquency, 1972).

The juvenile court was originally established in 1899 in Chicago as a choice court, which it remains today, in that the child may refuse to be heard in that court. If he chooses to be heard by the juvenile court, then he voluntarily waives the constitutional rights generally afforded an adult criminal in favor of the informal procedures intended to be in his interests. The principle of *parens patriae* originally placed the state in a position of responsibility for the welfare of its children, rather than in an adversary position, as would be the case with an adult offender. Subsumed under that principle was the concept of *non sui juris*, which meant that a juvenile court procedure was in equity and was not a contest.

The *Kent* case[2] had the effect of introducing counsel at the point of the waiver or at the point at which the child chose either to be heard or not in the juvenile court. This was based on the premise that, as Justice Abe Fortas wrote in his majority opinion, the child in the juvenile court "receives the worst of two worlds"—he receives neither the supportive treatment intended by the original juvenile court nor the protections guaranteed to a criminal offender by the Constitution of the United States. The *Gault* case[3] had the effect of introducing counsel *throughout* juvenile court procedure, bringing it closer to an adversarial procedure and separating out status offenses from delinquency by reserving acts that would be criminal were the offender an adult and able to relate to the constitutional guarantees, as opposed to those offenses that would not be a crime were the offender an adult (truancy, incorrigibility, violation of curfew laws, and similar acts that are offenses merely because the child is a minor). *Gault* eliminated the concept of *non sui juris*. *Winship* v. *New York*[4] moved the burden of proof in juvenile court from "preponderance of evidence" to "beyond a reasonable doubt," which is the burden of proof in adult criminal trials. *McKiever* v. *Pennsylvania*[5] held that the Fourteenth Amendment due process clause does not require a state to provide a jury trial in juvenile proceedings, as is provided for adults in the Sixth Amendment. The complications in due process introduced by the *Kent* and *Gault* cases, however, remain. The new juvenile court has become cumbersome, formalized, and the hearings have become protracted. The National Council on Crime and Delinquency recommends the Youth Service Bureau as an administrative device that could divert predelinquents and those children and youth without serious and

---

2 *Kent* v. *United States*, 383, U.S. 541-556, 1966.

3 *In re Gault*, 387 U.S. 1, L.Ed. 2nd 527, 1967.

4 *In re Winship*.

5 *McKiever* v. *Pennsylvania*, 403 U.S. S. 528, 1971.

dangerous behavior patterns from the juvenile court and let only the most serious cases be processed by the juvenile court.

THE YOUTH SERVICE BUREAU

The first recommendation for the Youth Service Bureau was by the President's Commission on Law Enforcement and Administration of Justice in 1967.[6] The purpose stated was that it should provide and coordinate programs for young people. In the same context, Youth Opportunity Centers and Neighborhood Youth Corps, sponsored by the Department of Labor, were seen as providing counseling and assistance. The primary need was seen as finding jobs for youth. In December 1968, the National Council on Crime and Delinquency received a grant from the Pinkerton Foundation to establish and publish nationwide guidelines for the Youth Service Bureau. The several youth service bureaus already in existence were sent letters of inquiry and questionnaires, ten youth service bureaus were visited, and a broad program of inquiry and consultation was instituted to determine the guidelines.

The first Youth Service Bureaus had been established in Chicago, Illinois, and in Pontiac, Michigan, in 1958. The Coordinating Service Center in Chicago was established under the Chicago Youth Commission with programs in high-delinquency areas. The Oakland County Youth Assistance Program (Pontiac, Michigan) was a citizen-oriented program jointly sponsored by the juvenile court, local municipal court, and the public school district. In 1964, a Youth Resources Department was sponsored and financed by the Town Meeting in Massachusetts in 1964 after a youth had been stabbed by a group of teenagers. About that time, a chief probation officer in Winston-Salem, North Carolina, was dismissed for using an ex-offender as a probation aide, a practice that has now become accepted and commonplace. Four other graduate probation officers resigned with him and secured funds from public and private places to establish a Youth Service Bureau sponsored by Wake Forest University. The first Youth Service Bureau to be initiated and funded by a state was in California in 1965, when four counties were funded by the State Delinquency Prevention Commission to the extent of $25,000 each.

A Youth Service Bureau must be (1) strictly nonauthoritative; (2) planned on a jurisdictionwide basis; (3) neighborhood-based for receiving referrals from law enforcement agencies, schools, and other sources; and (4) a coordinating agency to mobilize appropriate resources in behalf of the child or teenager and to follow through to assure appropriate service.

---

[6] *The Challenge of Crime in a Free Society* (Washington, D.C.: The President's Commission on Law Enforcement and Administration of Justice, 1967), p. 69.

PURPOSE

The magnitude of the juvenile delinquency problem can be demonstrated by the fact that the highest number of arrests in any age group in 1973 was at age 16, which is below the birthdates considered to be in the original jurisdiction of courts in all fifty states. The National Council of Crime and Delinquency recommends that the Youth Service Bureau make its services available to children 7 to 18 years of age.[7] The Youth Service Bureau has been organized under a variety of names, such as Youth Resources Bureau, Youth Assistance Program, Listening Post, Focus on Youth, and many other names. Because of the President's Commission on Law Enforcement and Administration of Justice, Youth Service Bureau is the name that has become more widespread. Its purpose is to provide help with solutions of problems before behavior reaches the point where judicial intervention becomes necessary.

The Youth Service Bureau can service all agencies in the community that work with youth.[8] It is available to youth at all times without appointment or other procedural delays. It relieves the courts of many minor cases and provides follow-up for troubled children who have not been adjudicated. It handles many informal adjustments in court cases, thereby relieving juvenile court counselors of much time-consuming work.

Police officers can use the Youth Service Bureau as an alternative to detention and court referral when detention is not really necessary. It facilitates communication between schools and the social agencies in the community, so that truancy and other school difficulties can be handled more effectively. It provides citizen volunteers with an opportunity to work constructively for youth and youth-serving agencies. Moreover, it provides an extension of services through citizen action for the private social agencies. The Youth Service Bureau provides an opportunity for the community as a whole to coordinate its services for children, rather than relying on the courts.

In short, the Youth Service Bureau is a brokerage agency in the community that assists in acquiring services of other agencies in behalf of the child. It can identify areas of need and develop resources not yet available by strengthening other agencies, pointing out areas of need, and monitoring services. This organization also assists in modifying attitudes and practices that discriminate against troublesome children in established agencies, such as the school, home, and other areas through consultation, demonstration, and political activities. It focuses on assist-

---

[7] Norman, *The Youth Service Bureau*, p. 8.

[8] Ibid., pp. 11–12.

Figure 13-1. Service Brokerage and Resource Development

Sherwood Norman, *The Youth Service Bureau: A Key to Delinquency Prevention* (Paramus, N.J.: National Council on Crime and Delinquency, 1972), p. 5.

ing children with beginning behavior problems in the home, school, and community. Suggested service brokerage patterns are shown in Figure 13-1.

ORGANIZATION

There is no single blueprint or prototype for a Youth Service Bureau.[9] Rather, the organization is dependent upon the agencies and other resources in the community. Each community has to determine what par-

_____
[9] Ibid., p. 13.

ticular type of organization can best divert its children and youth from the justice system and reduce the possibility of involvement in the courts. One suggested organization is shown in Figure 13-2 as a point of departure for organizing a Youth Service Bureau in which changes can be made in accordance with community needs and circumstances.

The Youth Service Bureau can be started by a citizen group or a private agency; it is possible to apply for funding from governmental or private foundations. The organization can be developed as a public agency or under private auspices. The National Council on Crime and Delinquency recommends that it not be run by an existing direct-service agency, either public or private. It should be a new and independent

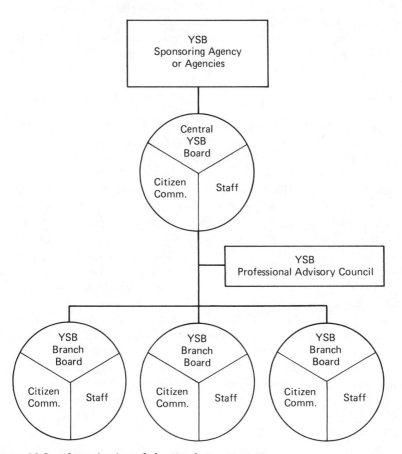

Figure 13-2.   Organization of the Youth Service Bureau

Sherwood Norman, *The Youth Service Bureau: A Key to Delinquency Prevention* (Paramus, N.J.: National Council on Crime and Delinquency, 1972), p. 28.

agency that is without existing prior contacts with other agencies. It needs sponsorship by state or local government or by a communitywide planning council if government sponsorship is not practical. A board should form a core of the citizen-action program that determines policies, target areas, and priorities. The size of the staff, of course, depends upon the area serviced. Volunteers to maintain close relationships with children, citizen committees to maintain contact with the community, and special committees on various projects are important. A variety of committees have been recommended by the National Council on Crime and Delinquency, mostly at the suggestion of Judge Arthur Moore of the Oakland County Probate Court (Pontiac, Michigan) who, in 1958, originated the idea of the Youth Service Bureau in its present form.[10] Some of these committees are nominating, membership, financing materials, needs, city and public relations, coordinating, education, case study, social resources, youth action, employment, recreation, organized faiths, juvenile justice, research, and volunteer pool committees.

EVALUATION

There have been several pertinent studies of the Youth Service Bureau. The Youth Development Program was established at Quincy, Illinois, by the University of Chicago's Committee on Human Development, to work with maladjusted, delinquent, and gifted children.[11] It opened in Quincy in February 1952 and was designed to last ten years to permit a longitudinal study to be made on children born in 1941–42. The population shifted so that an experimental group made up of 474 children at one time fluctuated and some new children were added, so 20 percent of the group had turned over during the first five years of the experiment. The control group was made up of 600 children not selected for the experiment. The results were considered to be most optimistic.

Five Youth Service Bureaus were evaluated in the publication by Sherwood Norman for the National Council on Crime and Delinquency.[12] While all the groups studied were different and from different parts of the country, the evaluations of all were consistently positive.

The Oakland County Youth Assistance Program at Pontiac, Michigan, began in 1958 with funds provided by the Oakland County Board of Commissioners. Grants from other foundations have supported it since.

---

10 Ibid., p. 27.

11 Paul H. Bowman, Robert F. DeHaan, John K. Kough, and Gordon P. Liddle, *Mobilizing Community Resources for Youth: Identification and Treatment of Maladjusted, Delinquent, and Gifted Children* (Chicago: University of Chicago Press, 1956).

12 Norman, *The Youth Service Bureau*, pp. 179–231.

TABLE 13-1   Problem Identification

In reviewing the reason for client referrals over the past
five years, we get the following breakdown:

School Truancy	1,346
Larceny	815
School Incorrigibility	542
Home Truancy	525
Breaking and Entering	404
Minor in Possession of Alcohol or Drugs	299
Neglect	255
Assault and Battery	167
Sex Violations	69
Other	2,092
Total	6,514

Five-year data from Oakland County Youth Assistance Program, Pontiac, Michigan.

Sherwood Norman, *The Youth Service Bureau: A Key to Delinquency Prevention* (Paramus, N.J.:
National Council on Crime and Delinquency, 1972), p. 213.

The problems with which it has dealt for a five-year period are shown
in Table 13-1.

A Youth Service Bureau was started in Pleasant Hill, California, in
1971 by the police department. It was funded by LEAA and is housed
in a building apart from the police headquarters.[13] It appears to have
achieved significant success, inasmuch as the number of young people
arrested in Pleasant Hill dropped from 360 in 1972 to 336 in 1973, while
referrals to the YSB increased from 236 to 443 during the same period.
At the same time, referrals to juvenile hall dropped from 167 to 140 and
referrals to probation decreased from 113 to 4.

CONCLUSIONS

A description and survey of fifty-eight programs that could be called
Youth Service Bureaus suggested a variety of level of effectiveness in
working with juveniles.[14] Three main influences in the development of
these programs were (1) the community; (2) the power base as a governmental unit funding source or an influential individual in the community; and (3) orientation of the staff, including the administration and
those individuals involved with the delivery of services. In other words,

[13] "Police Operate Diversion Program," *Target* (newsletter of innovative projects
funded by the Law Enforcement Assistance Administration), 4, No. 1 (January 1975), 1.

[14] *Youth Service Bureau—National Study—Final Report* (Sacramento: California Department of Youth Authority, 1972).

effectiveness most frequently depends upon interrelationships between the people involved in the community and the Youth Service Bureau.

Youth Service Bureaus have grown rather haphazardly in their focus, which centers on filling gaps in existing services. The role of such bureaus within the existing judicial–child welfare system has been a matter of concern.[15] Some have expressed fear that Youth Service Bureaus in some places have been used to get more money in some way, rather than conscientiously attempting to fill needs.

In general, the Youth Service Bureau has been evaluated as an agency having great potential for service for youth, and this potential has been constructively demonstrated in many places. Like many other small programs that are based locally and in the neighborhood, the personalities of the people operating individual groups often determine degree of success or failure. Most practitioners have concluded, however, that the Youth Service Bureau has provided considerable positive contribution to the youth and to the communities in which they function.

----

[15] J. A. Seymour, *Youth Service Bureaus—Current Status* (Chicago: University of Chicago Law School, 1971).

Chapter 14

Volunteers
in Community-Based Corrections

Volunteers have always been part of society's effort to help others in trouble, whether economically, in matters of health, in conflict with the law, or in any other type of debilitating circumstance. Man has always been a social animal, rather than a "loner," traveling in packs and tribes and families. Recent discoveries in Shanidar Cave in the rugged Zagros Mountains of northern Iraq have indicated that Neanderthals buried their dead with funeral rites, and other evidence suggests that human beings developed compassion and concern for one another as early as 60,000 B.C. It is obvious that people have volunteered to help other people since the dawn of history.

People have a basic need to be with other people. This explains lifetime monogamous marriage vows in most societies, the permanence of relationships, the predictability of credit ratings, and the confidence, trust, and the faith in fellow creatures that characterizes the lifestyle of civilized creatures. This is called socialization. People who do not live this way are called antisocial. A type of emotional interdependence, this also explains the need for pets, like dogs and cats—even the affection the old-time cowboy developed for his horse! This basic need to invest emotionally in others has given rise to the virtues of faith, hope, and charity and to the belief that man is, indeed, his brother's keeper. The familiar legend of the Good Samaritan suggests the value that people have long placed on assisting fellow beings in trouble without expecting compensation.

In criminal justice, the use of volunteers has accelerated vastly in the past few years. Municipal Judge Keith J. Leenhouts has been credited with organizing in 1959 the first volunteer group to work with misdemeanants in a Detroit suburb (see p. 245), although lay visitors and religious groups had been part of the volunteer movement in jails and prisons for a long time. In the 1960s, the volunteer movement grew rapidly, including the juvenile court, adult probation, and all other segments of the criminal justice system. By 1975, a group of volunteers in Virginia that had begun with jail visitation had evolved into a new system of jail management that placed control of the jail under control of citizens' board.[1]

EMERGENCE OF VOLUNTEERS IN CRIMINAL JUSTICE

Volunteer work has been an integral part of religious and philanthropic efforts throughout the centuries. In the field of criminal justice, probably the first organized volunteer groups involved prison visiting in England pioneered by John Howard (1773), Elizabeth Fry (1813), and the lesser known Sarah Martain (d. 1843).[2] After the death of Elizabeth Fry in 1845, a lay visitor's group for women was organized. However, there is no record of volunteers being allowed inside prisons until 1894, when the Ladies Visitors Association was formed and a small number of women were permitted to visit women prisoners. In the United States, such visiting was informal in a few prisons. On occasions, a "little old lady," sometimes considered to be "eccentric" and generally representing a religious denomination or group, would be permitted to visit older, long-term inmates who had not had visits or correspondence for a period of years. Some organized religious groups, such as the Salvation Army, of course, were permitted greater latitude.

Private individuals and groups have provided service to people in need when governmental agencies did not. Traditionally, the function of volunteers in private endeavors has been to fill gaps between governmental social services and the actual need. Only recently has the government concerned itself with the living conditions of citizens, beginning with the Child Labor Laws of 1912, which resulted from the first White House Conference on Children, called by President Teddy Roosevelt in 1910. In May 1854 a bill designed to provide government land for a mental health institution was vetoed on the basis that standards and conditions of living of individual citizens was not the proper concern of government. It was not until the Great Depression of the 1930s when, under

---

[1] "Civilians Manage Virginia Jail," *The VIP Examiner*, 4, No. 3 (Summer 1975), 1.

[2] Hugh L. Parsons, "The Prison Visitor in English Prisons," Proceedings of the Eightieth Annual Congress of Correction (St. Louis), October 8–13, 1950 (New York: American Prison Association, 1951), p. 4537.

Franklin D. Roosevelt, vast social changes that instituted Social Security and other governmental programs in welfare and mental health became a "proper concern of government." In the meantime, volunteer, religious, and philanthropic organizations filled these gaps.

The Citizens Participation Committee was organized in the American Prison Association in the late 1940s after World War II. In 1958, it listed the following volunteers' functions: (1) visiting correctional and penal institutions to understand their programs and purposes; (2) visiting individual offenders to offer constructive personal interest; (3) giving personal aid in institutional programs in recreation, education, vocational training, and religious activities; (4) giving services as sponsors or friendly advisors to parolees, probationers, and youth in trouble; (5) helping to expand existing programs in institutions and obtaining donations to purchase equipment for recreation and other activities within the institution; (6) promoting the development of new facilities and agencies for corrections as required by making the community aware of the need; (7) working with heads and staffs of institutions and correctional agencies, publicizing their programs to the public; (8) promoting legislation needed in correctional services; (9) working for improvement of neighborhoods and eradicating conditions that caused crime and delinquqency; and (10) working with organizations to promote correctional programs.[3] Even in 1958, volunteers in the criminal justice system were not well accepted and were sometimes seen by correctional administrators and practitioners as being "meddlesome." Prison personnel frequently viewed them as potentially dangerous to the safety and security of the institution, and volunteers were definitely not encouraged.

In 1959, eight citizens sat around a table to discuss the courts' problems with Judge Keith J. Leenhouts in Royal Oak, Michigan. The volunteer program was begun at that time with persons over 17 charged with misdemeanors.[4] Within nine months, there were thirty volunteers and seventy-five probationers. A chief probation officer was then hired to spend some overtime supervising the volunteers; he was paid by private donations from local businessmen. Additional coordinators of volunteers were hired on the same basis. By 1965, the city of Royal Oak provided a budget of $17,000 and private contributors contributed about $8,000. A staff of seven retirees administered the program, and twelve part-time professional chief counselors worked with the probationers and coordinated the volunteers. A part-time staff psychiatrist coordinated the efforts

---

3 Leon T. Stern, "Citizen Participation: A Record of Action," Proceedings of the Eighty-Ninth Annual Congress of Correction (Detroit), September 7–12, 1958 (New York: American Correction Association, 1959), p. 336.

4 Keith J. Leenhouts, "Royal Oak's Experience with Professionals and Volunteers in Probation," *Federal Probation*, 34 (December 1970), 45–51.

of thirty-five volunteer psychiatrists from nearby hospitals and private practices. Three retirees did pre-sentence investigations with assistance from volunteer psychiatrists and psychologists. About 20 percent of all probationers are assigned to volunteers. [Judge Leenhouts is now executive director of VIP-NCCD (Volunteers in Probation, Inc., a Division of National Crime and Delinquency) and spends all his time developing volunteer programs in the criminal justice system.] Other organizations also exist for this purpose. Conservatively estimated, the number of volunteer programs at all court levels in the United States has grown from 3 or 4 in 1961 to 2,000 or more in 1972.[5] The use of volunteers in the criminal justice system has continued to increase.

WHAT VOLUNTEERS DO

Volunteers can function in many areas and can provide many services. Many coordinators of volunteers have indicated that they could use anybody who volunteered in some way. A person who gets along well with other people, adults or juvenile, male or female, can be used by establishing a relationship with the offender. In essence, the volunteer becomes a "buddy," who can spend time with the offender in a variety of ways. For adults, such volunteers are generally probation aides or unpaid volunteers who assist probation agents or help with the supervision of specific members of his caseload. Many volunteers work with misdemeanants not on official probation. Probably the largest number of volunteers work with juveniles.

The volunteer in many cases can provide the family functions that have been missed, for both juveniles and adults. A substitute father is most important for the growing child, and a relationship with a strong "father figure" on whom they can depend is helpful for many adults who have missed that experience during childhood. A substitute mother is also important for a growing child and an adult—she can provide the compassion and emotional support that a person may have missed in growing up. One of the primary functions of a volunteer is to provide the growing child and the grown adult with meaningful relationship with a person he or she can trust. Few children and adults in trouble have had that experience.

If a volunteer has any deficiencies that might render him or her ineffective in working with children or adults, there are many other services that can be performed which do not require close contact with the offender. Clerical work, such as serving as a receptionist, answering the telephone, typing, filing, and similar tasks are necessary. Some volunteers

---

[5] Personal letter from Dr. Ivan Scheier, Director of the National Information Center on Volunteers in Courts (NOVIC), Boulder, Colorado, November 12, 1972.

are needed to canvass the job market. Many can write grant requests, participate in fund drives, and contact professional persons and agencies to generate volunteer professional services.

Volunteer professional services are constant needs. Many volunteer coordinators and their staffs spend a great deal of time enlisting the services of doctors, dentists, psychiatrists, psychologists, social workers, and other professionals in the field. Many persons in these professions will donate their services to a few offenders—particularly children—at the request of a volunteer. Many consider it to be good public relations and "goodwill."

Important functions of volunteers were identified in a project, Judicial Concern for Children in Trouble, sponsored jointly by the National Counsel of Juvenile Court Judges and the National Congress of Parents and Teachers in 1971–1972. This project was funded by the Sears Roebuck Foundation and the LEAA. (See Table 14-1.)

Realistically, there are many other jobs that a volunteer can do. One publication lists 192 separate jobs that have been assigned to volunteers.[6] For example, volunteer services provided at the Lane County, Oregon, Juvenile Department included (1) recreation and instruction in grooming, woodworking, sewing, cooking and baking, arts and craft, sport, and games; (2) special activities and entertainment in detention, such as variety shows, musical entertainment, dance and party arrangements, and programs for holidays and special occasions; (3) education, including library, field placement from the university of Oregon for education and special-interest speakers; (4) religious services, provided through the local ministerial association; (5) annual projects such as a Christmas project and open house; (6) counseling assistance; (7) clerical assistance; (8) administrative assistance in recruiting, screening, evaluating, trainnig, assigning, and supervising volunteers, public relations projects, a speakers' bureau, and coordination with other agencies; (9) donations of gifts, money, or equipment; (10) advisory functions to promote juvenile operations and develop community programs and community interest in the problems of youth.[7]

BEGINNING A VOLUNTEER PROGRAM

The beginning of a volunteer program is with planned action. This action should include the following steps: (1) gain the support of the

---

[6] Ivan H. Schier and Judith A. Berry, *Serving Youth as Volunteers* (Boulder, Col.: The National Information Center on Volunteers in Court, 1972), pp. 15–17.

[7] Jewel Goddard and Gerald Jacobson, "Volunteer Services in a Juvenile Court," *Crime and Delinquency*, 13 (April 1967), 537–43.

TABLE 14-1

1. Providing a child in trouble with a meaningful one-to-one relationship with an adult he can trust.
2. Private tutoring in school subjects to help the child learn academic and vocational skills away from the school setting, thereby allowing him to keep up in subjects he might be failing and to avoid school phobia that leads to dropping out of school.
3. Providing experience in the constructive use of leisure time, taking the child to ball games, fishing trips, and other acceptable recreational pursuits to replace his habitual leisure time pursuits that seem to bring him close to trouble.
4. Providing the child an image of normalcy in society in a meaningful way, including participation in socially accepted groups, such as organized athletic and other competion in leagues or with other long term experiences, Boy Scouts, and similar experiences with "establishment" groups that can be gratifying to him.
5. Obtaining volunteers from indigenous groups where the child in trouble lives can be of assistance in counseling delinquents, drug users, bitter children from minority groups, or any other indigenous group. Crisis rap sessions, bad trip counseling, and similar activities can help avoid more serious crises.
6. Implementing various programs in detention homes and other facilities for children in trouble.
7. Retired professionals can assist other working professionals and can work alone in volunteer services. These retired professionals in social work, psychology, psychiatry, dentistry, medicine, law, and other professions can work as general volunteers, or, probably better, serve the court or volunteer program in their specialties in service to the children and/or in training the volunteers.
8. Volunteers can maintain constructive liaison with the newspapers, radio, television, and other news media to interpret the available services, needs, problems, and objectives of the court to the public and to the political leadership.

There were other functions generally thought to be governmental services that could be rendered by volunteers, but which were questioned by some people responsible for volunteer programs in the juvenile court. Some wanted functions eliminated that others called essential. Functions accepted by most people were:

9. Responding constructively to the child's negative questions as to "What's your angle? What are you getting out of this? Getting your kicks?" To promote socially accepted approaches to constructive association, communication, and counseling without monetary reward as a normal form of social interaction. Help the child view the volunteer as not on the payroll of the establishment, but with wholesome and sincere concern for the child in trouble.
10. Accepting the child in the family so he can get a "new look" at men, women, and others in a normal family relationship. This keeps him from stereotyping all people in the image of his own father, mother, or other persons who might not fit society's role definitions or what the normal expectations are.
11. Provide the child with an improved self-concept by teaching him to be competent in some field, such as chess or auto mechanics, or by giving him a new look at authority or an adult that is supportive and friendly.
12. Provide leadership for parent group sessions. This was considered to be a must by some.
13. Provide leadership for group sessions for the children in trouble.
14. Help reduce the paranoid, picked-on feeling that emerges in some minority racial and ethnic groups. Social distance like this can be reduced or accepted by identification with pride to

TABLE 14-1   (Continued)

reduce or counteract the negative connotations associated with social distance.

15. Canvas the job market and serve as an employment coordinator. Getting jobs for children in trouble. This was considered to be "a must" by some.

16. Provide free charm school lessons for girls to learn the social graces and improve self-concept. Provide free beauty parlor and hairdo services.

17. Interpreting needs and problems to the public and to political leaders who can help provide resources for the court. This was considered to be classified information by some who thought volunteers should not be involved in this function.

Some of the functions suggested for volunteers in the four regional meetings, but which were rejected by two or three respondents as inappropriate for volunteers although they had enough support to warrant inclusion in the listing of functions as possible, depending upon local opinion and practice, were as follows:

18. Counseling after a trusting relationship has been developed in order to enhance insight in the child.

19. Serve as a confidant who will not "squeal" or "rat" on the child in trouble so he can develop the capacity to relate to others through trust, which provides the child with an alternative from the survival-of-the-fittest milieu to which he has become accustomed.

20. Front for the child in trouble as an advocate in court, school, and elsewhere to provide the child with a new look at authority that is supporting and accepting, rather than aggressive and hostile.

21. Promote acceptance of his father by the child, since the father-function is most important in delinquency situations that involve conflict with authority. Further, the volunteer may have become a threat to the father, a situation that must be made easier by bringing the father into a meaningful and acceptable relationship in some way.

22. Obtaining volunteer professional services, such as those involving an optometrist, dentist, physician, psychiatrist, psychologist, social worker, nurse, or other professional person. While three respondents said that this should be outside the function of the volunteer, three also wrote special comments that it was most important.

23. Expose the child in trouble to establishment institutions in an accepting way, such as museums, art galleries, the church, and other places where he will make cultural contacts in an accepting manner. There is considerable neglect of this exposure to many children in trouble, sometimes leading to outright hostility toward agencies and institutions representing "the Establishment."

24. Provide secretarial, receptionist, and clerical assistance in the office of the juvenile court, detention home, and other agencies concerned with children in trouble.

25. Provide constructive means of relieving tensions, such as boxing, swimming, debating, and other means of constructive competition.

26. Hold formal classes in volunteer education, whether academic, vocational, self-improvement, motivational, social problems, or other classes.

27. Assist the child in emotional maturation so he can learn to postpone immediate gratification for future reward.

28. Writing grant requests and participating in fund drives.

Vernon Fox, A Handbook for Volunteers in Juvenile Court, Special Issue of Juvenile Justice, 23, No. 4 (February 1973), 10–11. Also in the Juvenile Justice Textbook Series, National Council of Juvenile Court Judges, Reno, Nevada, 1973.

court staff and judge or the administration and staff of an institution that needs volunteers, (2) recruit volunteers, (3) select and train volunteers, (4) assign volunteers, (5) volunteer actions, and (6) give direction to volunteer programs.

Judge Leenhouts has what he calls his eleven "S" suggestions:

1. *Start.* There will always be thousands of reasons why you should delay. The key is to start.
2. *Start small.* It is easy to make adjustments if you start small.
3. *Selection.* Of the initial volunteers this is extremely important. You can start with the very best of the very best in your community. They will attract similar volunteers and ensure the excellence of your program. Quality is a must.
4. *Spirit.* Here it is important. A good feeling of spirit must be developed.
5. *Science.* It is critically important. While spirit is very essential, so are good techniques carefully utilized.
6. *Supervision.* Training and orientation are very important. On-going continuing supervision of volunteers is absolutely vital. So hence, support and supervision of volunteers are the keys to a good program.
7. *Selection of Mechanics.* Do your own thing in your own way. It is very important that you do not carbon-copy the mechanics of others. Learn from others but do not merely copy.
8. *Sweat.* Put your heart in the right place and then put your sweat where your heart is. Love and concern are very important and there is no such thing as a lazy love and concern.
9. *Superior.* Start a superior program from the very beginning. You may not do very much but do it very well. Perhaps you can only start out with shoplifters or those guilty of disorderly conduct. However, meet regular [sic] with your volunteers and do a superior job from the very beginning and you will gain the respect of others and, more important, self-respect.
10. *Screening.* As your program gets larger, be sure you have good screening program for volunteers.
11. *Staff.* Prepare them for the volunteers.[8]

Recruiting volunteers can be accomplished in several ways and is probably best done to accommodate local conditions and attitudes. Many prefer starting out by word of mouth and approaching three to six peo-

---

[8] Keith J. Leenhouts, "Thoughts on Beginning a Volunteer Program," *VIP Examiner*, 1, No. 3 (Fall 1972), 6.

ple individually. As the nucleus of the program stabilizes, other methods can be used. The advantage of informal, one-to-one recruiting is that people can be selected on the basis of personality and competence before they are approached—further, they tend to respond more favorably to personal invitations.

After the nucleus of the program has been established, broader approaches to recruiting can be initiated as needed. Volunteers generally come from civic organizations, church groups, persons already in "people-helping" occupations (such as social work and education), retirees, and friends of volunteers. Presentations before organized civic and church groups, and presentations and "commercials" in the newspapers, radio, and television can elicit volunteers. The PTA is a natural source for volunteers to work with children and youth.

Volunteers are frequently rejected because of (1) unsuitable personality characteristics, (2) overly authoritarian demeanor, (3) immaturity, (4) lack of transportation, (5) inability to make a dependable and durable commitment of time to the program, and (6) lack of daily or weekly availability.[9]

It is an advantage to have volunteers in a program—many experts in the field of volunteerism hold that any program should because (1) they help maintain a friendly climate, (2) they learn from the experience and become better citizens, (3) they help in propagating public understanding of the work of the agency for which they have volunteered, (4) they furnish greatly needed personnel, and (5) they make it possible for the agency to expand its service without increasing its budget.[10]

The personality of volunteers is of vital importance for relationships with people in trouble. It takes a dedicated, stable, and mature person to deal effectively with people in need. Many people with these qualities have experienced emotional trauma themselves.[11]

After volunteers have been selected, training is most important. In general, about 50 percent of the training period should be devoted to general education (psychology, social problems, communications, report writing, and public speaking.)[12] Approximately 25 percent should be

[9] *Supervisor Appraisal of Volunteer* form of the Volunteer Services Unit, Minnesota Department of Corrections.

[10] R. W. Tyler, "The Role of the Volunteer," *California Youth Authority* (California Department of the Youth Authority in conjunction with Stanford University), 18, No. 4 (1965), 15–23.

[11] *Guide for Associate Degree Program in the Community and Social Services* (New York: The Council on Social Work Education in cooperation with the American Association of Junior Colleges, 1970), pp. 19–20.

[12] Theresa Yancey, "Cook County Juvenile Court Augments Service," *Source* (publication of the Illinois Information Center on Volunteers in Courts), 1, No. 4 (1971), 3.

devoted to a study of social services—for example, social welfare, family, abnormal psychology, Black culture in America, the culture of poverty, and juvenile delinquency. And 25 percent of the training time should be devoted to technical skills, such as are involved in interviewing, group leadership, and social change. In addition, there should be some field experience outside the training classrooms, always with an experienced volunteer.

Some of the basic competencies to be learned in training for volunteer work in community-based corrections agencies must be the following:

1. Ability to understand and withstand provocative behavior without becoming punitive

2. Development of objectivity in accepting relationships with all clients in a nonjudgmental manner, without either punitive or sentimental emotional involvement

3. Ability to accept a person without personal involvement, with neither punitive nor sentimental views, much the same as a physician views a patient—this does not mean complete detachment but rather an empathic relationship

4. Knowledge of on-the-job counseling techniques

5. Ability to say "No"—with reasons when necessary, and ability to say "Yes" with equal reason

6. Sensitivity to pathological behavior as compared with normal random behavior, sufficient to permit intelligent referral to professional staff and/or agencies

7. Ability to assess strengths of an individual to determine what there is to build on in the treatment of an offender

8. Ability to make referrals to all staff, community resources, and other specialties with some understanding and sophistication

9. Ability to use tact to avoid creating or aggravating problem situations

10. Ability to use tact to ameliorate developing problem situations

11. Willingness to augment and support the staff of the agency or institution

12. Ability to observe and accurately record (a) individual behavior as pathological or manipulative and consequently might need referral to professional staff; (b) group behavior signaling the beginning of a potentially dangerous association; and (c) miscellaneous behavior that may be part of illicit activity or regression to earlier behavioral patterns

13. Ability to assess community and family attitudes toward the offender

14. Ability to constructively interpret agency or community attitudes and behavior toward the person on the volunteer's caseload
15. Ability to serve as an upward communicator from the offender to the agency or institution with a view toward improving services and policies
16. Ability to maintain discreet silence on some critical issues and "classified" information to maintain (a) staff morale, (b) caseload morale, and (c) good public relations
17. Ability to exert external controls by persuasion on individuals who need containment
18. Knowledge of specific procedures that might be modified or elaborated in training programs, consultations, or other ways by which the agency or institutional staff can assist the volunteer in understanding situations and desirable policy
19. Knowledge of the constitutional and civil rights of persons on the caseload and ability to incorporate that knowledge into the supervisory process
20. Ability to interpret the system of justice, including laws of arrest, judicial procedure, and a total correctional process, in order to answer correctly questions put by the offender.[13]

Volunteers can be trained at various times: (1) during screening of applicants, (2) after the screening, (3) during the orientation, (4) in the traditional training classes before assignment, (5) in small-group discussions, (6) through contact with staff, (1) in large-group meetings, (8) during periodic in-service training programs, and (9) through direct supervision.[14]

COORDINATION OF VOLUNTEERS

Because volunteers are unpaid and their services are based on their desire to serve, they cannot be *supervised,* but it is important that they be *coordinated.* Their identification with the court has to be recognized in some way, however, in order to sustain interest in and loyalty to the objectives and functions of the court or institution with which they are identified. In some cases, a certificate suitable for framing is given the

[13] Adapted from Vernon B. Fox, *Guidelines for Corrections Programs in Community and Junior Colleges* (Washington, D.C.: American Association of Junior Colleges, 1969), pp. 18–19.

[14] James D. Jorgensen and Ivan H. Scheier, *Training the Volunteer in Courts and Corrections* (Metuchen, N.J.: The Scarecrow Press, 1972).

volunteer, together with an identification card. When this is done, however, a termination date should be noted and a new certificate and card issued as the volunteer continues services. This protects the court or institution in case of termination of services for any of a variety of reasons.

The coordinator of volunteers is generally a full-time, paid employee of the pertinent court or institution. This person is responsible for recruiting, selecting, training, assigning, providing "supervision," evaluating, and termination of volunteers. Raising funds for various purposes from private and governmental sources is an important function of the coordinator, although much of this may be done by other people. It is important for this person to be well acquainted with civic groups and other community resources, just as it is for the community services officer or the administrator of community-based correctional facilities or programs.

The judge or the administrator is always boss. In a court, the volunteer coordinator must keep the judge and the chief probation officer informed of his or her activities, objectives, and intentions. Similarly, the administrator of an institution in which volunteers work must be so informed. In all cases, the coordinator must remain in concert with the policies of the judges and administrators. As an elected or politically appointed official, the judge is sensitive to attitudes and sentiments within his community—nobody in a position of responsibility likes to be surprised! When news reporters and prominent citizens ask the judge or the administrator about an incident or policy, the information should be available. It is just as much the responsibility of employees to keep the boss informed as it is the responsibility of the boss to keep employees informed about policy.

Liaison with schools and law enforcement is important in coordination of volunteers. Good working relationships with the police are important in any criminal justice activity, particularly community-based programs. School programs of all sorts, counseling, recreation, athletics, and other extracurricular activities can be a resource for the coordinator. The PTA—particularly the Childen's Protective Committee—can be helpful in a variety of ways.

Supervision of volunteers is the most important part of coordinating, even though the coordinator has no formal authority. Such "supervision" must be accomplished diplomatically and skillfully. Frequent consultation about cases and their progress is essential. Supervision is incorporated in all phases of relationships with the volunteers, including the training procedure.

Assignment of cases to volunteers is a matter of judgment based on assessment of personality compatibility between the offender and the volunteer, as well as other factors, such is capability and interest. On occasion, the coordinator may have to reassign volunteers to other cases. Sometimes it will be necessary to terminate the services of the volunteer. When this happens, the judge, chief probationer officer, and/or administrator must be consulted before termination. Most volunteers are stable and significant people in the community. This is why they make good volunteers. The danger of political repercussions because of the frustration and anxiety of an unwisely handled terminated volunteer could cause unnecessary problems for the agency.

The public relations function of the coordinator of volunteers includes not only presentations to civic groups and interviews with the news media, but also the all-important everyday one-to-one relationships in the community.

RELATIONSHIPS BETWEEN VOLUNTEERS AND OFFENDERS

The relationships between volunteers and offenders is a one-to-one partnership. They will spend considerable time together. The volunteer does not "lecture" or "moralize" to the offender, but functions as a friend. This is a relationship of interdependency. The volunteer must be strong, stable, and utterly dependable. He or she can serve as a friendly advocate on the side of the juvenile or adult offender in a crisis situation, whether it involves school, relationships on the job, law enforcement agencies, or court situations.

There are several basic principles that must be remembered by the volunteer in his relationship with the offender:

1. Listen to the juvenile or adult offender. Nothing can be learned about another person when somebody else is talking. The more the volunteer talks himself, the less he learns about the offender.
2. Accept the juvenile or adult offender as he is—without being judgmental. Nobody tries religiously to be bad and everybody wants to be accepted and loved. Deviant behavior is a failing attempt to resolve personal and social problems. Rejection aggravates the problem.
3. Give the juvenile or adult offender a meaningful relationship with an adult he can trust, probably for the first time in his or her life. Socialization is based on faith, trust, and confidence. Without experiencing trust of adults no person, juvenile or adult, can possibly be socialized. Rather, they have to deal with people at arm's length.
4. Develop the capacity to withstand provocative behavior, since juvenile and adult offenders who think they are being "picked on" tend to

fight back by baiting and taunting authority. Faced with the usual hostile responses, the offender's negative relationship with authority will be reinforced. An accepting reaction to hostility will provide a "new look" at authority and enhance the socialization of the offender who is in conflict with authority.

5. Don't give advice, because people asking for advice are "shopping" and compare opinions of various people. It is much more effective to respond with questions about what other factors are present and what would happen if various alternatives were taken. Advice places the counselor or volunteer in the position of being "an S.O.B." if the offender fails or encounters further problems while following that advice. Most important, the advice is not "his"—he has not worked through it, and is not committed to it. Rather than having thought through his problem with the questioning and suggesting help of his counselor or volunteer, he is "following instructions" as from a cookbook or manual, simply hoping the advice works. If it does not, the relationship will have been destroyed.[15]

A probation and parole supervisor must maintain close contact with the volunteer who works with him. It has been suggested that he (1) discuss plans for each case assigned to the volunteer; (2) develop specific goals for each case; (3) stay in contact with the volunteer, calling or telephoning him or her at least once a month; and (4) get to know the volunteer, since that person is willing to give his or her time and skills, so that the supervisor can be considered to be a friend.[16]

EVALUATION

Evaluation is the "bookkeeping" of any social program. No program can operate on a "faith, hope, and charity" basis. Adequate records must be kept as to what was done, when, why, with an evaluation of the results. Nearby colleges and universities can provide assistance in evaluation; graduate students are often available who can provide evaluation services as part of their supervised study. In fact, many have used these evaluations as theses and dissertations for advanced degrees.

Volunteer programs have been shown to significantly increase the

---

[15] Vernon Fox, *A Handbook for Volunteers in Juvenile Court*, Special Issue of *Juvenile Justice*, 23, No. 4 (February 1972), 23.

[16] "Get the Volunteers Involved or They Will Be Lost," *The Focus* (publication of the Florida Parole and Probation Commission), 9, No. 1 (January–February 1975), 7.

effectiveness of probation [17] and decrease the repetition of offenses. Success may relate to the frequency of contacts that enhance relationships, rather than a specific type of counseling or a particular person.

Although the San Francisco Project was originated for purposes of evaluation of caseloads in the probation office of the Northern District of California and is, therefore, beyond the scope of the definition of community-based corrections, it did point out that low caseloads can result in improved supervision.[18] It is reasonable, then, to conjecture that the one-to-one relationship between a volunteer and an offender in a community-based correctional setting could be more effective than supervision in a group of probationers or parolees.

SAMPLE VOLUNTEER PROGRAMS

As is the case with other community-based programs, the number of volunteer programs must be counted in the thousands. A few examples of these programs indicate the range of their services.

Probably 30,000 to 40,000 citizens throughout the United States are working as volunteers in jails.[19] The largest and most effective jail program is the Offender Aid and Rehabilitation Program (OAR) that exists throughout Virginia. It was begun in 1971 in Fairfax County as a one-to-one counseling program to prepare inmates to return to the community.

Partners, Inc., has been an integral part of Denver's juvenile justice system since 1968.[20] This group matches volunteers (senior partners) with juveniles between 10 and 18 years of age. They meet for a minimum of three hours per week. River rafting is a favorite recreation in this area, with trips lasting two to five days with four-partner teams. Since the partner River Raft Project began in the summer of 1971, over 500 partner teams have participated, at an annual operating budget of $30,000. An evaluation at the end of 1974 indicated that the project was successful in several ways, including reduced recidivism and concern for the environment.

---

[17] Gerald Rosenbaum, James L. Gisell, Thomas Koscheial, Richard Know, and Keith J. Leenhouts, "Community Participation in Probation: A Tale of Two Cities," Proceedings of the American Psychological Association, Seventy-Seventh Annual Convention (Washington, D.C.), 1969, pp. 863–64.

[18] William P. Adams, Paul M. Chandler, and M. G. Neithercutt, "The San Francisco Project: A Critique," Federal Probation, 35 (December 1971), 45–53.

[19] Law & Justice (New York: The Ford Foundation, 1974), p. 59.

[20] "Troubled Denver Youngsters Helped while Rafting," Target (newsletter of Innovative Projects Funded by the Law Enforcement Assistance Administration), 4, No. 5 (May 1975), 6.

Volunteers in Partnership, Inc., is located at the Family Court, Hall of Justice, Rochester, New York, to serve juveniles through one-to-one counseling with an adult. This is one of the hundreds of volunteer programs identified with juvenile courts in the United States.

The Connecticut Prison Association has a volunteer program at the adult level which works with men and women in prison and in the community. There are 275 volunteers working around the state. In this successful program, women work with men as well as women. Using a grant from the American Bar Association, young lawyers also work with parolees and others who have legal problems.

A volunteer group in Louisville, Kentucky, formed the organization called Families United for Hope in 1975.[21] The group is made up of mothers, fathers, wives, and others who have a relative incarcerated in Kentucky correctional institutions. They meet once a month to share and exchange ideas as to how to solve problems and to give each other support and assistance in understanding and helping their relatives in prison. The Kentucky Volunteers in Corrections, which was organized in April 1975, started simultaneously.

Volunteers in Tennessee Corrections, Inc., was formed in Nashville, Tennessee, in July 1973, with LEAA funding, when the Division of Probation and Parole assigned a counselor to serve as project director for the American Bar Association's Volunteer Parole Aide Program.[22] Thirty attorneys volunteer their time as aides to parole counselors to help find employment and housing for parolees and offer general emotional support as a "helping friend." By mid-1975, this group had sixty-five volunteers, including college students, housewives, professionals, and retired persons, in addition to the attorneys.

The National Center for Voluntary Action in Washington, D.C., was begun in 1972 at the national level to initiate and coordinate volunteer groups throughout the United States in all areas of endeavor. This program has been quite effective in some cities.

CONCLUSIONS

Volunteer programs have been growing rapidly in the 1960s and 1970s. They have helped citizens understand the objectives and problems of the criminal justice system and have involved them in attempting to help people in trouble. Existing programs are characterized by under-

---

[21] "Inmate Family Group Formed," *The Kentucky Inter-Prison Press*, 3, No. 5 (April 1975), 8.

[22] *Target* (newsletter of Innovative Projects Funded by LEAA), 3, No. 4, Issue 3 (March 1975), 4.

staffing, underfunding, and misunderstanding, so volunteers provide valuable and much-needed services.

In 1965, for example, there were 7,706 persons employed in community-based juvenile correctional programs (primarily juvenile courts), while the estimated need was 15,800 persons[23] to handle an average daily juvenile population in the community of 285,431. In 1968, there were approximately 900,000 cases of delinquency involving about 774,000 children.[24] In addition, there were 554,000 traffic cases and 141,000 dependency and neglect cases referred to juvenile court. Further, more than 500,000 runaways and other missing children are reported each year.[25] The number of children actually missing has been estimated as closer to a million.

It is obvious that the number of personnel employed in community-based corrections programs cannot possibly manage the many duties that must be performed for effective handling of cases. In fact, those available have all they can do to process cases administratively through the judicial system in terms of writing pre-hearing social histories, handling complaints, and other routine matters. There simply is not adequate time for counseling or casework. For example, the average workload for a staff member in a child guidance clinic is twelve to fifteen children with problems. Consequently, the use of volunteers is the only possible solution to a very difficult problem. Volunteers are indeed vital to an effective community-based corrections system.

---

23 *Task Force Report: Corrections* (Washington, D.C.: The President's Commission on Law Enforcement and the Administration of Justice, 1967), p. 97.

24 *Juvenile Court Statistics—1968* (Washington, D.C.: Office of Juvenile Delinquency and Youth Development, HEW, 1970), p. 3.

25 *The National Missing Youth Locater*, Vol. 1 (Hayward, Cal.: NMYL Publishing Co., 1971), p. 3.

Chapter 15

Problems
in Community-Based Corrections

Community-based corrections is so new as a recognized component of the criminal justice system that many problems have not yet been worked out. Governmental participation and recognition has come relatively recently. Halfway houses began to develop in the 1950s, volunteer programs started in about 1959, and full governmental recognition of community-based programs came with passage by Congress of the Prisoners Rehabilitation Act of 1965.

The diversion programs that began in the 1960s were a step beyond probation; they were intended to keep people out of the criminal justice system. More and more offenders were kept in the community, either at home or in halfway houses. Today community-based corrections has taken its place as a legitimate component of the correctional phase of the criminal justice system.

BEHAVIOR OF RESIDENTS

Persons with behavior problems serious enough to have attracted the attention of the criminal justice system through its law enforcement agencies understandably find it difficult to adopt a different lifestyle. A judgment has to be made as to the seriousness of the behavior patterns involved and what type of control is necessary to begin to neutralize deviant behavior patterns. It is at this point that the decision must be made by the courts, the police, and the probation agent representing the correctional phase of the criminal justice system, about whether to send the offender to prison, place him on parole, or use a halfway house or other community-based correctional program. It must be noted that the police, the courts, and correctional programs all have to share in this decision. In addition, the victim must agree if a diversion program is to be used. Usually only the most hopeful cases, generally involving non-violent property offenses, are admitted.

Even with this screening process, effort has to be made to help the offender handle his deviant behavior. The directors and program managers of community-based correctional facilities and agencies must use counseling, casework, and group methods involving peer-group pressure to help offenders learn to sustain responsible behavior.

Although the majority of people in these community correctional programs do not embarrass themselves or the administrator of the program, a few of them do. Probably the most frequent violation is in stopping for a drink, taking too many, and as a result not being able to report back to the facility. When this happens, many persons have just kept going, sometimes stealing a car and otherwise compounding the problem. Some have just made unauthorized trips. Others have used drugs in violation of their trust. Most serious, of course, are those instances in which a person, in the course of events, and frequently under the influence of alcohol or drugs, commits a serious offense, such as burglary or rape.

It is the problem of alcohol that has led many administrators and managers of community-based programs to suggest that Antabus and work release programs go together. Antabus is the drug that makes a person ill when it is combined with alcohol. Because it helps people avoid drinking, it prevents many behavior problems.

Variations in behavior must be recognized as part of the risk of such programs. Perfect prediction of behavior cannot be achieved. The responsibility for control, however, lies to a large extent with the peer group, the other residents in the facility. If a resident tells a supervisor that someone is planning to escape, the logical response should be, "What are you going to do about it?" Community-based facilities are non-authoritarian and without custody; any "rules" are made by the residents themselves to provide the environment for peaceful and responsible living. The police in the community should function around a community-based facility as they would around any other residence. If the approach that "Big Brother knows best" is used, the purpose of the corrections unit is defeated. This is why it is so important to select personnel who do not need to be authoritative.

The police, the prosecuting attorney, and the public defender or their counterparts in any community are all close to the activity of community-based facilities. When a resident gets drunk, doped, or for other reasons "keeps on going," the police pick him up and jail him or return him to the facility. If an offense, such as an automobile theft or burglary, has occurred, then the prosecuting attorney and the public defender become involved. This is why the administrator or manager of the community-based facility needs to develop and maintain open communication and good relationships with the police, the prosecutor's office, and the public defender. The final goal of all these agencies is the same—the protection of society and the restoration of the offender as a self-respecting, wage-earning, tax-paying citizen.

RELATIONSHIP WITH POLICE

Relationships of community-based programs with police are always delicate and tenuous. Because of the potential behavior problems associated with such agencies, the police have to remain alert and watchful.

The administrator or manager has to keep his relationships with the police open and above-board. In fact, he must make special efforts to interpret to police what he is trying to do, what his problems are, and how he is trying to handle them. He must keep the police informed. Only by open discussion can he gain the respect and help of the police.

On the other hand, he must keep this open communication without appearing to be a "cop" in the view of the participants in his facility. This can be partially accomplished by letting them know that he will do what he can within legal and ethical bounds to be of assistance to them. At the same time they must know that he will cooperate with the authorities when the welfare of his group is threatened by deviant behavior on the part of anyone. The best way to do this is to attempt to ameliorate problems between his residents, on the one hand, and law enforcement agencies, on the other, without being judgmental or threatening. It must be emphasized that the public safety is always a vital consideration.

JURISDICTIONAL PROBLEMS IN THE CRIMINAL JUSTICE SYSTEM

Jurisdictional problems sometimes arise between community-based managers and administrators and the traditional criminal justice services. A primary problem is that many probation and parole officers traditionally have had to do such things as find jobs, help people on their caseloads get legal advice, and perform other services that prevent them from spending a major part of their time on their primary job of counseling and supervision. The community services officer has as his job the mobilizing of community resources to assist offenders and exoffenders. In this service, he augments and supports the probation and parole services. But the provision of this service is sometimes threatening to an officer, who may feel his own job is being usurped. On the other hand, there have been community services officers who have become too aggressive and actually have become a threat to probation and parole agents or officers. Community services personnel must know exactly what their functions are. They do not *supervise* anybody, but attempt to facilitate the adjustment of offenders in their caseloads. They do not use force or weapons, nor do they perform surveillance. On occasion in a halfway house, they may have to transfer recalcitrant individuals back to a more secure institution, but even this is generally done by the peer group in the facility.

The probation or parole agent or officer has supervisory functions. Community-based correctional personnel support and augment these functions by mobilizing community resources to assist offenders and ex-offenders. The two should complement one another in a helpful way in the best interests of the offender and the public.

PUBLIC RELATIONS

Public relations presents a difficult problem. Many citizens favor community-based programs, but they want them situated "on the other side of town." The location of a halfway house, community correctional center, alcohol detoxification unit, drug treatment facility, or any other residence or center where offenders and ex-offenders are located thus becomes a public relations problem. In fact, this is one reason that most major prisons in the United States have been built in sparsely settled rural areas where the payroll may be considered to be a boon for the local economy and the presence of a prison is not a threat to large groups of people. The effort to locate a community-based correctional facility in an urban neighborhood, however, generally meets resistance.

Sometimes, halfway houses, drug treatment units, and other such facilities have been established in neighborhoods without letting the residents know what is happening. Essentially, the strategy in these cases has been to "tiptoe in at midnight." The residents awaken one morning suddenly to find an ongoing operation in their midst. Then the problem becomes one of trying to keep operating, at the same time pacifying the neighborhood and convincing citizens to accept the agency. Proponents of this strategy attempt to keep the residents quiet and provide services for them. For example, program participants may mow lawns without charge, or assist in painting or other maintenance of houses in the neighborhood. The difficulty with this type of activity is that, while the residents in the particular neighborhood may view the facility in a more favorable light and appreciate the free service, some people may have lost their income resources. The manager of the program must then determine the balance of advantages and disadvantages. The civic project approach, such as neighborhood beautification, assisting in facilitating garbage and trash disposal without disturbing city services, repairing old toys for the neighborhood children for Christmas, and similar projects, appears to be more innocuous.

Many managers of community-based facilities believe that the residents of the neighborhood should be contacted and made aware of the plans before they are executed. There are generally two ways by which this is accomplished. First, the person or group responsible for the facility could identify the significant people or leaders in the neighborhood. This could be done on an individual or a group basis, and the plans should be completely explained, including why this particular neighborhood was selected, and what the project hopes to accomplish. A free discussion of the advantages and disadvantages could ensue. Experience has been that mixed reaction continues; that some residents of the neighborhood will be accepting while others will object with varying degrees of vigor and intensity.

The second approach is the public hearing, frequently used by governmental agencies, such as those concerned with juvenile and youth services, adult institutional programs interested in halfway houses, and probation and parole services using community-based facilities. The public hearing is generally set up in the evening in an appropriate place in the neighborhood, sometimes in the building planned for eventual use. It is well advertised in the news media, including newspaper stories, radio and television announcements, and sometimes personal invitations are issued to neighborhood leaders. The experience in using this approach has been that two or three facilities may have been found and discussed before the final location is approved by the residents of the neighborhood.

One of the problems in locating a community-based center is the local zoning system. Areas zoned "residential" have to be avoided. Zoning is the legislative method of controlling the use of land through establishing certain standards and requirements. City or county land is divided into districts, each having specific conditions under which land and building may be legally developed and used. The community correctional program and facility must be located in accordance with zoning regulations. The community services coordinator or administrator must be acquainted with the regulations in his area before selecting a site for the community-based correctional operation. Facilities can be in areas zoned "residential-commercial," or some other designation indicating a mixed zoning status. In some cases, a desirable site in a residential area has actually been re-zoned by the city or county commission to permit the facility to be situated there. Some agencies have acquired abandoned stores downtown and renovated them for these purposes.

Finding housing for ex-offenders has been a persistent problem. Seldom do these people have funds for usual down payments or deposits. Persons under 18 years of age cannot receive social assistance on their own. In addition, many landlords do not want to rent to ex-offenders or recipients of public welfare assistance.

The continuing public relations problem, regardless of how the community-based program is established, is the behavior of the residents. The only real protection against problems is in the group counseling programs that emphasize peer pressure and peer responsibility for the maintenance of order in the facility and acceptable behavior on the part of fellow residents.

POLITICAL MISUSE

Unfortunately, many programs in community-based corrections and other areas have been started as "window dressing"—for the purpose of creating a good image for some political leadership. A good example was the New York City Youth Board, which was essentially inactive and certainly ineffective between 1966 and 1974. The National Center for Voluntary Action was also seen by some observers as a "window-dressing" venture when it began in 1972. Many private volunteer and helping programs have been devised as "fronts" through which money is obtained from governmental and private grants. Some have been incorporated as nonprofit organizations to qualify for tax-deductible contributions; some of these have had good intentions and others are distinctly shady. The political misuse of some programs without real intent to serve in good faith has plagued a few community-based programs.

FUNDING AND SUPPORT

Funding and support generally come from governmental and private sources. A majority of governmental support for community-based programs in recent years has come from the Law Enforcement Assistance Administration (LEAA) under the Omnibus Crime Control and Safe Streets Act of 1968, as amended through the State Planning Agency (SPA). (This latter agency goes under various names in different states, such as Governor's Commission on Criminal Justice or State Law Enforcement Commission.) Such funding begins with the writing of a grant request to LEAA, specifically to the SPA. The funding is then approved or disapproved depending upon the resources available and how favorably the projected program is viewed. Similar procedures are employed in projects that go through the Model Cities Program of the Department of Housing and Urban Development; the various programs in the Department of Labor; the Office of Economic Opportunity in the Executive Department; the Office of Education, National Institute of Mental Health, Office of Juvenile Delinquency and Youth Development, and other segments of the Department of Health, Education and Welfare.

Private funding is generally also done by grant requests to certain programs such as the Ford Foundation and other private foundations. The Stone Foundation, established by W. Clement Stone, has been active in the area of education and art for offenders and ex-offenders, as has his motivational course on Guides for Better Living. In the mid-1970s, however, the interests of the Stone Foundation shifted from corrections to child abuse. Although private foundations and contributors are generally more flexible than governmental agencies in terms of guidelines, they do have their own various interests.

Information about governmental agencies can be obtained by contacting them. There are directories that list the many private foundations and the types of projects they prefer to support; for example,

The Foundation Grants Index—1973, Lee Noe, Grants Ed. New York: Columbia University Press, 1974

Where America's Large Foundations Make Their Grants—1974–75, Joseph Dermer, ed. New York: Public Service Materials Center, 1974

Annual Register of Grant Support 1974–75. Chicago: Marquis Academic Media, 1975

The Foundation Directory, Edition 5, Marianna O. Lewis, ed. New York: The Foundation Center, distributed by Columbia University Press, 1975.

There are also booklets and other materials that provide instructions regarding how to find an appropriate foundation and how to write a grant request.[1]

COMPETENCY OF PERSONNEL

Competency of personnel is the most significant factor in community-based corrections operations. Programs have been influenced more by staff personalities than by the generic design or value of the projects.[2] It has often been said that the difference between a halfway house and a "flophouse" is in its management. This is one reason that evaluation

---

[1] For example, see Joseph Dermer, *How to Raise Funds from Foundations* (New York: Public Service Materials Center, 1972).

[2] Robert Martinson, *The Martinson Report* (New York: Praeger, 1974).

studies which compare success and failure rates in different community-based correctional programs are of questionable validity, because they erroneously assume that the personalities operating the programs are constant.

In planning for community resource centers, one of the first problems encountered has to do with attitudes and competence of personnel.[3] Because a person functions well in a maximum or medium custody prison does not mean that he or she can do well in a community-based facility, where custody is de-emphasized. Flexibility is important in community correctional programs, and some personnel have difficulty with this. If they are unable to tolerate ambiguous stimuli—to live with unanswered questions—and need "once-and-for-all" solutions, their needs will interfere with effective functioning within these programs.

FAILURE OF COMMUNITY-BASED PROGRAMS

A major problem with community-based programs is the fact that many of them are apt to be started with good intentions, but because they are not solidly funded or supported, or because they have not had adequate forethought and planning, they quickly fail and disappear.

The National Prisoners Alliance that began in Portland, Oregon, in 1972 was defunct by 1974, when Dave "Turkey" Turner was returned to prison and his associate fled from parole. The United Prisoners' Union began in 1970 and ceased to answer correspondence in 1975. Even some international organizations have gone the same way. Ex-Cons for a Better Society, Inc., which was an active and apparently successful group in Dayton, Ohio, folded in 1975 for lack of funding.

Even the well-meaning reform groups have difficulty in sustaining themselves. The Penal Reform Institute of Alexandria, Virginia, begun in the early 1970s, did not sustain itself and was "merged" into the National Prison Project of the American Civil Liberties Union. The Murton Foundation for Criminal Justice, Inc., was founded at the University of Minnesota in the early 1970s, but it died in 1974 for lack of funding.

Many good programs stagnate in about two years. They start with enthusiasm, then tend to become custodial in some cases, which defeats their purpose. All too many disappear after having given promise. Sometimes they fail because of improper management and/or planning;

3 Authur V. Huffman, "The Process of Planning For Community Resources Centers," Proceedings of the One-Hundred-Third Annual Congress of Correction (Seattle), August 12–17, 1973 (College Park, Md.: American Correctional Association, 1974), pp. 106–10.

sometimes they disappear because of lack of financial and/or community support. Many potentially good projects tend to be transitional and temporary.

CONCLUSIONS

It is apparent that the problems of community-based corrections programs are many. Adequate control of the behavior of residents is one major problem—its solutions remain primarily among the group itself. Relationships with police and the public always need attention, particularly when illegal or annoying behavior is exhibited by the participants in the facility. Funding and support also represent a never-ending source of concern. Personnel determines the success or failure of a community-based program

One of the problems in community-based corrections is what Norval Morris has called "Balkanization," referring to the political divisions and heterogeneous cultures in the Balkans.[4] Fragmentation divides interest and effort, and the phenomenal diversity and variety of governmental authority and private functioning frequently results in confusion, overlapping of services, and gaps in services. It complicates police planning and administration, impedes expeditious processing through the courts, and divides responsibility among agencies and organizations. This great diversity precludes in many cases the pinpointing of responsibility for failure, credit for success, or coordination of services.

Another problem is that ex-offenders' residency programs, both private and public, need more thorough study; there should be a re-evaluation of the indices used to match types of offenders with types of programs.[5] There is a need for greater specification of program elements and a more sophisticated classification system for offenders to make halfway houses and other community-based corrections successful.

Aid and assistance without custodial control must be emphasized in community correctional programs. There must be no "giveaways" or financial assistance without contingent conditions. Neither love nor successful adjustment can be bought. Any such program is only a delivery system by which people are brought together with people who need them—nobody has ever been "rehabilitated" by a *program.* Interpersonal relationships are basic to community-based corrections.

---

[4] Edith Elizabeth Flynn, "Planning For Community Corrections," Proceedings of the One-Hundred-Third Annual Congress of Corrections, p. 97.

[5] Edward M. Koslin, Warren A. Kass, and Marguerite Q. Warren, "Classification, Evaluation and Treatment Models in Community Ex-Offenders Residency Programs," Proceedings of the One-Hundred-Third Annual Congress of Corrections, pp. 133–37.

Many of the problems of the community-based program involve the image of orderliness and systematic approaches, which tend to conceal the actual processes in organizing and operating the programs.[6] Innovation of any type tends to arouse the suspicions of and become threatening to the established bureaucracy in the subject area. Creating committees to get action is less effective than using committees for dissemination of information. The relationships between planning, action, and "activism" are sometimes confused to the point that some organizers spend most of their time planning, and little actually gets done. Others first get started and then plan later, and that approach has equally unhappy results. The relationships between competition, cooperation, and compromise are likewise confused. Official programs functioning side by side with private or ex-offender programs sometimes have difficulty communicating. In many cases, for example, administrators of official pre-release programs operated by governmental agencies have difficulty in accepting and working with the nonprofessional private halfway houses and pre-release programs operated by ex-offenders. And, too, accountability as compared with control is frequently a confusing problem, particularly when a funding agency wants certain goals met, which would impinge on control, and the final evaluation or accountability merely gives the funding agency justification rather than reflecting an effective program. For these many reasons, all too many programs start out with great sincerity and enthusiasm and even promise, and then fail within a short time.

[6] Gary J. Faltico, "Organizing Drug Abuse Treatment and Training Programs for the College and the Community," in Richard L. Rachin and Eugene H. Czajkoski, eds., *Drug Abuse Control* (Lexington, Mass.: D. C. Heath, 1975), pp. 99–106.

Chapter 16

The Future
of Community-Based Corrections

Although the future of community-based corrections remains tenuous, the trend of correctional programming in this direction is steady and clear. The National Council on Crime and Delinquency has recommended that no new prisons be built until all other alternatives have been examined. Governmental acceptance of community-based programs began in the 1950s and became fully accepted with the Prisoners Rehabilitation Act of 1965 that authorized the establishment of work release and other community-based programs in the United States Bureau of Prisons.

On the other hand, some political leaders have called for "stiffer sentences and longer prison terms." Mandatory minimum sentences have been passed by some state legislatures. Some political leaders have been calling for fixed sentences to replace the indeterminate sentences, which would have the effect of eliminating parole and many community-based correctional programs with it.

An evaluation of some of the phases of community-based corrections might be appropriate, together with a look at some of the factors that bear upon the future of these programs.

DISSATISFACTION WITH PRISONS

Dissatisfaction with prisons has been a primary theme of professional criminologists and correctional administrators in recent years. The bad effects of institutionalization have been central concerns of persons involved in correctional treatment programs. In spite of the belief of many

270

criminologists that the last large institution had been built, and their recommendations that no more be built for over 600 persons, it appears that the "big-prison" period is not yet over. It has sometimes been called the "Edifice complex." Ohio built a large institution at Lucasville in 1972, and in 1975, Texas began constructing a prison unit for 2,000 persons.

On the other hand, the closing of several major prisons has been announced. California has tentatively announced the closure of the California State Prisons at Folsom and San Quentin "as soon as practicable." Wisconsin announced the closing of the Reformatory at Green Bay but did not close it. In 1973 Michigan announced the gradual closing of the largest walled prison in the world, the State Prison of Southern Michigan at Jackson, but has had to delay the close. Pennsylvania closed the old Eastern State Penitentiary in Philadelphia in 1970.

Thus, many major prisons are being closed at the same time some large prisons are being built and a few political leaders are calling for longer sentences—the field of corrections appears to be confused. There is, however, a definite trend toward community-based correctional programs and facilities. Yet, a record high of 25,000 prisoners was reached in 1976.

Closing large institutions stimulates new thinking with regard to community-centered programs for helping people who cannot benefit from conventional community structures or traditional prisons. It is the thesis of this book that deinstitutionalization of the correctional process holds greater promise for success in the protection of society through the rehabilitation of the offender than traditional institutional procedures.[1] Institutions are financially and socially expensive. Professionals in youth services, health, and correction have arrived at the conclusion that society can be served by alternatives to incarceration within the society to which the offenders ultimately return. On the other hand, prison populations are more sensitive to unemployment rates than they are to crime rates. There is no point of placing people on probation, parole, or community-based, work-oriented programs when they have no visible means of support. For prison populations and community-based corrections, crime rates are less important than unemployment rates.

Closing prisons is believed to be beneficial to the correctional effort because it reduces the damage done to some people. Sociological criminologists have in recent years become concerned with the "labeling process" by which a person is stigmatized as a prisoner. Moreover, research in several prisons indicates that socialization within the prison commu-

---

[1] Yitzhak Bakel, ed., *Closing Correctional Institutions: Strategies for Youth Services* (Lexington, Mass.: D. C. Heath, 1973), p. 186.

nity supports deviant norms, making the inmates less amendable to socialization than they were before the prison experience.[2]

The National Campaign against Prisons (NCAP) was initiated by John O. Boone, former Commissioner of Corrections in the District of Columbia and State of Massachusetts, for the purpose of reducing significantly the use of prisons in the criminal justice system.[3] His belief is that only a small percentage of convicted offenders represent a clear and present danger to society and thus need institutionalization. The vast majority can be released in community-based programs and minimum security institutions.

Some scholars have called for change in correctional programs simply because the traditional methods have not worked sufficiently well to satisfy either the criminal justice system or the public.[4] Further, the current interventions aimed at crime reduction are faulty in theory and procedures are caught between the concept of caused behavior on the part of social and behavioral sciences and "free will," "intent," and *mens rea* basic to the law. Sometimes, procedural law has impeded substantive law to the extent that plea bargaining has been accepted by both the prosecution and the defense, as an escape from the dilemma.

The American Assembly, headquartered at Columbia University and begun in 1950 when Dwight Eisenhower was president of that university, publishes authoritative books to illuminate issues of policy in the United States. It is a national educational institution designed to provide information, stimulate discussion, and evoke independent conclusions in matters of vital public interest. In meetings throughout the country, the issues in corrections have been consistently toward breaking down large prisons and emphasizing community-based facilities and programs. In the Chicago meeting in February 1975, the Assembly recommended greater use of alternatives, including pretrial diversion and diversion from jail, as well as greater use of community-based facilities, stating that the concept of large institutions should be abandoned.[5]

In the absence of some formal programs, courts have avoided sentencing to institutions by assigning duties in the community. In 1975, for example, a woman in Miami found guilty of killing her husband

---

[2] Stanton Wheeler, "Socialization in Correctional Communities," *American Sociological Review*, 26 (October 1961), 697–712.

[3] National Campaign Against Prisons, P.O. Box 8902, John F. Kennedy Station, Boston, Massachusetts 02114.

[4] Walter C. Bailey, "Correctional Outcome: An Evaluation of a Hundred Reports," *Journal of Criminal Law, Criminology and Police Science*, 57, No. 2 (1966), 153–60.

[5] *Prisoners in America*—Report on Midwest American Assembly (Illinois), February 9–11, 1975 (New York: American Assembly of Columbia University, Graduate School of Business, 1975), p. 11.

under extenuating circumstances was sentenced to teach Sunday School for fifteen years. There have been many examples of lesser offenses being disposed of by lesser time in performing other community services. In England, the Criminal Justice Act of 1972 provided for alternative sentences that had the offender complete a specific number of hours of unpaid, voluntary community work under the supervision of the Probation Service. Some examples of sentences are as follows:

Helping run a youth club.

Assisting staff and patients in geriatric or mental hospitals.

Helping run weekend projects for youth clubs.

Helping the local Ambulance Service (cleaning and checking equipment).

Painting and decorating houses for the elderly, the handicapped, and the housebound.

Landscaping derelict sites and clearing redevelopment areas.

Driving for organizations for the handicapped or taking them on short trips.

Helping run a day center for the elderly, a preschool play group, or a junior football team.

Bookkeeping, filing, and typing, as well as fund raising for an organization.

Helping to preserve buildings of historic interest, as well as nature trails and footpaths.

Entertaining old people or children in homes.

Helping the handicapped in swimming and games.

Making and repairing furniture and toys.

Helping in projects for tenants associations, housing associations and nature conservation groups.

Helping run a community newspaper.

Gardening for the elderly.[6]

As we have indicated throughout this book, the most hopeful trend in education for offenders has become community-based programs outside institutions.[7] Programs of education, counseling, and work seem to have better chances in halfway houses where peer-group discussions and counseling are available. This is a much less expensive procedure

---

[6] Howard Standish Bergman, "Community Service in England: An Alternative to the Custodial Sentence," *Federal Probation*, 9, No. 1 (March 1975), 43–46.

[7] K. E. Kerle, "Educating in Prisons," *New Society*, 25 (1973), 13–15.

than imprisonment and provides a better atmosphere in which the offender can readjust with far fewer difficulties than those found in prisons.

A comparison of male delinquents 10 to 17 years of age in Louisville and Jefferson Counties, Kentucky, during the fiscal year 1967–1968, on the basis of their treatment in institutions or community-based programs, concluded that the latter treatment was more successful.[8] Of 367 delinquents, 12 were on probation, 31 were in the halfway house program, and 324 went to the maximum custody institution. A disproportionate number of blacks and inner-city juveniles were institutionalized. Juveniles with a higher degree of social pathology and lower interpersonal maturity level were more likely to be institutionalized. Juveniles with a higher economic status, better school attendance records, and a higher mean grade of education were more likely to receive community treatment. The type of offense was not a determinant in treatment disposition, but delinquency history and prior institutionalization was related to institutional treatment. The better correctional treatment programs are directed toward the more hopeful cases. The selection process affects every stage of the procedure from apprehension to disposition, which biases the outcome in many ways. Even so, it was apparent that institutional treatment is more damaging than community-based treatment.

PREVENTION PROGRAMS

Delinquency prevention programs, such as the Chicago Area Projects, the New York City Youth Board's program using detached workers, Mobilization for Youth, and some private religious projects have generally been viewed positively. Some have been called failures because of the lack of rigid research methodology, but even so, clinical observation in many of these projects has been positive. The original results of the Cambridge-Somerville Project in Massachusetts indicated failure, but McCord and McCord several years later re-evaluated this project and considered it to be a success. It is obvious that better research methods are needed that take into account the clinical judgment as well as easily collected demographic data.

There are many uncontrolled variables in evaluating community-based programs. Consequently, even a disappointing evaluation cannot be accepted as unquestioned fact. One project in Chicago, for example, carried on by the Center for the Study of Law and Criminal Justice at the University of Chicago, had an experimental neighborhood and a

8 *Comparative Analysis of Community and Institutional Treatment* (Louisville, Ky.: Louisville and Jefferson County, Metropolitan Social Services Department, 1971).

control neighborhood next to each other. Delinquency prevention programs were established in the experimental neighborhood and none were established in the control neighborhood. After a year, the delinquency rate in the experimental neighborhood was higher than that in the control neighborhood, suggesting that not only was the program a failure, but that it made matters worse. Closer examination, however, pointed out that the delinquency prevention programs were so successful that families were able to mobilize themselves and move out of the neighborhood to better areas and were replaced by more disorganized families who had had neither the advantages of the program nor the stability that existed even in the control neighborhood. Consequently, the delinquency prevention program was, in fact, considered to be successful.

A prevention program that works with youth in the city can be successful. As was mentioned in an earlier chapter, the New York City Youth Board, for example, used street workers who were successful with aggressive and resistant delinquent youth. Conclusions that were drawn from that program indicated that it was very effective. Some of the conclusions were as follows:

1. The children whose behavior is such that they are likely to become problems to themselves and to the community can be identified at a comparatively early age and reached before they arrive at a point of overwhelming crisis (average age of 310 children was 10.7 years).
2. Even though the majority of these children are presenting problems predominantly of an aggressive nature and are thus considered by some clinics less amenable to treatment, they can and do respond to appropriate help (58.6 percent presented difficulties in aggression).
3. While much needs to be learned about effective methods of working with these resistive children and families, both the referral units and the agencies have found ways of communicating with them and helping them to use available services.
4. Basic to the methods used both by the referral units and the contract agencies is the belief that a family's initial refusal of service is not a reason for discontinuing agency effort.[9]

Prevention programs have been established in several places based on encouraging citizens to report crime when they see it. Although citizen participation in crime prevention in the form of vigilantes or the

---

[9] *How They Were Reached: A Study of 310 Children and Their Families Known to Referral Units*, New York City Youth Board, Monograph No. 2 (November 1954), pp. 89–90.

sheriff's posse appeared to be usual during pioneer days, such reporting in the modern urban city has been found to be less usual and less successful. A survey of several of these programs in 1975 indicated that these "Help Stop Crime" programs have been essentially unsuccessful.[10] Probably the most classical example occurred on the evening of March 26, 1964, when Catherine "Kitty" Genovese was raped and stabbed to death while thirty-eight residents watched without intervening or even reporting it to the police.[11] A subsequent study by social scientists reported that some people just did not want to become involved. Reporting of organized crime and white-collar crime, of course, is virtually nonexistent. It is obvious that crime prevention and delinquency prevention programs have to be formally organized and administered.

DIVERSION PROGRAMS

Dissatisfaction with prisons and the criminal justice system in general has resulted in the implementation of diversion programs. As we saw earlier in the book, these diversion programs are of two general types: (1) pretrial diversion that takes an alleged offender completely from the criminal justice system, and (2) diversion from jail and bail, which means that the accused person does not have to be confined while awaiting trial. Diversion from the criminal justice system is accomplished when the alleged offender is placed under probation supervision on a voluntary basis. This is usually done when a minor property offender indicates that he is guilty and the prosecution, judge, defense, and police agree that there is no real point in sending that person through the traditional procedures. Instead, the handling becomes informal. The United States Courts and some states refer to this as "deferred prosecution." Pennsylvania calls it "accelerated rehabilitative disposition." Florida and some other states refer to it as "probation without adjudication." Originally, this procedure was just for misdemeanants, but felons (generally restricted to nonviolent property offenders) now participate as well.

In 1961 and 1962, Justice Douglas indicated that a person should not be kept confined because he could not afford bail. Interest was then focused on release on one's own recognizance without bail. The Manhattan Bail Project began in 1961, financed by the Ford Foundation and the Vera Foundation. Its studies and experience indicated that

10 Lorelei A. Vaughn, *Florida's Model Rape Investigation Guidelines: An Analysis of a Crime Prevention Program* (Tallahassee: Florida State University, unpublished master's thesis, 1975), p. 67.

11 *The New York Times*, March 27, 1964, p. 1:4.

Release on Own Recognizance (ROR) could successfully be used. Again, it was first used for misdemeanants and later for felons.

It is much better for the criminal justice system to accomplish justice or resolve social problems than it is to gain a victim.[12] The logjam in the courts has resulted in a breakdown of the process of justice so that people can be in jail awaiting trial for eighteen months or more. This situation is what led in the 1970s to the massive revolt in several of New York City's Detention Centers, including the famous Tombs.[13] Primitive peoples use compensation and restitution rather than punishment for crime. Basically, this idea is conducive to a more harmonious society under a consensus model, rather than the conflict model that exists in modern criminal justice systems.

HALFWAY HOUSES AND GROUP HOMES

Halfway houses have been in existence in relatively large numbers since the 1960s under governmental auspices and the 1950s under private auspices. Their success has been mixed, apparently depending largely upon the personnel in charge. Like other community-based facilities and programs, the halfway house is a reflection of the people who run it. If they can provide subtle leadership so that peer-group pressure is conducive to responsible behavior on the part of the residents, then the program will work successfully. On the other hand, a careless or incompetent management that provides no leadership or attempts to be authoritarian results in failure.

A review of programs designed to ease the transition from prison to the free community has revealed two contradictory discoveries: (1) with minor reservations, the majority of agencies administering the programs report that graduated release is beneficial to the offender and to society and should be expanded; and (2) of the research and experiments undertaken in the areas of work release, pre-release, and halfway houses, the more rigorous the methodology used, the more ambivalent or negative are the findings regarding the efficacy of these programs.[14] It took the nations of the West two centuries to realize that penitentiaries do not make penitents, and it took a generation to see that correctional institutions do not correct. Future analysis of graduated release programs also may point to the painful conclusion that well-intentioned efforts

12 David L. Bazelon in a lecture, December 7, 1972, at the University of Cincinnati. Also Paul H. Hahn, *Community Based Corrections in the Criminal Justice System* (Santa Cruz, Cal.: Davis Publishing Co., 1975), p. 103.

13 "Logjam in Our Courts," *Life*, August 7, 1970.

14 E. Doleschal, "Graduated Release," in *Information Review on Crime and Delinquency*, 1, No. 10 (1969), 1–26.

were misplaced and that more efficient methods of achieving the same ends are available to the community. One unexpected outcome of experience with graduated release programs has been that as judges have become aware of the practicability of releasing offenders under supervision, they have placed larger numbers directly on probation rather than committing them to correctional institutions. At least one work release program is reported to be decreasing—paradoxically, a sign of its success. On the basis of the limited reliable information available, this development may be indicative of things to come. There is no question that partial release is better than no release at all—better for society and better for the offender. But it is only second best. The time has come to acknowledge that the social and psychological effects of the prison or the jail are often more harmful to society and the offender than the offense itself. Thus many of the inmates who find the road from prison to freedom painful and difficult should never have been exposed to the prison setting in the first place. A review of completed research studies on the effectiveness of correctional programs shows that it is difficult to escape the conclusion that the act of incarcerating a person at all will impair whatever potential he has for crime-free future adjustment; and regardless of which "treatments" are administered while he is imprisoned, the longer he is kept there, the more deteriorated and recidivistic he will become. Based on the preliminary evidence presented here and on the experience gathered from community treatment schemes, conclusions indicate that supervision and treatment in the free community of those offenders eligible for partial release are at least as effective, often more effective, always more humanitarian, and far less costly than the more drastic measure of imprisonment.

According to the General Accounting Office Report to Congress on halfway houses, they are a viable alternative to prisons.[15] A review of fifteen such facilities in the United States found that they were not systematized and did not constitute a unitary component in the criminal justice system. The conclusion was that the productivity of halfway houses was not worse than probation, prison, and parole, and appeared in some cases to be better—as well as cheaper.

Group homes have been received with more consistent optimism. The typical group home is a small residence usually operated by a man-and-wife team and designed to hold a small number of children or youths. Because of the small number of cases involved and the informal atmosphere, better management procedures can be brought to bear. It has been called one of the most significant movements in the field of juvenile justice in the last decade.

---

[15] "A New, Coordinated Effort Needed to Make Halfway Houses a Viable Alternative to Prisons—GAO Report Concludes," *Corrections Digest*, 6, No. 12 (June 11, 1975), 1.

WORK RELEASE AND FURLOUGHS

The considerable research on work release indicates that it is beneficial on a short-term basis. Six months to a year on work release assists people to readjust to society and keep jobs when they go home, and it provides a gradual re-entry into society. Over a year on work release, however, seems to impair self-esteem and self-concept because the individual lives in two worlds, one representing confinement and the other representing freedom in the community. Over a period of time, the individual may become almost schizoid, feeling that there is no real identity with either. In the beginning, the freedom granted by work release is a welcome respite from confinement. By the time six months or longer have passed, however, the confinement at night and weekends becomes embarrassing and self-depreciating.

Studies of work release programs, however, have shown that though selection plays a role, participation in a work release program can be a major variable in post-release success.[16] Work release groups have shown significantly better adjustment in all areas.

Every month in the United States approximately 30,000 furloughs are granted to adult prisoners and about 6,000 to juveniles. There is intense controversy around furloughs, however.[17] Inmates and staff of most prisons agree that the furloughs are beneficial. On the other hand, police, prosecuting attorneys, and some other officials, already angry because some suspects were not found guilty or were placed on probation, frequently object strenuously to seeing an offender on the streets when they think he should be behind bars. They contend that even if only one furloughed offender commits another serious crime, then the correctional officials have abdicated their primary responsibility of protecting the public. Once an unfortunate incident breaks into news headlines, the furlough program is immediately cut back. With all the difficulties, however, the furlough programs are growing.

VOLUNTEERS

Evaluations of volunteer programs have generally been favorable, if only because they bring sufficient personnel to a court or institutional setting to bring some type of counseling or interpersonal relationships to the program. Citizen participation programs preceded volunteer pro-

---

16 *Evaluation of Work Release* (Montgomery, Ala.: Rehabilitation Research Foundation, 1975).

17 Michael S. Serrill, "Prison Furloughs in America," *Corrections Magazine*, 1, No. 6 (July/August 1975), 57–58.

grams to support existing programs. Volunteer programs have grown from 3 or 4 in 1961 to over 2,000 in 1972 in court settings alone. Such programs provide one-to-one counseling *and* support existing programs. A good volunteer program is an asset, not only for the offenders and ex-offenders but also for public relations and peripheral political support at budget time.

DEPENDENCY PROGRAMS—ALCOHOL AND DRUGS

Community-based programs concerned with alcohol and drug problems have also had mixed evaluations. In some drug programs, particularly those under private auspices, a relatively high success rate can be seen. One of the reasons, of course, is that the persons motivated to go to a private treatment program are more hopeful than those who have to be committed to other programs. The peer support that comes from these programs is also a beneficial factor. Certainly, these programs take much pressure from other governmental programs by working with people who are motivated to control their dependency, leaving the poorer risks to some of the governmental programs.

Alcohol dependency programs, including detoxification units, have experienced similar results. People motivated to abstain from alcohol volunteer to go to treatment units, while those who have to be picked up because of drunkenness are less apt to have successful results.

In all dependency programs, the difficulty is in sustaining emotional support to neutralize psychological dependency on the drug or alcohol. Some personalities are more vulnerable to alcohol and drugs than are others. Psychiatrists have indicated that some differences in vulnerability are due to differences in the types of relationshps in the parental family, particularly with the father. Other physicians have suggested a biological vulnerability as well.

Although the knowledge of personalities and other factors relating to alcohol and drug dependency is inadequate, enough is known so that several courts have indicated that such dependency should not be considered to be criminal. The *Driver* v. *Hinnant* case in 1966 in North Carolina, for example, indicated that sentencing an alcoholic for a crime is tantamount to sentencing a sick person for showing evidence of his symptoms.[18] The *Robinson* v. *California* case in 1962 posited that drug addiction is an illness and that laws making addiction a crime are cruel and unusual punishment in violation of the Eighth Amendment.[19] Of course, the majority of states still have public drunk-

---

18 *Driver* v. *Hinnant*, 356 F.2d 761 (4th Cir. 1966).
19 *Robinson* v. *California*, 370 U.S. 660 (1962).

enness and narcotic addiction in the criminal statutes, and it would take a court case in each state to overturn these laws or legislative action to repeal them. In most progressive jurisdictions, however, police have ceased to arrest people for public intoxication, but generally take them home or to a detoxification center; they frequently take addicts to a hospital, particularly if he is in withdrawal.

COST BENEFIT ANALYSIS

When it is realized that for the same amount of money thirteen persons can be supervised in a community setting as compared with one in a prison or correctional institution, the cost factor becomes obvious. The fact that the recidivism rate from prisons and correctional institutions is higher than that from community-based programs makes the advantages even more obvious. On the other hand, the most serious cases are sent to the prisons and correctional institutions, so an exact comparison in favor of the community-based program would be unfair to the prison and correctional institution. Even so, the cost benefit analysis seems to be favorable to community corrections programs.

There is a growing interest in cost benefit analysis in corrections, but the use of "new correctional costs," rather than recidivism rates, appears to permit more precise measurement.[20] Stuart Adams' report of six controlled experiments carried out between 1955 and 1967 have shown the highest gains per caseload.[21] There is an obvious lack of interest in providing intensive supervision programs in prisons, although there have been reduced caseloads in probation and parole among specialized groups, but it could be argued that these groups should have been diverted from the criminal justice system in the first place.[22] The evidence is accumulating that cost benefit analysis in corrections favors community-based programs.

THE MOVE TOWARD COMMUNITY-BASED CORRECTIONS

It is clear that society will not continue to tolerate the ever-increasing costs of imprisonment in support of a system utilizing mass custody without effective treatment as its primary focus.[23] The development of personality problems that spill over into behavioral problems that encroach on the rights and property of others can be detected early.

---

20 *Community Based Correctional Programs: Models and Practices* (Rockville, Md.: National Institute of Mental Health Crime and Delinquency Topics, 1971), p. 35.

21 Ibid.

22 Ibid.

23 Hahn, *Community Based Corrections*, p. 14.

Ethically and pragmatically, they should not be permitted to develop into serious behavioral problems in a society as sophisticated and knowledgable in social and psychological areas as modern America. Failure to apply what is known tends to accompany clumsy efforts at empirical evaluation of "innovative" projects while leaving the most significant factors uncontrolled. Personality and factors involving interpersonal relationships are much more important in evaluating successful or unsuccessful social adjustment than are such demographic factors as race, age, nationality, per capita income—these are only peripherally related to successful adjustment. Even the rudimentary evaluations obtained from these research projects that only control solid demographic data indicate that reduced caseloads *can* permit greater personal attention in the treatment-supervision process and *can,* therefore, produce better results. Administrative procedures and "projects" are only delivery systems by which people are brought together with people who need them. People are changed by other people, not by "programs" or "projects." It is in this area that community-based correctional programs can make a contribution as compared with the traditional massive institution concerned with regimentation and security.

Policy decisions based on the success or failure of rehabilitative programs have been viewed as impossible to justify because rehabilitation as a goal can hardly be supported by sociological theory or empirical statistics.[24] This means that society is confronted with a continuing need for a prison of some sort and no way to make it presentable. Because criminal and delinquent activity occur in the community, it is the most logical correctional base. Therefore, probation and parole, halfway houses, work release programs, group homes, and community correctional centers have been established to provide alternatives to incarceration. Although there is not an overwhelming amount of evidence to show that these programs are more effective than the prisons, they are certainly no worse. Further, they are less costly and damaging.

The National Advisory Commission on Criminal Justice Standards and Goals published recommendations in 1973 concerning the entire field of criminal justice. Focusing on community-based corrections, Standard 4.1 recommended that each criminal justice jurisdiction immediately develop a comprehensive plan for improving the pretrial process, including pretrial diversion, pretrial release, and organization of pretrial services.[25] The use of community-based corrections is recom-

---

[24] John P. Conrad, "Corrections and Simple Justice," *Journal of Criminal Law and Criminology,* 64 (1973), 208–17.

[25] *Corrections* (Washington, D.C.: National Advisory Commission on Criminal Justice Standards and Goals, 1973), pp. 111–40.

mended by the National Advisory Commission on Criminal Justice Standards and Goals.[26] Pointing out that community-based corrections is not yet well organized and not well planned as a program, it is a goal for the future. Community alternatives to confinement, foster and group homes, community correctional centers, work release programs, family visits, pre-release programs, and other similar approaches are recommended in Standards 7.1 to 7.4.

That some change is needed has been agreed upon by almost everyone in the criminal justice system, but the direction and degree of that change remains at issue. Hahn has suggested twelve steps toward arriving at effective change:

1. Establish goals to arrive at some consensus as to the objective of the system. This means that the community must decide what it expects from the criminal justice system.

2. Professional self-evaluation to relinquish the vested interest and status that is enjoyed by the professional community to obtain realistic treatment effectiveness. There seems to be more research that raises questions than answers them and greater concern with diagnosis than the treatment process itself.

3. Share decision-making responsibility so that elected officials and all those in responsible positions in the criminal justice system need to examine organizational policies and administrative requirements and maintain dialogue with the community at large.

4. Eliminate "veils of secrecy" so that operation of the criminal justice system should not be in secrecy or semi-secrecy. The public should be brought into the system in a participative way through public relations or other methods.

5. Develop community tolerance to enable the criminal justice system to discontinue some traditional but nonfunctioning services and develop new approaches together with evaluation components.

6. Minimize professional "feuding" in which the various segments of the criminal justice system are in conflict. A truly functional criminal justice system is a cooperative one, mutually supportive, and aimed at the protection of society.

7. Re-align funding priorities in the criminal justice system. "If such an evaluation should reveal, for example, that we are spending 80 cents on 'mopping up the bathroom floor' at the end of the correctional cycle, and only allocating 25 percent of that amount to

---

26 Ibid., pp. 221–46.

'turning off the faucet' through preventive measures," then a cost effectiveness approach would demand reallocation of some funds.

8. Establish criminal justice council as recommended over 50 years ago by Roscoe Pound and Felix Frankfurter in the report on criminal justice in Cleveland, Ohio, and reinforced by the Report of the National Commission on Causes and Prevention of Violence. Such a council in each community could serve as a clearinghouse for reports issued by other branches of government and take advantage of research from universities and consulting organizations. It would involve commitment from many agency heads in the criminal justice system and in the community at large.

9. Implement systems-wide approaches to reduce conflict and provide free communication so that influence is based on technical competence and knowledge rather than on personal whims within the power structure.

10. Establish priority ranking for decision making to achieve a step-by-step determination of goals, objectives, means to reach goals, alternatives, constraints, problems, and implementation. A properly planned approach would broaden the perspectives and extend the horizons of all involved.

11. Orient research to practical needs so that these efforts can be focused on program evaluation and problem solving.

12. Develop alternatives to traditional programs. Segregation in institutions obviously does more harm than good in most instances, its justification being protection of the public from dangerous people. Incarceration of nondangerous people generally works against the public safety and interest because of the bad effects of institutionalization.[27]

A planned and orderly move from maximum custody institutions to community-based correctional programs appears to be in the public interest.

It must be noted, too, that there is place for compromise in making changes. An administrator who is a "crusader" needs the motivation and enthusiasm to do the job, but he must also work within the community and in harmony with existing programs. An adamant person who will not compromise to effect a program frequently ends up without a program. A person too dictatorial for the democratic process is unable to consider the opinions and interests of others. Only a few "benevolent dictators" have made constructive changes in corrections. Most changes have been made by enthusiastic and capable leaders.

---

[27] Hahn, *Community Based Corrections*, pp. 29–37.

CONCLUSIONS

Conclusions in evaluating community-based programs, as well as many other programs in the criminal justice field, can sometimes be better drawn by quality of judgment than by statistical evidence. The reason for this is that there are so many uncontrollable factors in the lives of people and in community settings that it is difficult to make a complete evaluation on a statistical basis. Although this can be done in the laboratory, it cannot be done in the free community.

Hahn sees ten advantages to community-based settings:

1. They tend to place subtle pressure on the citizens of the community to recognize that they have a role to play in restoring offenders to useful citizenship.

2. Greater responsibility for adequate decision making is placed on the offender.

3. Placement in open-type, community-oriented facilities eliminates the "ritualistic responses and forced conformity" observed in prisons.

4. Opportunity for decision making and responsibile choice removes the "excuse" that "I never had a chance."

5. They constantly present the opportunity to "hold up the mirror" in which the offender must recognize his real motives.

6. They present regular opportunities for more frequent ego-supportive experiences such as volunteer work in hospitals and assisting in the community.

7. Life in the community presents many more role models and real-life situations.

8. They permit the offender to depart from the medical model and interact with a variety of helping figures.

9. Correctional workers find themselves in new roles and begin to function as "brokers for services."

10. Individual rights of the offender are more easily safeguarded in these settings.[28]

LeMar Empey pointed out in 1967 that community-based programs have the potential to provide viable alternatives to corrections, but they must be systematized in an orderly fashion.[29] No single innovation—

---

[28] Ibid., p. 158.

[29] LeMar T. Empey, *Alternatives to Incarceration* (Washington, D.C.: Office of Juvenile Delinquency and Youth Development, 1967), p. 87.

whether halfway house, work release, diversion program, use of volunteers, and so forth—and no single program can comprise a solution to the correctional problem. Rather, a systematic and balanced correctional program that includes many approaches and methods appears to be needed.

The systematic and balanced correctional program must include private *and* public facilities and services. Integral to the effective operation of community correctional facilities is a good relationship with the private sector. There are many resources within the community that can be purchased or placed on contract cheaper than the center can support; further, these provide good contact with the community.[30] Also, private community-based correctional programs must maintain good relationships with public services and agencies in order to coordinate their assistance to the offenders and ex-offenders with whom they work.

The advantage private programs have over tax-supported or public programs is flexibility. Though this flexibility may sometimes be unfortunate because of lack of control, it also affords the opportunity for innovative programs that might not easily receive funding by a state legislature, state planning agency, or other governmental body responsible for dispersing public funds.

Community-based correctional programs have no single pattern. They are reflections of the personalities operating the programs.

Successful programs in any field dealing with people cannot be produced piecemeal from a headquarters cookie cutter.[31] Many alternatives to traditional programs are in reality traditional programs with an additive of more of the same, not sufficiently sustained to be effective; and some have missionary overtones that favor the underachiever at the expense of the achiever. Consequently, many innovative programs become a channel for demonstrating the effectiveness of traditional programs, altering dialogue, and introducing some new ideas. Alternative programs should not be seen as a "salvage and reclamation" component of the old order, but as part of a sustained approach to learning and communicative efforts evaluated to be productive.

It must be remembered that community-based corrections can be only a part of the correctional system. Prisons and institutions will always be necessary. Total reliance on community-based corrections would be

---

[30] R. M. Minkoff, "Purchase of Services from the Private Sector: New Methods of Correctional Management and Administration," *American Journal of Correction*, 33, No. 2 (1971), 12–19.

[31] Diane Ravitch, "Programs, Placebos, Panaceas," *The Urban Review*, 2, No. 5 (April 1968), 11.

naive.[32] There are dangerous offenders who need maximum security imprisonment, but their number is small.

Many groups have moved toward encouraging expansion of community-based corrections. Some members of the bar contend that the individual attorney can and should play a multifaceted role in shaping the future of working with offenders in community-based corrections.[33] The First National Conference on Alternatives to Incarceration was held in Boston in September 1975 under the leadership of the National Task Force on Higher Education and Criminal Justice of the National Council of Churches.

By 1972, twenty-one of twenty-eight departments making use of community treatment programs indicated that special legislation had been required, while four states started these programs administratively and without special legislation.[34] The evaluation was that community-based programs obviously enhanced re-entry into the community by providing continuity with the community, assisting in finding adequate employment, and providing needed support during the difficult initial period of adjustment in the community. Skoler has identified seven innovative programs in the forefront of corrections: (1) youth service bureaus, (2) court diversion projects, (3) volunteer and paraprofessional services, (4) community custody, (5) community or regional correctional centers, (6) foster care or substitute homes, and (7) new uses for correctional manpower.[35]

The central task of corrections has been viewed as bringing the offender into contact with the opportunity system of the community and integrating him or her with the socializing institutions of society.[36] To accomplish this, corrections must alter those systems and institutions that have a tendency to reject and eliminate people. Regardless of how many resources are provided and in whatever setting, the problem of reintegration into society requires the participation of the community.

---

[32] Milton Luger and Joseph S. Lobenthal, Jr., "Cushioning Future Shock in Corrections," *Federal Probation*, 38 (June 1974), 19.

[33] Lawrence P. Wilkins, "Community-Based Corrections: Some Techniques Used as Substitutes for Imprisonment," *Capital University Law Review*, 2, No. 1 (1973), 101–25.

[34] Bertram S. Gruggs and Gary R. McCune, "Community-Based Correctional Programs: A Survey and Analysis," *Federal Probation*, 36, No. 2 (June 1972), 19–23.

[35] Daniel Skoler, "Future Trends in Juvenile and Community-Based Corrections," in Gary R. Perlstein and Thomas R. Phelps, eds., *Alternatives to Prison: Community-Based Corrections* (Pacific Palisades, Cal.: Goodyear, 1975), pp. 3–15. Originally published in *Juvenile Court Judges Journal*, 21 (Winter 1971), 98–103.

[36] Robert M. Carter, Daniel Glaser, and Leslie P. Wilkins, eds., *Correctional Institutions* (New York and Philadelphia: J. B. Lippincott, 1972), p. 423.

The evaluations of community-based programs have been positive and neutral rather than negative. On the basis of the evidence available, the conclusions can be drawn that such programs (1) cost less than institutionalization, (2) are reported in many places to be more effective than institutions, and (3) are certainly less damaging to the people participating in them. It is apparent that the most optimistic way of working with offenders and ex-offenders in their readjustment to society lies in community-based corrections.

Bibliography

ADAMS, STUART, *Evaluative Research in Corrections: A Practical Guide.* Washington, D.C.: U.S. Department of Justice, Law Enforcement Assistance Administration, National Institute of Law Enforcement and Criminal Justice, 1975.

ALBRIGHT, E., *Example Evaluation Component: A Community Based Rehabilitation Project—National Impact Program Evaluation.* Washington, D.C.: U.S. Department of Justice, Law Enforcement Assistance Administration, National Institute of Law Enforcement and Criminal Justice, 1972.

ALEDORT, S. L., and M. JONES, "Euclid House: A Therapeutic Community Halfway House for Prisoners," *American Journal of Psychiatry,* 130, No. 3 (March 1973), 286–89.

ALEXANDER, M. E., *Residential Center: Corrections in the Community.* Washington, D.C.: U.S. Department of Justice, Bureau of Prisons, 1970.

ALLEN, ROBERT F., HARRY N. DUBIN, SAUL PILNICK, and ADELLA C. YOUTZ, *Collegefields: From Delinquency to Freedom.* Seattle: Special Child Publications, Inc., 1970.

ALPER, BENEDICT S., *Community Residential Treatment Centers.* Washington, D.C.: National Parole Institutes, Department of Health, Education and Welfare, 1966.

————, *Prisons Inside-Out: Alternatives in Correctional Reform.* Cambridge, Mass.: Ballinger, 1974.

AMOS, WILLIAM E., RAYMOND L. MANELLA, and MARILYN A. SOUTHWELL,

Action Programs for Delinquency Prevention. Springfield, Ill.: Thomas Books, 1965.

Analysis of Extent of Applicability of Standard Minimum Rules for the Treatment of Prisoners to Community-Based Supervision and Residential Care for Convicted Offenders. Washington, D.C.: American Bar Association, 1974.

Analysis of the Group Residence for Hard-to-Place Juvenile Boys, March 1971 to February 1972. St. Paul: Minnesota Department of Corrections, 1972.

Analysis of Work Release for Felons in Minnesota. Chicago: Chicago University Law School, 1971.

Annual Report. The Status of Current Research in the California Youth Authority. Sacramento: California Youth Authority, 1972.

ARCAPI, B. A., *Work Release in Minnesota, 1969.* St. Paul: Minnesota Department of Corrections, 1970.

Assessment of Junior College Programs for Youthful Offenders in an Institution. Sacramento: California Youth Authority, 1973.

AUSTIN, K. M., and F. R. SPEIDEL, "Thunder: An Alternative to Juvenile Court Appearance," *California Youth Authority Quarterly,* 24, No. 4 (Winter 1972), 13–16.

BACHMAN, D. D., *Work-Release Programs for Adult Felons in the United States: A Descriptive Study.* Tallahassee: Florida Division of Corrections, 1968.

BAKAL, YITZHAK, ed., *Closing Correctional Institutions: New Strategies for Youth Services.* Lexington, Mass.: D. C. Heath Co., 1973.

BALCH, R. W., "Deferred Prosecution: The Juvenilization of the Criminal Justice System," *Federal Probation,* 38, No. 2 (1974), 46–50.

BARON, R. and F. FEENEY, "Preventing Delinquency Through Diversion: The Sacramento County 601 Diversion Project," *Federal Probation,* 37, No. 1 (March 1973), 13–18.

BARTHOLOMEW, CAROLE L., JAMES J. RYAN, and NATHAN G. MANDEL, *Analysis of Work Release in Minnesota.* St. Paul: Minnesota Department of Corrections, 1970.

BELLASSAI, J. P., and P. N. SEGAL, "Addict Diversion: An Alternative Approach for the Criminal Justice System," *Georgetown Law Journal,* 60 (1971–72), 667–710.

BELLASSAI, J. P., *District of Columbia Superior Court—Operating Procedures, Pretrial Diversion Project.* Washington, D.C.: District of Columbia Superior Court, 1972.

BERECOCHEA, J. E., and G. E. SING, *Effectiveness of a Halfway House for*

Civilly Committed Narcotics Addicts. Sacramento: California Department of Corrections, 1971.

BERLEMAN, W. C., "Value and Validity of Delinquency Prevention Experiments," *Crime and Delinquency*, 15, No. 4 (October 1969), 471–78.

BILES, D., "A Proposal for Work Release of Prisoners in Victoria," *Australian and New Zealand Journal of Criminology*, 3, No. 3 (1970), 156–65.

BOONE, JOHN O., *A Study of Community-Based Correctional Needs in Massachusetts.* Boston: Massachusetts Correctional Department, 1972.

BORUM, E. A., "Day Treatment Center: A Program for Girls from Problem Families," *Journal of the California Probation, Parole and Correctional Association*, 8 (Spring 1972), 23–24.

Boys Residential Youth Center, Final Report, 1969. New Haven: Boys Residential Youth Center, 1969.

BRADFORD, MACK E., *A Study of the Community Treatment for Recidivist Offenders Project of Oakland County Circuit Court Probation Department,* paper submitted to the School of Criminal Justice, Michigan State University, East Lansing, 1972.

BRADY, J., and R. GRELUTTI, *Study of Community-Based Correctional Needs in Massachusetts.* Boston: Massachusetts Correctional Department, 1972.

BRAKAL, S. J., "Diversion from the Criminal Process: Informal Discretion, Motivation, and Formalization," *Denver Law Journal*, 48 (1971), 211–38.

BRAKAL, S. J., and G. R. SOUTH, *Diversion from the Criminal Process in the Rural Community: Final Report of the American Bar Foundation Project on Rural Criminal Justice.* Chicago: American Bar Foundation, 1969.

BRAUTIGAM, RICHARD K., "Work Release: A Case Study and Comment," *Prison Journal*, 52, No. 2 (1973), 20–35.

BRODERSON, R. E., "San Joaquin County: A Day Care Treatment Center," *California Youth Authority Quarterly*, 24, No. 3 (Fall 1972), 20–24.

BROWN, B. S., and J. D. SPEVACEK, "Work Release in Community and Institutional Settings," *Corrective Psychiatry and Journal of Social Therapy*, 17, No. 3 (1971), 35–42.

BUSHER, WALTER H., *Ordering Time to Serve Prisoners: A Manual for the Planning and Administering of Work Release.* Washington, D.C.: U.S. Department of Justice, Law Enforcement Assistance Administration, 1973.

————, *Work Release: A Compilation of Enabling Legislation—Work*

Release Resource Document No. 3. Washington, D.C.: U.S. Department of Justice, Law Enforcement Assistance Administration, 1972.

————, *Work Release: A Directory of Programs and Personnel—Work Release Document No. 2.* Washington, D.C.: U.S. Department of Justice, Law Enforcement Assistance Administration, 1972.

Busher, W. H., and D. Tompkins, *Work Release: A Bibliography of Work Release Resources, Document No. 1.* Washington, D.C.: U.S. Department of Justice, Law Enforcement Assistance Administration, 1972.

California Standards for Juvenile Homes, Ranches and Camps. Sacramento: California Youth Authority, 1972.

Carter, R. M., "The Diversion of Offenders," *Federal Probation*, 36, No. 4 (December 1972), 31–36.

Case for the Pretrial Diversion of Heroin Addicts from the Criminal Justice System, report by Special Committee on Crime Prevention and Control. Washington, D.C.: American Bar Association, 1972.

Cavan, R. S., *Juvenile Delinquency: Development, Treatment, Control,* 2nd ed. Philadelphia: J. B. Lippincott, 1969.

Chatfield, J. F., "Pre-trial Diversion in the Twin Cities," *American Bar Association Journal*, 60 (1974), 1089–92.

Clarke, S., *Contributions of Juvenile Offender Treatment and Service Programs to the Reduction of Juvenile Delinquency.* Chapel Hill: North Carolina University, 1973.

Coates, Robert B., and Alden D. Miller, *Neutralization of Community Resistance to Group Homes.* Boston: Center for Criminal Justice, Harvard University Law School, 1972.

Collins, G. R., and M. S. Richmond, *Residential Center: Corrections in the Community.* Washington, D.C.: U.S. Department of Justice, Bureau of Prisons, 1971.

Community-Based Correctional Programs Models and Practices. Rockville, Md.: National Institute of Mental Health, 1971.

Community-Based Corrections in Des Moines: A Coordinated Approach to the Improved Handling of Adult Offenders. Washington, D.C.: U.S. Department of Justice, Law Enforcement Assistance Administration, National Institute of Law Enforcement and Criminal Justice, undated.

Community Correctional Centers. Washington, D.C.: District of Columbia Department of Corrections, undated.

Community Corrections in Des Moines: A Coordinated Approach to the Handling of Adult Offenders—A Handbook. Des Moines: Division of Court Services, Iowa Fifth Judicial District, undated.

Community Corrections Programs and Facilities for Maryland: Summary. Baltimore: Maryland Governor's Commission on Law Enforcement, 1971.

Community Pre-Release Programs, Annual Report, 1970–71. Columbia, S.C.: South Carolina Department of Corrections, 1971.

Community Services Manual. Washington, D.C.: District of Columbia Department of Correction, undated.

Comparative Analysis of Community and Institutional Treatment. Louisville: Louisville and Jefferson Counties, Kentucky, Metropolitan Social Services Department, Office of Research and Planning, 1971.

Connecticut Department of Correction: An Introduction. Hartford: Connecticut Department of Correction, 1973.

CONRAD, JOHN P., "Corrections and Simple Justice," *Journal of Criminal Law and Criminology,* 64, No. 2 (1973), 208–17.

————, "Counties and the Correctional Crisis," *American County,* 37, No. 10 (November 1972), 15–19.

COOPER, W. D., "Employers and Employees in the Work-Release Program in North Carolina," *Crime and Delinquency,* 16, No. 4 (1970), 427–33.

Corrections: Report of the National Advisory Commission on Criminal Justice Standards and Goals. Washington, D.C.: National Advisory Commission on Criminal Justice Standards and Goals, U.S. Department of Justice, Law Enforcement Assistance Administration, 1973.

COUGHLIN, J., "Counties Can Lead Community-Based Corrections," *American County,* 37, No. 10 (November 1972), 13–14.

COUGHLIN, C. J., *King County Sheriff's Department Work Release Program: Final Report.* Seattle: King County Sheriff's Department, 1968.

Courts: Report of the National Advisory Commission on Criminal Justice Standards and Goals, 1973. Washington, D.C.: National Advisory Commission on Criminal Justice Standards and Goals, U.S. Department of Justice, Law Enforcement Assistance Administration, 1973.

COX, G. F., *Project Intercept: Eighteen Months Progress Report, April 13, 1971–October 13, 1972.* North Bay, Cal.: North Bay Human Development Coporation, 1972.

CRESSEY, D. R., and R. A. McDERMOTT, *Diversion from the Juvenile Justice System.* Ann Arbor: University of Michigan, 1973.

Criminal Justice System in Polk County, Iowa, Vol. 4: Juvenile Justice—Description and Analysis. Des Moines: Drake University, 1973.

DASH, S., and R. J. MEDALIE, *Demonstrating Rehabilitative Planning as a Defense Strategy.* Washington, D.C.: Georgetown University Law Center, 1968.

DEEHY, P. T., *Halfway House in the Correctional Sequence: A Case-Study of a Transitional Residence for Inmates of a State Reformatory*, unpublished dissertation. Ann Arbor: University Microfilms, 1969.

Deferred Prosecution and Deferred Acceptance of a Guilty Plea. Honolulu: Honolulu Law Enforcement Planning Office, 1971.

DENTON, G. J., and N. GATZ, "Ohio's Work Furlough: College for Felons," *American Journal of Corrections*, 35, No. 3 (1973), 44–45.

Description of North Carolina Work Release Program and Pre-Release Program. Tallahassee: Florida State University, undated.

A Description of the Function and Procedures of the Polk County Department of Court Services. Des Moines: Polk County, Iowa Court Services Department, 1972.

Descriptive Profiles on Selected Pretrial Criminal Justice Intervention Programs: Portfolio. Washington, D.C.: American Bar Association, 1974.

Design for an Evaluation of the Pre-trial Intervention Program of the Manpower Administration. U.S. Department of Labor, Vol. 1, ABT Associates, May 31, 1973.

The Des Moines Community Corrections Project: An Alternative to Jailing. Hackensack, N.J.: National Council on Crime and Delinquency, 1972.

Des Moines Model Neighborhood Corrections Project Research Evaluation Report No. 1 (Feb. 3, 1970 to Dec. 16, 1970). Hackensack, N.J.: National Council on Crime and Delinquency, 1971.

Directory of Halfway Houses and Group Homes for Troubled Children. Tallahassee: Florida Youth Services Division, 1973.

DOLESCHAL, E., and G. GEIS, *Graduated Release*. Rockville, Md.: Center for Study of Crime and Delinquency, National Institute of Mental Health, 1971.

DOLESCHAL, E., "Graduated Release," *Information Review on Crime and Delinquency*, 1, No. 10 (1969), 1–26.

Drug Diversion Program: An Initial Report. Sacramento: California Bureau of Criminal Statistics, 1973.

DUNLAVEY, D., Work Release in Minnesota," *American Journal of Corrections*, 31, No. 4 (1969), 28–29.

EMPEY, L. T., "Contemporary Programs for Convicted Juvenile Offenders: Problems of Theory, Practice and Research," *Crimes of Violence*, National Commission on Causes and Prevention of Violence, 1969.

EMPEY, L. T., and M. L. ERICKSON, *The Provo Experiment: Evaluating Community Control of Delinquency*. Lexington, Mass.: D. C. Heath, 1972.

EMPEY, L. T., and S. G. LUBECK, *The Silverlake Experiment: Testing Delinquency Theory and Community Intervention.* Chicago: Aldine Publishing Co., 1971.

Evaluation and Program Monitoring Project: A Study Prepared for the Columbia Region (or) Association of Governments. Portland: Portland State University, 1972.

Evaluation of the Effects of Alternatives to Incarceration on Juvenile Offenders: The Cohort Analysis in the Study of the Massachusetts Department of Youth Services by the Center for Criminal Justice, Harvard University. Washington, D.C.: U.S. Department of Justice, Law Assistance Administration, National Institute of Law Enforcement and Criminal Justice, 1974.

Evaluation of Youth Service Bureaus. Sacramento: California Youth Authority, 1973.

Ex-Convict Motivation and Recovery Center (X-MARC): First Year, Final Report, July 1, 1971–June 30, 1972. Washington, D.C.: California Council on Criminal Justice, U.S. Department of Justice, Law Enforcement Assistance Administration, National Institute of Law Enforcement and Criminal Justice, 1972.

Expansion of Self-Financed, Locally Planned and Activated Pre-Trial Intervention Programs for Early Offenders Based on Department of Labor Pilot and Demonstration Project Experience. Washington, D.C.: American Bar Association, 1972.

Explorations in After-Care. London: Home Office Research Unit, Her Majesty's Stationary Office, 1971.

First Year Santa Clara County Day Care Center Evalution. Washington, D.C.: American Justice Institute, U.S. Department of Justice, Law Enforcement Assistance Administration, National Institute of Law Enforcement and Criminal Justice, undated.

FISCHER, R. G., *Maryland: Analysis of Comprehensive Plans to Develop a Statewide Community Corrections System,* Maryland Governor's Commission on Law Enforcement and Administration of Justice, 1973.

FLACKETT, JOHN M., "Criswell House: An Alternative to Institutional Commitment for the Juvenile Offender," *Federal Probation,* 34, No. 4 (December 1970), 30.

————, "Juvenile Offenders in the Community: Some Recent Experiences in the United States," *The Howard Journal of Penology and Crime Prevention,* 14, No. 1 (1974), 22–36.

Florida Bureau of Group Treatment. Tallahassee: Florida Bureau of Statistics, Research and Planning, undated.

FOGEL, D., and B. GALAWAY, "Restitution in Criminal Justice: A Minnesota Experiment," *Criminal Law Bulletin*, 8, No. 8 (October 1972), 681–91.

Follow-up Study of 166 Juveniles Who Were Released from State Group Homes from July 1, 1969 through June 30, 1972. St. Paul: Minnesota Department of Corrections, 1973.

FREEDMAN, M., and N. PAPPAS, *Training and Employment of Offenders.* Washington, D.C.: President's Commission on Law Enforcement and Administration of Justice, U.S. Department of Justice, Law Enforcement Assistance Administration, 1967.

FRIEDLANDER, WALTER A., *Introduction to Social Welfare.* Englewood Cliffs, N.J.: Prentice-Hall, 1955.

FRIEDMAN, S., and G. G. HOSKINS, *Long-Range Juvenile Correctional Program for San Joaquin County, Final Report.* Stanford Research Institute, October 1969.

GAGLIARDO, A. J., "Are Youth Bureaus the Answer?" *Juvenile Court Journal*, 22, No. 3 (Fall), 57–59.

GARRETT, JAMES E., and PETER O. ROMPLER, *Community Resocialization: A New Perspective.* Washington, D.C.: The Catholic University of America Press, 1966.

GAY, M., *Pretrial Release and Diversion for Alcoholism Treatment and Rehabilitation*, paper presented at NCAE Seminar on Alcoholism Within the Criminal Justice System, Arlington, Va., October 18–19, 1973.

GEMIGNANI, R. J., "Youth Service Systems: Diverting Youth from the Juvenile Justice System." *Federal Probation*, 36, No. 4 (December 1972), 48–53.

GILLIAM, J. L., *Project First Chance: An Experimental and Demonstration Manpower Project—Final Report.* Columbia, S.C.: South Carolina Department of Corrections, 1969.

GODBY, G.D., *Work Release Six-Year Report, July 1, 1966–June 30, 1972.* Portland: Oregon Corrections Division, 1972.

GOLDBERG, N. E., "Pre-trial Diversion: Bilk or Bargain?" *National Legal Aid and Defense Association Briefcase*, 31, No. 6 (November–December 1973), 490–93, 499–501.

GOLDFARB, R. L., and L. R. SINGER, *After Conviction.* New York: Simon and Schuster, 1973.

GRIGGS, BERTRAM S., and GARY R. MCCUNE, "Community-Based Correctional Programs: A Survey and Analysis," *Federal Probation*, 36, No. 2 (1972), 7–13.

GRISHAM, ROY A., JR., and PAUL D. MCCONAUGHY, *The Encyclopedia of*

U.S. Government Benefits. Union City, New Jersey: William H. Wise Co., 1968.

Grupp, S. E.. "Work Furlough and Punishment Theory," *Criminology,* 8, No. 1 (1970), 63–79.

————, "Work Release: Some Issues and Needs," Proceedings of the Ninety-Eight Annual Congress of Correction, American Correctional Association, College Park, Md., 1968.

Guidelines and Standards for Halfway Houses and Community Treatment Centers. Washington, D.C.: International Halfway House Association, U.S. Department of Justice, Law Enforcement Assistance Administration, 1973.

Guidelines for the Administration and Implementation of the Federal City College, Lorton Extension College. Washington, D.C.: District of Columbia Department of Corrections, 1972.

Gunn, J., "Rehabilitation Workshop for Offenders," *British Journal of Criminology,* 12, No. 2 (April 1972), 158–66.

Halfway House Specification. Columbus: Ohio Adult Parole Authority, undated.

Halfway House Tips. Honolulu: Halfway House, October 1, 1960.

Hamberg, R. L., *Family House Program Evaluation.* Seattle: Washington Law and Justice Planning Office, 1973.

Haragadine, J. E., *Attention Homes of Boulder, Colorado: Community-Sponsored Group Foster Homes for the Care of Delinquent and Problem Youth.* Washington, D.C.: U.S. Department of Health, Education and Welfare, undated.

Harding, J., "The Offender and the Community: Some Change Aspects of an Old Relationship," *Social Work Today,* 5, No. 16 (1974), 478–81.

Harlow, E., and J. R. Weber, *Diversion from the Criminal Justice System.* Hackensack, N.J.: National Council on Crime and Delinquency, 1971.

Harlow, E., "Intensive Intervention: An Alternative to Institutionalization," *Crime and Delinquency Literature,* 2, No. 1 (1970), 3–46.

Hawryluk, A., *Treatment Strategies for Juvenile Delinquents: A Survey of Current and Experimental Programs and Their Implications.* American Judicature Society, Report No. 34, 1971.

Hecht, J. A., *Effects of Halfway Houses on Neighborhood Crime Rates and Property Values: A Preliminary Survey.* Washington, D.C.: District of Columbia Department of Corrections, 1970.

Herron, L., "Rehabilitation of Prisoners, Reforms and Innovations in the Penal System," *Australian Journal of Forensic Sciences*, 3, No. 2 (1970), 40–43.

HOARE, M. B., and C. R. BEVAN, "Alternatives to Imprisonments and Progressive Variations in Current Practices," *Australian and New Zealand Journal of Criminology*, 5, No. 1 (March 1972), 15–34.

HOLAHAN, J. F., *Benefit-Cost Analysis of Project Crossroads*. Washington, D.C.: National Committee for Children and Youth, Manpower Administration, U.S. Department of Labor, 1970.

HOLDER, H.D., and D. S. ALBERTS, *Taking Corrections Into the Community: An Evaluation Design*. Raleigh: Institute of Human Ecology, North Carolina Department of Correction, 1971.

In Lieu of Arrest: The Manhattan Bowery Project, Treatment for Homeless Alcoholics. New York: Vera Institute of Justice, undated.

IRWIN, JOHN, "The Trouble With Rehabilitation," *Criminal Justice and Behavior*, 1, No. 2 (1974), 139–49.

JEFFREY, ROBERT, and STEPHEN WOOLPERT, "Work Furlough as an Alternative to Incarceration: An Assessment of Its Effects on Recidivism and Social Cost," *Journal of Criminal Law and Criminology*, 65, No. 3 (September 1974), 405–15.

JOHNS, DENNIS, and TED PALMER, *Atmosphere and Activities in a Community Center Dayroom for Delinquent Adolescents*. Sacramento: California Youth Authority, 1970.

JOHNSON, E. H., "Report on an Innovation: State Work-Release Programs," *Crime and Delinquency*, 16, No. 4 (1970), 417–26.

————, *Work Release: A Study of Correctional Reform*. Carbondale, Ill.: Southern Illinois University, 1973.

————, "Work Release: Conflicting Goals Within a Promising Innovation," *Canadian Journal of Corrections*, 12, No. 1 (1970), 67–77.

————, *Work Release: Factors in Selection and Results*. Carbondale, Ill.: Southern Illinois University, 1969.

JOHNSON, E. H., and K. E. KOTCH, "Two Factors in Development of Work Release: Size and Location of Prisons," *Journal of Criminal Justice*, 1, No. 1 (1973), 43–50.

JOHNSON, J. L., and E. B. McCUBBIN, *Taking Corrections Into the Community: A Way to Begin*. Raleigh: Institute of Human Ecology, North Carolina Department of Corrections, 1971.

Justice for Children, Vol. 2: How to Set Up a Group Home. New York: National Council of Jewish Women, 1973.

Juvenile Court: A Status Report. Rockville, Md.: National Institute of Mental Health, 1971.

Juvenile Diversion: A Perspective. College Park, Md.: American Correctional Association, 1972.

KAHN, ALFRED J., *Planning Community Services for Children in Trouble.* New York: Columbia University Press, 1963.

KELLER, O. J., and B. S. ALPER, *Halfway Houses: Community-Centered Correction and Treatment.* Lexington, Mass.: D. C. Heath, 1970.

KEYES, D., and S. ROBINSON, "Inmate Vocational Training: A National Overview," *Correctional Education,* 25, No. 2 (Spring 1973), 15–24.

KINZER, J. G., *Evaluation of Criminal Justice Programs: Guidelines and Examples.* Washington, D.C.: U.S. Department of Justice, Law Enforcement Assistance Administration, National Institute of Law Enforcement and Criminal Justice, 1973.

KIRBY, B. C., "Crofton House: An Experiment with a County Halfway House," *Federal Probation,* 33, No. 1 (March 1965), 53–58.

———, *Crofton House Final Report.* San Diego: San Diego State College, 1970.

———, "In-Between Correctional Facility," *Police,* 16, No. 7 (March 1967), 52–55.

KLAPMUTS, N., "Diversion from the Justice System," *Crime and Delinquency Literature,* 6, No. 1 (March 1974), 108–31.

KLEINDIENST, R. G., "The New Approach to Corrections," *Carolina Law Review,* 22, No. 6 (1972), 32–39.

KNOWLES, C. D., *Alternative Programs: A Grapevine Survey.* Hackensack N.J.: National Council on Crime and Delinquency, 1973.

KONOPKA, G., "Our Outcast Youth," *Social Work,* 15, No. 4 (1970), 76–86.

KRAUSE, K., "Denial of Work Release Programs to Women," *Southern California Law Review,* 47, No. 4 (1974), 1453–90.

KUPERSMITH, G., *High Impact Anti-Crime Program: Sample Impact Project Evaluation Components.* Washington, D.C.: U.S. Department of Justice, Law Enforcement Assistance Administration, National Institute of Law Enforcement and Criminal Justice, 1974.

LAYMAN, V. L., "Prison to Community Via Oregon's Project Newgate," Proceedings of the One Hundredth Annual Congress of Correction, American Correctional Association, College Park, Md., 1970.

LEEKE, W. D., "A Successful Strategy in the War Against Crime," *FBI Law Enforcement Bulletin,* 39, No. 9 (1970), 25–29.

———, *Community-Based Corrections Programs: Alternatives to Failure.* Columbia, S.C.: South Carolina Department of Corrections, 1971.

Legal Issues and Characteristics of Pretrial Intervention Programs—Monograph. Washington, D.C.: American Bar Association, 1974.

LEJINS, P. P., and T. F. COURTLESS, *Justification and Evaluation of Projects in Corrections.* College Park, Md.: Maryland University, 1973.

LEJINS, P. P., "Modern Concepts of Imprisonment in the USA," in *Education to Freedom by Deprivation of Freedom,* M. Busch and G. Edel, eds. Neuweid: Hermann Luchterhand Verlag (1960), pp. 293–308.

LEMERT, E. M., *Instead of Court: Diversion in Juvenile Justice.* Rockville, Md.: National Institute of Mental Health, 1971.

LEONARD, R. F., *Prosecutor's Manual on Screening and Diversionary Programs.* Chicago: National District Attorneys Association, 1972.

LEONARD, R. F., and J. GARBER, *Screening of Criminal Cases.* Chicago: National District Attorneys Association, 1972.

LONERGAN, B., "Community Treatment Services," *American Journal of Corrections,* 34, No. 5 (1972), 34–35, 46.

LONG, E. V., "Prisoner Rehabilitation Act of 1965," *Federal Probation,* 25, No. 4 (December 1965), 3–7.

Lorton Prison College Program: Third Year Final Report. Washington, D.C.: District of Columbia Department of Corrections, 1973.

LOWE, C., "Contra Costa County: The Guide Program for Girls," *California Youth Authority Quarterly,* 24, No. 3 (Fall 1972), 35–36.

LUGER, M., and J. S. LOBENTHAL, JR., "Cushioning Future Shock in Corrections," *Federal Probation,* 38, No. 2 (1974), 19–23.

MCARTHUR, V., and B. CANTOR, *Cost Analysis of the District of Columbia Work Release Program.* Washington, D.C.: District of Columbia Department of Corrections, 1970.

MCARTHUR, VIRGINIA A., *From Convict to Citizen: Programs for the Woman Offender.* Springfield, Va.: National Technical Information Service, 1974.

MCCARTT, JOHN M., and THOMAS J. MANGOGNA, *Guidelines and Standards for Halfway Houses and Community Treatment Centers.* Washington, D.C.: U.S. Department of Justice, Law Enforcement Assistance Administration, 1973.

MCCREA, TULLY L., and DON M. GOTTFREDSON, *A Guide to Improved Handling of Misdemeanant Offenders.* Washington, D.C.: U.S. Department of Justice, Law Enforcement Assistance Administration, National Institute of Law Enforcement and Criminal Justice, undated.

MCGEECHAN, W., "Penal Evolution: Corrective Services," *Australian Journal of Forensic Sciences,* 3, No. 4 (1971), 148–56.

MCLAUGHLIN, G. T., "Prisoners Are Home for Christmas: A Swedish

Experiment in Penology," *New York State Bar Journal*, 44, No. 4 (June 1972), 211–14.

MANDELL, W., "Making Correction a Community Agency," *Crime and Delinquency*, 17, No. 3 (1971), 281–88.

Manhattan Court Employment Project. New York: Vera Institute, New York City Criminal Justice Coordinating Council, 1970.

Manual of Correctional Standards, rev. ed. College Park, Md.: American Correctional Association, 1966.

MARGOLIN, R. J., "Postinstitutional Rehabilitation of the Penal Offender: A Community Effort," *Federal Probation*, 31, No. 1 (March 1967), 46–50.

MILLER, F. P., "The Reintegration of the Offender Into the Community (Some Hopes and Some Fears)," *Canadian Journal of Corrections*, 12 No. 4 (1970), 514–25.

MILLER, O. T., *Massachusetts Correctional Institution, Concord: Characteristics of Men Accepted and Rejected for Day Work*. Boston: Massachusetts Department of Correction, 1970.

MINKOFF, R. M., "Purchase of Services from the Private Sector: New Methods of Correctional Management and Administration," *American Journal of Correction*, 33, No. 2 (1971), 12–19.

MONTILLA, M. P., *Model Community Correctional Program—Report 2: Community Organization for Correctional Services*. Institute for the Study of Crime and Delinquency, California, undated.

MORRIS, A., *Correctional Administrator's Guide to the Evaluation of Correctional Programs*. Boston: Massachusetts Correctional Association, 1971.

MORRISON, E., and J. P. HEFFERAN, "A Carefully Administered Work Release Program Does Work," *Washington Law Enforcement Journal*, 4, No. 2 (1974), 17.

National Conference on Criminal Justice, January 23–26, 1973. Washington, D.C.: U.S. Department of Justice, Law Enforcement Assistance Administration, 1973.

New Approaches to Diversion and Treatment of Juvenile Offenders. College Park, Md.: Institute of Criminal Justice and Criminology, Maryland University, 1972.

NewGate Model. Hackensack, N.J.: National Council on Crime and Delinquency, undated.

New Model of Juvenile Justice System. Pima County, Ariz.: Pima County Juvenile Court Center, 1972.

NIMMER, R. T., *Alternatives to Prosecution: Diversion from the Criminal*

Justice Process—Draft of Final Report of American Bar Foundation Study of Non-Criminal Disposition of Criminal Cases, Draft 2. Chicago: American Bar Foundation, undated.

NORMAN, SHERMAN, *The Youth Service Bureau: A Key to Delinquency Prevention.* Hackensack, N.J.: National Council on Crime and Delinquency, 1972.

O'LEARY, V., "Current Issues in Community-Based Corrections," Proceedings of the One Hundredth Annual Congress of Correction, American Correctional Association, College Park, Md., 1970.

Operations Review and Monitoring System for the Pre-trial Intervention Program of the Manpower Administration, Vol. 2. Washington, D.C.: ABT Associates, Manpower Administration, U.S. Department of Labor, 1971.

PALMER, JOHN W., "Pre-Arrest Diversion: The Night Prosecutor's Program in Columbus, Ohio," *Crime and Delinquency,* 21, No. 2 (April 1975), 100–108.

PALMER, TED B., *Bibliography of Community Treatment Project Publications.* Sacramento: Community Treatment Project, California Youth Authority, undated.

————, *California's Community Project: A Brief Review of Phases I and II (1961–1968) and Overview of Phase III (1969–1974).* Sacramento: California Youth Authority, 1970.

————, *The Community Treatment Project in Perspective, 1961–1973.* Sacramento: California Youth Authority, 1973.

————, *Differential Placement of Delinquents in Group Homes, Final Report.* Sacramento: California Youth Authority, 1972.

————, *The Phase III Experiment: Progress to Date.* Sacramento: California Youth Authority, and Rockville, Md.: National Institute of Mental Health, 1971.

————, "The Youth Authority's Community Treatment Project," *Federal Probation,* 38, No. 1 (March 1974), 3–14.

PEARCE, W. H., "Reintegration of the Offender into the Community— New Resources and Perspectives," *Canadian Journal of Corrections,* 12, No. 4 (1970), 466–81.

Pennsylvania Community Treatment Services: An Evaluation and Proposed Evaluation Information System—Final Report. Informants, Inc., Pennsylvania Bureau of Correction, 1972.

PETTIBONE, J. M., "Community-based Programs: Catching Up With Yesterday and Planning for Tomorrow," *Federal Probation,* 37, No. 3 (1973), 3–8.

PLATT, ANTHONY M., *The Child Savers*. Chicago: University of Chicago Press, 1969.

PLECK, J. H., and S. I. SIMON, *Effectiveness of a Correctional Halfway House*. Washington, D.C.: U.S. Department of Justice, Law Enforcement Assistance Administration, National Institute of Law Enforcement and Criminal Justice, 1969.

Police: Report of the National Advisory Commission on Criminal Justice Standards and Goals, 1973. Washington, D.C.: National Advisory Commission on Criminal Justice Standards and Goals, Law Enforcement Assistance Administration, 1973.

POOLEY, R., "Work Release Programs and Corrections: Goals and Deficits," *Criminal Justice and Behavior*, 1, No. 1 (1974), 62–72.

Pre- and Post-Trial Correctional Processes in Philadelphia. Hackensack, N.J.: National Council on Crime and Delinquency, 1972.

"Pretrial Diversion from the Criminal Process," *Yale Law Journal*, 83, No. 4 (March 1974), 827–54.

Pre-trial Intervention Project: A Rehabilitative Program for First Offenders, January 17, 1972–April 17, 1972. Washington, D.C.: Dade County Pretrial Intervention Program, Dade County, Fla., U.S. Department of Justice, Law Enforcement Assistance Administration, undated.

Project Crossroads, Final Report. Washington, D.C.: National Committee for Children and Youth, Manpower Administration, U.S. Department of Labor, 1971.

Providence Educational Center: An Exemplary Project. Washington, D.C.: National Institute of Law Enforcement and Criminal Justice, Law Enforcement Assistance Administration, undated.

RACHIN, R. L., "So You Want to Open a Halfway House?" *Federal Probation*, 36, No. 1 (1972), 30–37.

RECTOR, M. G., *Corrections in the United States: A Survey for the President's Commission on Law Enforcement and Administration of Justice*. Hackensack, N.J.: National Council on Crime and Delinquency, 1966.

Reintegration of the Offender into the Community. College Park, Md.: Institute of Criminal Justice and Criminology, Maryland University, and Washington, D.C.: U.S. Department of Justice, Law Enforcement Assistance Administration, National Institute of Law Enforcement and Criminal Justice, 1972.

RICHMOND, M. S., "The Practicalities of Community Based Corrections," *American Journal of Corrections*, 30, No. 6 (1968), 12–18.

RISKIN, L. L., "Removing Impediments to Employment of Work Release Prisoners," *Criminal Law Bulletin*, 8, No. 9 (1972), 761–74.

ROBERTS, ALBERT R., *Correctional Treatment of the Offender: A Book of Readings.* Springfield, Ill.: Charles C. Thomas, 1974.

ROBERTSON, J. A., "Pretrial Diversion of Drug Offenders: A Statuatory Approach," *Boston University Law Review*, 52, No. 2 (Spring 1972), 335–71.

ROOT, L. S., "State Work Release Programs: An Analysis of Operational Policies," *Federal Probation*, 37, No. 4 (1973), 52–58.

————, "Work Release Legislation," *Federal Probation*, 36, No. 1 (March 1972), 38–43.

ROVNER-PIECZENIK, ROBERTA, *Pretrial Intervention Strategies: An Evaluation of Policy-Related Research and Policymaker Perceptions.* Washington, D.C.: American Bar Association, 1974.

————, *Project Crossroads As Pre-trial Intervention: A Program Evaluation.* Washington, D.C.: National Committee for Children and Youth, Manpower Administration, U.S. Department of Labor, 1970.

RUDOLFF, A., T. C. ESSELSTYN, and G. L. KIRKHAM, "Evaluating Work Furloughs," *Federal Probation*, 35, No. 1 (1971), 34–38.

RUDOLFF, A., and T. C. ESSELSTYN, "Evaluating Work Furlough: A Follow-up," *Federal Probation*, 37, No. 2 (1973), 48–53.

————, *Jail Inmates at Work: A Study of Work Furlough, Final Report.* Sacramento: California Department of Rehabilitation, 1971.

Rupert Crittenden Center (A Community Correctional Center): A Status Report. Sacramento: California Department of Corrections, undated.

RYAN, M. G., and K. L. JOHNSON, *Omaha-Douglas County Metropolitan Criminal Justice Center-Base Line Data Collection, V. 4, Sec. 2—The Separate Juvenile Court.* Omaha: Nebraska University, 1973.

SALEEBEY, GEORGE, ed., *The Non-Prison: A New Approach to Treating Youthful Offenders.* Rockville, Md.: Institute for the Study of Crime and Delinquency, 1970.

SANDHU, HARJIT S., *Modern Corrections: The Offenders, Therapies and Community Reintegration.* Springfield, Ill.: Charles C. Thomas, 1974.

SANTA CRUZ, LUCIANO A., and RICHARD J. SHELDON, *Evaluation of the Work Release Program at the Federal Correctional Institution, Tallahassee,* MSW thesis. Talahassee: Florida State University, 1967.

SCHOEN, KENNETH F., "PORT: A New Concept of Community-Based Corrections," *Federal Probation*, 36, No. 3, (1973), 35–40.

SCHRAG, C., *Crime and Justice—American Style.* Rockville, Md.: National Institute of Mental Health, 1971.

SCOTT, E. M. and K. L. SCOTT, *Criminal Rehabilitation: Within and Without the Walls*. Springfield, Ill.: Charles C. Thomas, 1973.

SCOTT, R. J., *Work Release: Toward an Understanding of the Law, Policy and Operation of Community-Based Corrections, National Directory, State Work Release Centers, Summer 1972*. Carbondale, Ill.: Southern Illinois University, 1972.

Seattle—King County Corrections Development Project for January 1 through April 30, 1972. Seattle: Corrections Development Project, 1972.

Selected Project Evaluations. Washington, D.C.: U.S. Department of Justice, Law Enforcement Assistance Administration, undated.

SEYMOUR, J. A., *Youth Service Bureaus*. Chicago: Chicago University Law School, 1971.

SHERIDAN, W. H., "Juveniles Who Commit Noncriminal Acts: Why Treat in a Correctional System?" *Federal Probation*, 31, No. 1 (March 1967), 26–30.

SIEGEL, H. H., *Alcohol Detoxification Programs: Treatment Instead of Jail*. Springfield, Ill.: Charles C. Thomas, 1973.

SINGER-DEKKER, H., "Work Rather than Imprisonment: Here and Overseas," *Process*, 53, No. 4 (1974), 79–85.

SKIDMORE, S., "Evaluation of Short-Term Intensive Treatment in the Lightning Treatment Unit for Younger Boys and Their Parents," *Journal of the California Probation, Parole and Correctional Association*, 8 (Spring 1972), 17–22.

SKOLER, D., "Future Trends in Juvenile and Adult Community-Based Corrections," *Juvenile Court Journal*, 21, No. 4 (1971), 98–103.

———, "Protecting the Rights of Defendants in Pretrial Intervention Programs," *Criminal Law Bulletin*, 10, No. 6 (1974), 473–92.

SMITH, ROBERT R., JOHN M. McKEE, and MICHAEL A. MILAN, "Study Release Policies of American Correctional Agencies: A Survey," *Journal of Criminal Justice*, 2, No. 4 (Winter 1974), 357–64.

So You Want to Start a Community Corrections Project? Hackensack, N.J.: National Council on Crime and Delinquency, undated.

SPECTER, A., "Philadelphia's Accelerated Rehabilitative Disposition Program," *American Bar Association Journal*, 60 (1974), 1092–96.

SPERGEL, IRVING A., *Community Problem Solving: The Delinquency Example*. Chicago: The University of Chicago Press, 1969.

STEGGERDA, ROGER O., and PETER S. VENEZIA, *Community-Based Alternatives to Traditional Corrections: The 1973 Evaluation of the Fifth Judicial District Department of Court Services—State of Iowa*. Hackensack, N.J.: Research Council, National Council on Crime and Delinquency, 1974.

STEWART, D. D., *Absconders from the Misdemeanant Work-Release Program: Preliminary Study*. Washington, D.C.: District of Columbia Department of Corrections, 1968.

STONEMAN, KENT, *A Prototype for a Community Correctional Center in Burlington, Vt.* Burlington, Vt., 1971, mimeographed.

Study of Florida's Halfway Houses: Their Benefits, Costs, and Effectiveness, Part I. Tallahassee: Florida Division of Youth Services, undated.

SULLIVAN, D. C., and L. J. SEIGEL, "Halfway House, Ten Years Later: Reappraisal of Correctional Innovation," *Canadian Journal of Criminology and Corrections*, 16, No. 2 (April 1974), 188–97.

SULLIVAN, S., "Convicted Offenders Become Community Helpers," *Judicature*, 56, No. 8 (1973), 333–35.

SWANSON, RICHARD M., *Work Release: Toward an Understanding of the Law, Policy and Operation of Community-Based State Corrections*. Carbondale, Ill.: Southern Illinois University, Center for the Study of Crime, Delinquency, and Corrections, 1973.

SWITZER, A. L., *Drug Abuse and Drug Treatment*. Sacramento: California Youth Authority, 1974.

TAGGART, R., III, *Prison of Unemployment: Manpower Programs for Offenders*. Baltimore: Johns Hopkins University Press, 1972.

Task Force Report: Corrections. Washington, D.C.: President's Commission on Law Enforcement and the Administration of Justice, U.S. Department of Justice, Law Enforcement Assistance Administration, 1967.

Task Force Report: Juvenile Delinquency and Youth Crime. Washington, D.C.: President's Commission on Law Enforcement and the Administration of Justice, U.S. Department of Justice, Law Enforcement Assistance Adminstration, 1967.

TREGER, H., and J. H. COLLIER, "Deferred Prosecution: A Community Treatment Alternative for the Non-Violent Adult Misdemeanant," *Illinois Bar Journal*, 60, No. 12 (August 1972), 922–31.

TURNER, E., *Girls' Group Home: An Approach to Treating Delinquent Girls in the Community*. Sacramento: California Youth Authority, 1969.

VENEZIA, P. S., *Pre-Trial Release to Supportive Services of High Risk Defendants: The Second-Year Evaluation of the Des Moines Community Corrections Projects*. Hackensack, N.J.: National Council on Crime and Delinquency, 1972.

VENEZIA, P. S., and R. D. STEGGERDA, *Residential Corrections—Alternative* to Incarceration: An Empirical Evaluation of the Fort Des Moines Corrections Component of the Iowa Fifth Judicial District Department of Court Services. Hackensack, N.J.: National Council on Crime and Delinquency, 1973.

WALDO, G. P., T. G. CHIRICOS, and L. E. DOBRIN, "Community Contact and Inmate Attitudes: An Experimental Assessment of Work Release," Criminology, 11, No. 3 (1973), 345–81.

WARREN, M. Q., "Case for Differential Treatment of Delinquents," Canadian Journal of Corections, 12, No. 4 (1970), reprinted from Annals of the American Academy of Political and Social Sciences, 1969.

————, Correctional Treatment in Community Settings: A Report of Current Research. Rockville, Md.: National Institute of Mental Health, 1972.

WATERS, J. P., Annual Report of Community Release Programs for the Period Ending June 30, 1972. Hartford: Connecticut Department of Corrections, 1972.

WEBER, J. ROBERT, and MARY MAYER, A Strategy for Action in Establishing Alternatives to Training Schools. Hackensack, N.J.: National Council on Crime and Delinquency, 1968.

WEEKS, H. ASHLEY, Youthful Offenders at Highfields: An Evaluation of the Effects of the Short-Term Treatment of Delinquent Boys. Ann Arbor: University of Michigan Press, 1958.

WEIS, C. W., Diversion of the Public Inebriate from the Criminal Justice System: Prescriptive Package. Washington, D.C.: Pennsylvania Governor's Justice Commission, U.S. Department of Justice, Law Enforcement Assistance Administration, National Institute of Law Enforcement and Criminal Justice, undated.

WETTERGREN, DAVID, MARGARET THOMPSON, and O. RUSSELL OLSON, PORT Handbook: A Manual for Effective Community Action with the Criminal Offender. Rochester, Minn.: PORT of Olmsted County, 1972.

WHITLATCH, W. G., "Toward an Understanding of the Juvenile Court Process," Juvenile Justice, 23, No. 3 (November 1972), 2–8.

WILGOSH, L., "Study of Group Home Placements as a Possible Correction of Delinquent Behaviour," Canadian Journal of Criminology and Corrections, 15, No. 1 (January 1973), 100–108.

WILKINS, LAWRENCE P., "Community-Based Corections: Some Techniques Used as Substitutes for Imprisonment," Capital University Law Review, 2, No. 1 (1973), 101–25.

WILSON, C. G., and E. A. LEWIS, Overview of Correction in North Carolina: A Description of the State System and Characteristics of Prison

Inmates. Raleigh, N.C.: North Carolina Department of Correction, undated.

Wisconsin Division of Corrections: Work Release/Study Release Program, Calendar Years 1971 and 1972. Madison: Wisconsin Division of Corrections, 1973.

WITHERSPOON, A., "Foster Home Placements for Juvenile Delinquents," *Federal Probation,* 30, No. 4 (December 1966), 48–52.

WITTE, A. D., *Work Release in North Carolina: The Program and the Process.* Chapel Hill: North Carolina University, 1973.

Work-Pass Program: 20-Year Report. Lansing: Michigan Department of Corrections, 1971.

"Work Release," *Correctional Sidelights,* 12, No. 2 (1968), 13.

Work Release for Felons: A Summary of Five Years Experience. St. Paul: Minnesota Department of Corrections, 1973.

Work Release in Minnesota, 1970. St. Paul: Minnesota Department of Corrections, 1971.

Work Release/Study Release Program, 1970, and First Five Year Trends. Madison: Wisconsin Department of Corrections, 1972.

YARYAN, R. B., "Community Role in Juvenile Delinquency Programs," paper presented for the Fourth National Symposium on Law Enforcement, Science, and Technology. Huntsville, Texas: May 1972.

Youth Services Bureau in California: Progress Report No. 2. Sacramento: California Youth Authority, 1971.

ZALBA, SERAPIO R., "Work Release—A Two-Pronged Effort," *Crime and Delinquency,* 13, No. 4 (October 1967), 506–12.

ZIMRING, F. E., "Measuring the Impact of the Pretrial Diversion from the Criminal Justice System," *University of Chicago Law Review,* 41, No. 2 (1974), 224–41.

Index